"

Very funny and entertaining... Too many books about Scotland as po-faced and serious as my own are craving attention. **The Scottish Ambassador** will amuse readers of every political stripe and will be popular with both Scots patriots and their critics.

ALASDAIR GRAY,
author of Lanark

"

AEFA MULHOLLAND

THE SCOTTISH AMBASSADOR
Learning How To Be Scottish in America

PONIES+HORSES**BOOKS**

PONIES + HORSES BOOKS

Published by Ponies + Horses Books

Ponies + Horses Books (Scotland), 7b The Hidden Lane, 1103 Argyle Street, Glasgow, G3 8ND

Ponies + Horses Books (Canada), Box 271, Stn C, Toronto, ON, M6J 3P4

www.poniesandhorsesbooks.com

First published by Ponies and Horses Books in 2015

I

Font: Gotham

Design: Craig Design Studio

ISBN: 978-1-910631-09-6

In memory of my beloved brother, Brian,
my beloved sister, Ciara,
and my beloved mother, Claire.
Mission accomplicated.

CONTENTS

Towering in gallant fame,
Scotland my mountain hame,
High may your proud standards gloriously wave,
Land of my high endeavour,
Land of the shining river,
Land of my heart for ever,
Scotland the brave.

Far off in sunlit places,
Sad are the Scottish faces,
Yearning to feel the kiss
Of sweet Scottish rain.
Where tropic skies are beaming,
Love sets the heart a-dreaming,
Longing and dreaming for the homeland again.

Cliff Hanley, 'Scotland the Brave'

1. THE SCOTTISH AMBASSADOR:
PORTLAND, OREGON

I'm on board a rickety, 70s-colour schemed, 50-seater plane. It looks like a tan and cream prop left over from an early disaster movie. It looks untouched by developments in aviation of the past 40 years. It looks like the odds of it making it to the end of the runway are something of a long shot.

It's the kind of hulking antique they still use on routes rarely travelled by senior airline executives, such as from Glasgow and Edinburgh to non-Glasgow and non-Edinburgh parts of Scotland, and from many places to my destination this morning, Portland, Oregon. To really underline the fact that this is not a priority route, the gate for Portland flights is hidden away in a forgotten corner of the airport behind a graveyard for expired plastic furniture and an artificial plant display so tired and grey that you could successfully hide several layers of dense morning fog and a medium-sized leopard seal among its wrinkled fronds.

We're buckled up, crosschecked and nestled in our cracked fake leather seats, when the cabin maître d' cheerfully pipes up:

'Wellllll... it's time for the safety demo, folks. All eyes on Feather up at the front of the cabin.'

Feather stomps up the aisle and into position. She swipes the air grimly. It's hard to tell if this was an attempt at a wave or a vain effort to block out the sight of our cursed faces. A perfunctory smile briefly rumples her cheeks. Her eyes skim the cabin and fix on me. I drop my gaze under her hawk-like glare.

I imagine going through life called Feather: those teenage years of cursing cruel parents for inflicting such a fate upon you, the decades of having to state over and over again, 'No, not Heather...,' the refusing to be ruffled by jokes about winging it and other such avian banter. Luckily Feather looks quite light on her feet. If she wasn't, the name would be an even heavier burden to bear. If she didn't seem quite so fierce, I might feel some empathy for her and her distinctive name. After all, I spent my teenage years telling anyone outside family earshot that my name was Ann.

Forty-five minutes later, we haven't moved an inch along the runway and my seatmate, a severe, navy-business-suited woman, is forced to talk to me out of sheer boredom.

Discussing our time on tarmac, she hears my accent and says, 'You are Scottish. Will you get independence?'

Suddenly I am in the position of spokeswoman for my people. This is surprising; I'm not usually a person people consult about such topics. After spending two decades as a travel writer, I've been asked to weigh in on best places for mule racing in Montana, the where-abouts of the world's largest doughnut and other matters of such crucial importance, but national politics, no. But it's a more pertinent question than many I've had during the 20 years I've been away from Scotland. Over the years, I've found myself breaking the seemingly startling news that yes, we do have schools and electricity; yes, we speak English; no, we are not part of Russia (a surprisingly common misconception); and, no, we do not often use donkeys as a mode of transport. Obviously we only use them on special occasions when we fancy a wee change from badger-drawn carts. Other than these international revelations, my previous experience of diplomacy has been limited to once making the guest list for the Australian Embassy's Melbourne Cup snail racing party.

My seatmate looks at me seriously.

'We will do our best,' I inform her gravely.

Three animated 20-somethings in the row behind me shriek 'jazz hands' and throw their palms in the direction of the oxygen mask storage spaces every time they see an Air Canada Jazz plane. We're in Seattle, just an hour's flight from Air Canada's main western hub. There are a lot of Air Canada Jazz planes. By the time we finally lurch to the end of the runway, their enthusiasm has become far less endearing. One of them starts describing a dream, a movie or a vision attained with the assistance of hallucinogenics. His sentences all sound like questions, lurching upwards at the end?

'Weird, whale-like creatures that could, like, fly? Like, weird bug-like creatures that lived in the, like, mud? It was, like,' he pauses to search for a word capable of conveying maximum effect and finishes triumphantly, 'Weird?'

By the time we're out over the Puget Sound, the summer sun glinting off cobalt waters below, the threesome behind is lamenting the loss of the Portland contender on TV game show, *Rockstar Supernova*. All three sigh dramatically, only perking up when whale-bug guy suggests they amuse themselves by picking drinks off a well-stocked, imaginary in-flights drinks cart.

'It's got whatever you want? It's got it all? Banana lassi with rum?' he queries, and the others tumble quizzically into the conversation with their own orders.

I'm just contemplating my own fantasy drinks order when Feather's superior bounds back behind the mike and chirps up again to tell us how glad he is to be here. I'm about to tune him out when he mentions the happy fact that Feather is about to come through the cabin offering, as well as the usual run of the mill hot beverages, complimentary Pinot Gris from Firesteed Cellars, Oregon, and Hefeweizen Ale from Pyramid Breweries, Seattle. I am impressed. There's nothing quite like a refreshing plastic beaker of wine for breakfast. This is my kind of airline. Several thousand feet above the Gulf Islands, I gratefully sip my 10 am tumbler of Pinot Gris.

It's the next morning and the imperious-sounding Portland Oregon Visitor Authority, in the form of an enthusiastic Frenchwoman called Vero, is taking two other travel writers, Andrew from New Mexico and a delightful Michigander called Dan, and me to see the city's big event, the Rose Festival Parade. In our capacity as travel writers for an assortment of newspapers and magazines, the three of us have been invited here by the city to experience Portland.

Born out of the world's fair that celebrated the centennial of the 1804-1806 Lewis and Clark Expedition, it turns out that this parade is a very big deal in Portland.

The first I ever heard of Lewis and Clark was from my friend Jenn Jones from Montana. We were tramping along an overgrown path beside a Lanarkshire waterway, ducking under branches and narrowly avoiding eddies of cow manure.

'We're just like Lois and Clark!' I heard her exclaim.

I looked perplexed, unsure as to why Superman and his ladylove would have been stumbling about a Scottish riverbank, ankle-deep in heifer dung. It wasn't until I lived in the Pacific Northwest myself that I finally understood that Jenn was in fact referring to Lewis and Clark, the intrepid duo that explored west of the Mississippi and made it through to the Oregon Coast in 1806. Their efforts laid the trail for thousands of others to tackle the 8,000-mile journey along what became known as the Oregon Trail. It is unfortunate, however, that I've never subsequently been able to think of their accomplishments without first imagining them bravely attempting to skirt puddles of cow poo.

A hundred and some years after the initial event, Portland's Rose Parade now coincides with Rose Festival Fleet Week, a week where white-clad sailor boys and girls from the US and Canadian navies roam Portland's streets in packs, getting hit on by lustful locals. Or, at least, that's what it looks like to an innocent bystander.

Vero hands us programmes for today's shenanigans. A heavily made-up Beauty Queen pouts from a page advertising last night's

Junior Parade. She's twirling her mariachi skirt and simpering provocatively at the camera. She's about seven.

For years Portlanders have been returning to their chosen spots along the route, many marking off their patch with duct tape, paint or chalk, or chaining chairs to lampposts. But this year things have turned ugly. There have been shocking headlines in *The Oregonian* about tape being ripped up, padlocked chairs being forcibly removed. Tensions are running high and desirable corners are hotly contested. Today, on the big day itself, streets around the parade route are cordoned off, with hundreds of police barricades blocking all vehicles from interfering with this century-old tradition.

Dan, Andrew, Vero and I wait in the hotel lobby for our driver, the city having generously provided us with one for the day. Our chauffeur is a former teacher who was relieved of his post after inviting Darcelle IX, Portland's octogenarian drag queen, to a school function. Now he helms limousines through the city. We met earlier and he was very taken with my Scottish accent. He comes in from the barricaded streets.

'The cops stopped me a few times,' he says nonchalantly. 'But you got me through,' he says with a mischievous wink.

I am puzzled.

'They waved me through once they heard that it was the Scottish Ambassador I was picking up.'

I am delighted and take to my new role immediately. Becoming the Scottish Ambassador instantly becomes my new ambition. Scotland doesn't currently have any ambassadors and I know next to nothing about my country's politics, but I throw a mean cocktail party and know a thing or two about snail racing. Surely that will snag me the job?

As we crawl through the streets of downtown Portland, we pass half a dozen roadblocks. Our driver tells the first officer just whom he has in back. The officer straightens up, nods to his partner to slide back the barricade, and we're through. As we pass, he looks through the window. I give a regal wave and on we sail. The word goes ahead and we glide through downtown Portland saluted and unchallenged. Once outside the arena where the parade kicks off, I pose for photos with a troop of pipers as they tune up, and practice my ambassadorial wave in the rain.

Seated in the front row of the 13,000-seat Memorial Coliseum, we consult the programme. It promises all sorts of spectacles from the parade's 5,000 participants. I'm most looking forward to the Oregon Association of Mounted Posses, which is due to trot out 'more than 75 horses and riders representing 18 different posses from throughout the State of Oregon.' I don't really know what they mean by a 'posse,' but I'm excited anyway.

In between flower-decked cars and rodeo queens, high school marching bands strut through the stadium. I am perplexed to see that most of the white wooden rifle-twirling and flag-waving teenage girls who act as an eye candy intro for the musical chunk of each band are wearing tartan miniskirts. One band is also preceded by a flamboyant pipe major in an impressively bouffant feather bonnet and kilt combo. The kilt is the slightly less bouffant of the two. I am amazed at my country's influence on the youth of America. What did we do to provoke this? I search for a word to summarise my bewilderment about this phenomenon and finally hit on it... weird. I watch as band after band troop through in their tartans, dancing gun-toters leading the way. It's a pleasant change when a Washington State high school sashays into the stadium to the cheesy strains of 1969's sunny pop song 'Age of Aquarius.' The kids blow bubbles and wave cartoonish peace signs, while their teachers embarrass themselves alongside with Afro wigs and shockingly bad dance moves.

We're sitting in the front row. It's an appropriate position for Scotland's Ambassador. I pretend I deserve the prestigious seat and wave to yet more rodeo queens, to a hundred or more Oregon mayors, to countless flower-strewn corporate floats. I stand with the arena's thousands for various floatloads of American war vets and military branches, including the intriguingly named US Coast Guard Silent

Drill Team, wondering whether they have a Raucous Drill Team as well. As the commentator lists the numbers of Oregonian dead in America's recent wars, a riderless horse is lead through a suddenly silent and stilled arena.

Then we're back to the cheerleaders, marching bands and inexplicable tartan. Dozens of cheerleaders, flag dancers and marching band members from Pleasanton, California, prance through. The cheerleaders' tight red turtlenecks are tartan-free, but have 'SCOTS' emblazoned across their breasts. Have we sartorially brainwashed a nation?

There are a lot of cheerleaders. There is also a lot of horse poo. People scurry in each equine-accessorised group's wake, hurriedly shovelling horse muck out of the way before the next contingent waltz into it. It is an extremely well organised production, and the floral floats are really quite inventive. I'm picking up some useful tips for around the house. I would never have thought of creating a 38-foot-long tiger entirely out of carrots before now.

A rose falls off Ms Thunder Mountain Pro Rodeo's saddle and a wee girl dashes from her seat, into the path of oncoming floats. She skirts hoofs and dollops of manure and gleefully snatches up the fallen bloom. Back in her seat, an official remonstrates with her. Her mother continues gossiping with a woman in the row behind her. The child could have attempted to clamber aboard her pick of the Southwest Washington Llama Association's beasts or tried to arm wrestle any number of colourfully attired members of Guadalajara's Ballet Folklorico and her mother probably still wouldn't have registered. The girl concentrates on viciously ripping apart and squashing the rose she has carefully saved from death by hoof. Neither child nor mother pays any attention to the official. He retreats, frustrated.

Our limo is waiting outside to shepherd us off to our next booking, but obviously, as the Scottish Ambassador, I have to wait for my people. Finally, the Oregon Vietnamese Community Association band's cheerful cha cha begins to give way to the plaintive sound of pipes and drums, and I'm taken aback to find tears in my eyes as

Clan McLeay and the Portland Police Highland Guard file into the stadium. Dan chooses that moment to remember that he has both a camera and an evil streak, and gleefully captures my blinking cultural confusion.

He asks, 'What does this mean to you?'

I manage an 'it's very emotional' and for some reason, it actually is. It's also perplexing. I've never been a fan of the bagpipe. Who knew it would take only 20 years for me to find their bray bearable? Dan goes for the close-up.

'It makes me miss... things,' I sniff.

Dan gets it all on tape. I surreptitiously wipe my eyes, give a final wave and reluctantly vacate the front row. As we clamber up the stairs, I feel somehow simultaneously engulfed by homesickness and quite at home. The sound of the pipes wafts after me, out into the drizzle.

Three days later I'm still in Portland, having stayed on after the other writers left to see friends, consider my new diplomatic career and puzzle over the delayed emotional punch of the bagpipe. While wandering round the Northwest neighbourhood I discover that the stately historical drama *The Queen* is playing at a second-run cinema and go in. But halfway through the film, something happens. Brooding Scottish mountains loom as a bagpiper starts to play under the Queen Mother's Balmoral bedroom window—a suitably regal and impressively hard-to-ignore alarm clock—and I am startled to find tears welling up again. I am taken aback. What is happening? Over the years I've been quite vocal about my dislike of the bagpipes. They cannot possibly hold any emotional sway over me. Yet, the pipes play, Helen Mirren and various jowly extras loll about looking stoic on-screen and I sit in the dark on a sunny Oregon afternoon, tears rolling down my face.

Why now? Why bagpipes? Why that particularly queasy hue of tartan? I've always dismissed such stereotypical symbols of home.

Despite having a Scottish accent, I'm not the cliché that the tourist board, television and Mel Gibson have prepared the world for. Like most of my friends, I never had any interest in tartans or Highland Games, Gaelic and golf. They just weren't any part of my life growing up in Scotland.

But while I never paid any attention to Scotland's more post-card-popular pursuits during my teenage years, my sister Orla did.

Orla hunted down a tutor so she could do Scottish Gaelic as an extra subject for exams. She spent summers in the Outer Hebrides speaking Gaelic. To Hebrideans! She joined a traditional Scottish fiddle orchestra! Voluntarily! She had kilts. Plural! And a flouncy wee black velour waistcoat and big puffy white blouse to go with them! I remember her being on television a few times in that outfit. Any envy I might have had at her getting more than her fair share of attention was swiftly dispelled by the fact that I wouldn't be seen dead wearing a get-up like that in public. Yet, there she was, week after week, her earnest bow slicing its way through assorted jigs and reels, a legion of similarly attired and equally earnest, 60- and 70-somethings fiddling away in a phalanx behind her.

There were so many great things to do in Scotland that didn't involve wearing tartan or being in close proximity to bagpipes, why would Orla choose to put herself through such things? Why were they so important to her? Why did the blouses have to be so puffy? It was very puzzling.

My parents led a similarly tartan-free existence and were perplexed but proud that one of their brood of five was developing such a tra-ditional streak. They exhibited this pride by inflicting Orla's annual fiddle orchestra album upon the entire family every Saturday night as we tucked into that true Glaswegian delicacy, deep-fried pizza and chips. The rest of us writhed and squirmed at each thud of the bass drum, each saw of the bow, each whoop from the cheery band members. The 14-track CDs seemed to go on forever, and essentially did once my dad accidentally jammed the repeat play button on our hulking brute of a stereo. To her credit, Orla had the decency to appear equally unhappy about being subjected to the endless repeat plays and was otherwise an excellent wee sister, always up for whatever devilment she or I could concoct, so I didn't torment her terribly much over her kilty shenanigans.

It's not that I didn't care about Scotland—if I'd ever stopped and thought about it I might have realised that I just cared about a different side of Scotland. The Scotland I loved didn't have such an easily identifiable pattern, dress code or soundtrack. It wasn't the Scotland that made it onto postcards or got celebrated overseas. It was grittier. It was down to earth. It was the only place I knew that threw pizzas into deep fat fryers. But I didn't stop and think about it. I just took my Scottishness for granted, left a few months before my 20th birthday and didn't look back.

I leave the cinema, unsettled, with a niggling sense that something is missing. I feel as if I've mislaid my keys, forgotten something important, lost my sense of direction or a significant portion of a really good night out.

That night, at a dinner party, I am still disconcerted, but chat away with my hosts and fellow guests. Soon after I am complimented on how well I speak English for a Scottish person and reveal that my countrypeople are reasonably familiar with the concept of the light bulb, I say, 'lee-sure' mid-sentence. Not 'leh-sure,' as I've said for the first 30-something years of my life, but an all-out, blatantly Americanised 'lee-sure.' I don't say it ironically or as part of some clever comment about welcoming the return of polyester leisure suits to my weekend wardrobe, I merely say it to explain that I stayed on in the city for fun, not for work. I am horrified.

I first moved over to this side of the Atlantic as part of a brisk Transatlantic trade in teen lobster servers. Back then, Scotland's hotel schools and universities provided an annual summer supply of clambake attendants, buffet minions and housekeeping underlings to the hotels and resorts on the island of Martha's Vineyard. The Gulf War had quashed all graduate job offers with the Scottish,

English and Irish companies I'd spent the year courting, and it was either serve and clear lobster loads on Vineyard lawns or go back to the haddock hatch in the Highland chip shop where I'd worked the previous year for another oil-saturated summer.

It wasn't a hard decision. Lobster trumped haddock. The thrill of this fantasyland that I'd glimpsed in books, television and movies easily eclipsed the cosy familiarity of home. Scotland would always be there. The opportunity to wear high-waisted beige slacks while serving seafood to Carly Simon and James Taylor might not. I practically galloped on board the first flight out.

Martha's Vineyard was my introduction to the US; its white shingled whaling captains' mansions, colourful gingerbread cottages, chowder shacks and 25-miles-per-hour speed limit added up to an almost fairy-tale take on the US. The Vineyard's quaint distillation of 1950s Americana might be a US unrecognisable to most Americans, but it offered a delightful first take on this land before I graduated to the mainland and the realities of the modern-day US. And lobster really did trump haddock, although it was much harder to get rid of the green snail trail of lobster goo that slimed down my work shirts each day.

In between stocking up on useful Portuguese phrases, courtesy of the hotel's disgruntled Brazilian dishwashers, my fellow Scots seafood servers and I would scornfully say that people had 'gone over to the dark side' if they slipped into North American pronunciation instead of their usual Glaswegian or Ayrshire versions. How we mocked these turncoat utterances! We would never forget where we were from or who we were. We had the sureness of youth. We had the best shifts. We had the accents that brought in the most tips. These were not things to give up lightly.

In Oregon, all these years later, I hear what I've just said and lurch to a stop mid-sentence. I'm 19 again and back on the Vineyard, practicing how to say 'You dance like John Travolta's grandmother' in Portuguese. It is happening to me, and it feels shockingly dark. This would have provoked infinite mirth, had it been heard by any of my compatriots. Luckily, I am among Americans, who are far too polite a people to make a scene when a Scot has an identity crisis before dessert.

I'm saved from immediate public ridicule, but not from the hours of consternation and self-examination that then follow. Yes, I've been away a long time. Yes, I've written for North American magazines for what feels like a lifetime. Yes, I've watched *Saturday Night Fever* more times than I'll admit to in company. But 'lee-sure'? It is a startling slip.

The next morning I'm still disconcerted and am worrying the day away when I get an e-mail from my Aunt Martha, one of those forwarded quizzes that are a crucial and time-consuming part of a self-employed person's day. Today's missive is called 'How Scottish Are You?' After last night's linguistic debacle, this seems like perfect timing to receive such a thing and I confidently set to it. Three short minutes later I am taken aback to tot up my score and discover myself officially only 86% Scottish. Where has the other 14% gone?

One of the very many things I didn't know when I was 19, carting crates of crustaceans and worrying about whether the Room Service Captain preferred me, my roommate Susy or Stuart from housekeeping, was that I wouldn't go home to Scotland after that long, lobster-scented summer. In fact, other than for visits, I've never gone back. Five countries later, my mum is still waiting for me to come home. When my sentence faltered last night, almost two decades had passed since I'd got on that Continental flight from Glasgow to New Jersey, my parents waving till long after the plane had left the tarmac.

I've always taken my Scottishness for granted. I didn't think anything—not even the fact that I now qualify for three different nationalities of passports—could ever change the fact that I'm Scottish. True, I've now spent more years outside the country than I spent living there, but I always viewed my national identity as a crucial constant. Have I been away so long that my Scottishness is fading?

I hadn't realised it was something that could be lost. Is this what the bagpipes are sounding the alarm about?

The more I think about it, the more I fear that the quiz and the bagpipes are right and I've been away so long that I'm no longer a 100% Scot. It is a serious blow.

Unable to concentrate on my day's work, I pick up an old copy of *The Scottish Banner,* a Scottish-American newspaper that a friend got me as a joke. Flipping through, I am surprised and delighted to see an ad for Gatlinburg, East Tennessee's annual Scottish Festival and Highland Games, the first such exhibition of Transatlantic tartanry that I've heard of in the US. I flick through the rest of the paper and am amazed by all the Scottishness going on in the US. There are celebrations, festivals and events; books, videos and shops; lessons, courses and clubs. It seems that, all this time my Scottishness has been ebbing, I've been surrounded by people utterly committed to maintaining theirs.

I've never been to a Highland Games. Or discovered the delights of Scotch whisky, worn a kilt or feather bonnet or spoken Scottish Gaelic. Or done a jig or so many of the Old Country things so often considered mandatory for Scots by Americans I've met over the years since I left. It's time to change that.

Gatlinburg's major event is a parade down the Parkway, the Smoky Mountains town's main street. The ad informs me that 'anyone Scottish' can march the length of it. Anyone Scottish. I know what I have to do. I'm going to go to Gatlinburg and join that parade.

But first I have work to do. It's time to rediscover my Scottishness. It's time to fill in the gaps in my Scottish education. The next Gatlinburg Scottish Festival is 11 months away. In those months, I'll learn how to do Scottish country dancing and how to toss a caber. I'll learn Gaelic. I'll discover what my clan tartan looks like and swathe myself in it. I'll hit Highland Games wherever I can find them. I'll take bagpipe lessons, play golf and down Scotch. I'll befriend posses of Scottie dogs and herds of Highland cows. I'll find out what Tartan Day is all about and see if I can uncover the secrets of the Scottish psyche. I'll do all that and more. Whatever it takes, I'll leave no Scottish stone unturned. I'll become entirely Scottish, make my way to Gatlinburg and walk down the main street in that parade, a fully fledged, 100% Scot.

But I'm not in Scotland. I'm in the US, so I'll have to work on this tartan transformation over here. I'll have to learn how to become Scottish in America.

I call Orla and ask to borrow a kilt.

2. CLOAKED IN TIME:
PORTLAND AND
GRESHAM, OREGON

I study the mural on the wall of my room at the Ace Hotel for some time and am not entirely sure what it is telling me. It details the plight of 'The Oregonian Gentleman,' who is 'alert, wide-eyed, ear to the tree and hand on the ground,' and pleads with the guest to save him. Portland is refreshingly eccentric—and proud of it. Even car bumper stickers proclaim, 'Keep Portland Weird' and Portlanders really do seem to make impressive efforts to keep things off-kilter.

This is a city where evening class offerings include Sculpting Horses in Clay, Visioning Collage and Cement Leaf Casting. Since the 24-hour Church of Elvis—the reason for my very first visit to Portland years ago—closed down, Voodoo Doughnuts has stepped up to fill the Church's place as Top Quirky Wedding Location. Sadly, the grungy donut emporium had to stop selling Pepto Bismol donuts, since the indigestion aid is considered medication and therefore not appropriate for pastry filling, but they still serve person-shaped Voodoo Donuts with stakes in their hearts and tasty dribbles of jam blood.

The city is as eco-conscious as it is offbeat. The best way to horrify a Portlander is to mock their attempts to build a solar oven or to express mirth at them having a rainwater tank and a flock of free-range chickens on their roof.

Now that the Rose Parade has run its course, Portland is once again pleasantly free of heavily made-up 7-year-olds, edible, tram-sized tigers and platoons of over-sexed sailors. Since this is where I realised that I've lost a crucial chunk of my Scottishness—and since my flight to Chicago doesn't leave for another few days—I decide that this is as good a place as any to start looking for my missing pieces.

I prospect in Portland's Scottish Country Shop, confused by their array of imported chocolate bars, kippers, Irish black puddings and jars of Sharwood's curry. Looking in the freezer is like peeking into the cupboards of an eccentric, elderly Scottish aunt who hasn't added to her shopping list since the 60s.

Still, it's definitely less disconcerting than peering into my parents' freezer back home in Glasgow. While, radically, I now view a freezer as a convenient place to keep a few frozen dinners, a couple of tubs of impulse-bought ice cream and a teetering skyscraper of ice trays, my parents' freezer has always carried way more weight. You might open up that ancient chest in the hopes of locating an overlooked Popsicle and instead find anything from an entire deer to a carefully packaged 18th-century Persian rug and matching cushions, deposited into the icy depths to thwart moths. My mum always makes a bit extra when she's cooking and tucks leftovers into wee plastic boxes that she then piles on top of unwieldy stacks of other wee plastic boxes to save cooking a couple of nights a week. The fact that she likes a bit of a surprise and so doesn't label the boxes means that the menu on such nights is a dangerous game of culinary roulette that could easily see carrot soup served alongside chocolate mousse or stewed pears paired with stuffed eggplant. Her subsequent slightly apologetic, but mostly highly amused expression is one of my favourite things to look at. These are among the best nights to visit—there's a delicious suspense in not knowing until the first spoonful whether the mossy green substance waiting in your bowl started life as pureed peas or gooseberry sorbet.

When I was wee, all remaining room round the carcasses and carpets was taken up by vast quantities of vegetables grown by Miss Hamilton, an elderly artist who lived four doors away in a roomy apartment that had no space for such trivialities as a freezer. Miss Hamilton considered such an item unnecessary and too unsightly for her own home, but filled half of ours for most of my childhood. She would appear most often when we were in the middle of dinner, announcing, 'Mulhollands, I am in desperate need of rhubarb' or 'I must count my cauliflowers' and then stay for half a dozen glasses of sherry and the entire evening. While she was our most regular such visitor, many unusual neighbours arrived and stayed in a similar manner. My parents' sense of hospitality was known to extend far beyond hosting generous quantities of frozen vegetables. They threw dinner and drinks parties frequently and, on nights in between, it seemed perfectly normal to have a reclusive Canadian photographer, a former Slovene presidential contender or a world-renowned harpist pop round whilst we were tucking into our stewed pears and eggplant. Cousins, school friends and even a stern Russian icon painter lived with us for months at a time. Growing up there, much like trips to the freezer, you never knew who was going to be there when you opened the door—or how well they were going to go with whatever company was already assembled. The house was often very full, but it was never dull.

Sadly, the Scottish Country Shop is not as surprisingly stocked as my parents' freezer. I examined its website before setting out. It promised, 'all manner of things Scottish,' as well as 'ghillies, Scottish accessories and other items of Scottish attire,' but apart from an impressive shortbread aisle and a generous supply of Cadbury's Curly Wurlys, I am underwhelmed. I should have been prepared: the site did also inform visitors that the store's best selling items included 'College of Piping Green Tutor Volume 1' and 'Rimmed Soup Bowls.' Those two were narrowly beaten out for top place by an 80-pack of breakfast tea. If this is what it takes to be officially Scottish, I'm in trouble. Beyond the tea I am in alien territory here. I try on a tartan golf visor, but just look even more out of place. I find a lot of music that is guilty of overusing the word 'bonnie,' but find out nothing about how to be a better Scot or any explanation of what a ghillie is. Disappointed, I stock up on chocolate, head back out and give up for the day.

It's the next morning and there's a murky sky overhead as my Wisconsinite friend Erin and I drive towards Gresham, Oregon for the annual Portland Highland Games. Erin's pretty much a Portland local at this stage, having lived in Oregon long enough to vote here and to think it's perfectly normal for people to tether miniature plastic horses to telephone poles, but not quite long enough to adopt any free range poultry.

I'm quiet this morning. I was quick to exclaim that good fortune would surely follow in the wake of the black cat that dashed across my path on the way to the car. It may still, but it wasn't such good fortune for the tiny, fat baby bird the cat then pounced upon and scoffed for breakfast. I feel somehow responsible, despite Erin's attempts to assure me that it was merely nature taking its course.

Minivans, SUVs and pick-up trucks trundle alongside as we turn onto the I84 towards The Dalles. Mashed potato clouds loom to the east, while sudden shards of sunlight light up the foothills of the Cascades ahead. I look out the window at the double decker freight train racing alongside us. A huge Stars and Stripes is painted on the yellow ochre engine, with 'We Will Deliver' proclaimed largely underneath. We keep pace with the train for a mile, then leave the highway and find ourselves on a rural road, wheat fields waving on either side. A sign welcomes us to Troutdale, where it's raining in a very Glaswegian manner. Soon, we turn off into the grounds of Mount Hood Community College, the site of today's Scottish events, and I am astounded by the number of people here. The vast car park is absolutely crammed. We trawl round in a slow caterpillar of cars in the hopes of a space and eventually find a slot in Section X. There are easily five thousand cars. Hordes of people spill out of vehicles and head purposefully to the right. We follow a trail of people in kilts, the faint strains of bagpipes and a woman with a Lion Rampant Scottish flag umbrella.

'What a lot of very white people,' says Erin, a resident of decidedly multicultural Portland, as we wait at the entry gate for our friends, Michelle and Adam.

I look around at all the white faces around me and notice how very much whiter this is than Glasgow.

The other night, Michelle and Erin were out together and texted me a succession of questions about this excursion.

'Will everyone be wearing kilts?'

There was a pause before the next text message landed.

'Even the dogs?'

Online, I found Heelan Hound dog coats and kilt-coats in 'five popular authentic Scottish tartans for the well-dressed hound' and sent Michelle and Erin the link. I was glad to see there are some classy canines that only wear the real thing, unlike those cheap trashy schnauzers in the dog park in their knock-off, faux-plaid rain attire. Michelle and Erin were delighted. Now we are all hoping to see plaid-clad hounds gallivanting about the college playing fields.

Next they wanted to know whether women wear kilts. I looked up women's kilts online and found a selection of longer, 'hostess kilt' options available. Other questions followed, but their biggest concern seemed to be about the kind of sustenance we could expect today. The Games' site indicates only that we will not be short of either shortbread or jam. There's also the possibility that there will be pots of stew on sale. From the lack of text messages back after I delivered this answer, I suspect they were unimpressed. Perhaps they'd gone off to stock up on more appealing fare while they still could.

Michelle finds us and I thank her for coming to celebrate my culture with me.

She leans forward and says confidentially, 'I've already spotted a hostess kilt.'

Once through the entrance gates we are met by a raffle ticket table. This year's prize, like last year, is a trip to Scotland. Somewhat suspiciously, the woman selling the tickets turns out to be the lucky winner from last year. I ask her where she went for her prize trip.

'All over! England, Wales...'

'Oh, lovely.' I try again, 'Where in Scotland did you go?'

'Oh, England, Wales...' She turns to sell raffle tickets to someone else and the conversation is over.

They're not too strict about what qualifies as 'Scotland' and 'Scottish' here. It seems that pretty much anything 'Celtic' goes and there are almost as many Irish items for sale as there are Scottish. In one of the college halls a stand sells English Toffee. I forgive them, however, since they're giving out free samples and have gone to the bother of stuffing the toffees into tartan tins.

We make our way to the main field and arrive as a couple of dozen assorted clan members are doing a plodding lap around the running track. They are followed by a troop of men in Civil War-era uniforms and kilts, representative of the thousands of Scots who fought on both sides of the American Civil War. Four female re-enactors in bonnets and long frocks trek subserviently in their wake. They all halt and hold a practised pose near the queue for 'Scottish Meat Pies' until the hungry herds threaten to absorb them into the pie line and they are forced to disband. The meat pie line is at least four times as long as the beer line. This makes me feel very far from home. Alerted by the ever-vigilant Michelle, I have my first sighting of a tie-dye kilt and feel the distance even more keenly.

According to historian Jenni Calder in the book *Scots in the USA*, the first 'Scotch Fair' was held in 1783 in Laurel Hill in the Cape Fear area of North Carolina. It featured all sorts of good, virtuous fun, such as wine and whisky guzzling, horseracing and betting booths. The local Presbyterian minister was much dismayed that both 'sober piety' and 'respect for law and order' were left off the programme. He really would be delighted to see what the games have been tamed down to. It's ironic that the Scots' celebrations in the US started out as drink-fuelled rambunctiousness that has now been toned down to today's well-behaved events, while Saint Patrick's Day parades first appeared on the calendar as temperance processions. Now look.

I draw the others' attention to a man silhouetted on the brow of the hill beside a fishermen's sweater booth. He is sporting a kilt, full metal visor and chain mail. A sword hangs downs his back and he clutches a blue and white golf umbrella with a leather-gloved hand. Minutes later, as Erin and Michelle are debating whether to hit the pie or the beer stand, I notice the knight standing nearby and scamper over to question him.

His eyes peek out from behind his gleaming, silver helmet and he tells me his name is Thomas. I guess he must be about 20, although it's hard to tell. He seems fairly good-humoured about my enquiries. Again, I could be wrong. After all, the only bits of the man on display are his eyes and knees. Unlike the visors I am familiar with from *Scooby Doo* and other such reliable educational resources, Sir Thomas' visor is an all-in-one number, without that bit that pivots up when the knight wants to scoff a pie, have a quick cigarette or reveal that he is actually the evil, double-crossing villain. There will be none of that kind of frivolity for this young knight. This is obviously not a man who cuts corners when it comes to standing about in fields on rainy afternoons in Oregon. There will be no easy pie eating or beer guzzling today. Well, when you've decided to stand and look enigmatic in suburban college grounds, there are sacrifices that you have to make, golf umbrellas aside.

I come up with the brilliantly insightful question, 'Do you dress like this often?' It's not my best line, but I'm not particularly used to accosting men in head armour. Luckily, the full face cover means I can't see from his expression that he thinks I'm a complete moron.

He answers politely, 'No, not often. You know, just at things like this. Highland Games. Renaissance Faires. You know.'

I don't know and am just about to ask him what renaissance faires are when the others bound up and we get distracted smirking and setting up photo opportunities. I shall have to discover my country's contribution to the mysterious world of mock medieval pageantry at a later date.

I really hadn't known the scope of Scotland's influence on America today. Never mind that approximately half of the signatories of the US Declaration of Independence were of Scottish descent. Forget that cultural forces from Donald Trump to Eminem are of Scottish blood.

The Scots have contributed so very much more than liberty, luxurious hotels and homophobic rap to this land. What would renaissance faires, dungeons and dragons conventions, cheerleading practice and high school bands do without us? Our influence has been truly great.

Nearby, around a dozen kilted contenders for the Kilted Mile race are warming up. Erin and Michelle are betting on a blond guy in his early 20s. His kilt hangs long and shapeless.

'Is he wearing a hostess kilt?' asks Michelle.

We look and think she may have hit on something. I'm about to bet on the exhibitionist with the flowing ginger, early 1980s rock drummer hair and the red, white and blue headband, when I spy a stocky man who must be in his late 60s. While the young lads are stretching and the drummer is doing extravagant star jumps at the starting line, this character is swigging pints. The runners walk in a sprightly manner to take their places. The sexagenarian lags behind the group, chugging his pint and swinging a Blackthorn walking stick. He is still strolling round the course 15 minutes after the last straggler has loped home and washed down his disappointment with a few pies and a couple of tins of English toffee.

Meanwhile, the official opening ceremony is getting underway. A kilted woman is belting out a song on stage.

'Which anthem is this?' asks Erin.

'Um...' I say assertively.

I don't know. I'm not sure that Scotland has an official anthem and wonder whether 'Flower of Scotland' or 'Scotland the Brave' might do in a pinch. I'm sure I'd recognize those two thanks to years of pub revelry after international rugby matches. Michelle, Erin and I all strain to catch some lyrics to work out which Scottish classic it might be.

Slowly, Erin asks, 'Did she just sing 'O Canada?'

We listen and it is, in fact, the Canadian national anthem.

'We didn't see that one coming,' Erin comments.

'O Canada' is swiftly followed by 'God Save The Queen' and 'The Star-Spangled Banner.' I'm relieved to recognize them, but I am a tad disappointed not to get to warble along with something Scottish.

Scottish-American Highland Games seem to have a very definite pro-monarchy/British Isles slant to them. Why British, not Scottish? Soon we get an answer.

Oregon's Honorary British Consul, Andy MacRitchie, takes to the stage and Michelle exclaims with dismay, 'Oh no, someone's already got your job!'

After sizing up this diplomatic upstart, I assure her that my plans shouldn't have to be revised too much, as I'm planning on being the ambassador to the entire country. Doubtless, this honorary chap will end up as one of my minions. The Consul gestures at the relentless drizzle and says that we're experiencing 'a wee bit of Scottish weather.' The crowd in the bleacher seats cheer.

While the Consul is speaking, our friend Adam finds us amid the hordes, arriving clutching the handwritten invite that Erin made in order to persuade him to join us for this outing. He tells us he brought it with him in case it was discovered that he has no Scottish credentials at all and needed to pass tartan security on his way in. I inspect it and am delighted to discover that under the enticing line, 'Cabers tossed here,' Erin, borrowing enthusiastically from the Games' website, has promised Adam not only 'leaping ladies' and 'the finest piping, drumming, fiddling, dancing, clan garb and other Celtic tomfoolery this side of the Orkneys,' but that 'Actual Scot Will Be On Hand.'

We inspect some of the stands around the running track.

Adam examines an array of tartan items and says, wistfully, 'I wish we had clans back in Kansas.'

Booths sell a baffling array of items. I am particularly confused by the existence of the Cloaked in Time operation. It sells, well, cloaks. Dozens of them. We watch as several people are fitted for 'traditional Scottish cloaks.' Another stand has banks of swords. Erin, Michelle and Adam turn to me with questioning looks as we pass. I assure them that we were all given swords as toddlers.

The queue for pies is as long as ever, so we head for another food tent, passing some urchins whose t-shirts declare, 'Tartan is my favourite colour.'

As I'm downing a welcome imported can of Glaswegian carbonated classic, Irn Bru, I ponder a number of pressing concerns. Why are people wearing chain mail and knights' visors with their kilts? Surely visors had been long prised off by the time Scotland's tartans wove their way into fashion? Furthermore, here in a land where the wearing of burkas is frowned upon, I'm not sure that the donning of slitty-eyed metal balaclavas is a fashion statement likely to win too many fans in Homeland Security. And what's so Scottish about plastic dragons and cloaks? I think people may have mixed up Scotland with *Harry Potter*. Most importantly, though, which t-shirt is more amusing, the one asking passers-by whether they 'Wanna Pet My Sporran?' or the one getting all attitude-y and informing its readers that 'That's Ms Celtic Bitch To You'?

I am wrestling with these questions when Erin suggests we go and check out the Border Collie demonstration. Off we canter in the entirely wrong direction and are frowned at by a security guy with 'Harbor Patrol' emblazoned on his shirt. The fact that we are over 100 miles from the ocean makes me wonder if we should trust his directions. Traipsing back across the main field, through a sea of kilt-wearing bagpipe bands and hordes in Hard Rock Café Edinburgh t-shirts, we spy a banner in the far corner declaring 'COLLIES.'

The Scottish Border Collie demo is surprisingly popular. People are clinging to a makeshift metal fence around the sheepdog pen. Around two hundred people jostle for a view of the sheep, braving the prickly perils of the poison ivy-covered hillside. Cameras flash and people cram in tighter to the fence. On the other side, the dogs sit alert and ready for action. At the point that we find ourselves, the fence is at least nine feet high. Perhaps we've underestimated the five confused and trembling Cheviot North Country lambs from Brooks, Oregon that are huddled in the corner.

The MC and shepherdess warns the surging crowds, 'If the sheep hit the fence, that means they can hit you.'

She doesn't say, 'and you'll have no-one to blame but yourself and it will serve you right,' but her tone leaves little doubt that it would give her a considerable amount of satisfaction should this happen.

'If the sheep hit the fence?' What are the collies going to be doing with these poor sheep? I picture the sheep being tossed viciously against the fence, sailing through the air, bleating.

The three-month old lambs are much larger than I expected and they look terrified. They are shepherded about the place by eight-year-old collie Vic and his relations. He follows his mistress's whistled commands to do full 360-degree turns circling the bewildered lambs, to 'lock on' one beastie and to round them all up. He has them in their pen in 30 seconds. The crowd claps politely.

Adam whoops and yells, 'Go Vic! Yeah!'

People nearby look round at Adam and cling even more tightly to the fence.

The shepherdess lets an unruly gaggle of children into the pen and sets them to the task of trying to corral the sheep into the pen. It's supposed to show us how much cleverer the dogs are, but it really just demonstrates how vindictive children can be. The four of us watch the primal joy on the brat pack's faces as they chase the frightened animals around and around. I suppose it really is just nature taking its course.

Although Adam continues to whoop and holler at various dogs' performances, we're all a bit uncomfortable watching the shivering and shuddering lambs and are relieved when the demonstration is over and it's time to head for the heavy athletics field.

The programme tells us that, 'Men in kilts—and ladies too—will show their strength in competing with the elements of the High-lands.' We wonder about these elements. Having spent a summer working in the Highlands, I suggest that the elements might be air, earth, water, heating (it can get pretty nippy up there) and criminal. Or perhaps they mean Carbon, Oxygen and Hydrogen. I'm pretty sure that last time I checked the periodic table, cabers weren't on it. Or maybe they mean the weather. Looking up at the cloudy sky, I begin to wonder if events might get cancelled and the elements will chalk up yet another a victory. Those elements have certainly been the undisputed victors on many of my Highland outings.

At the athletics field, four-dozen clan tents stretch in rows. Clan members at deserted stands look up hopefully as we pass. The most popular stand by far is Doctor Stinky's, a clan I was previously unaware of, where Scottish, and presumably authentic, dragon puppets are going a bomb.

On the field, some burly chaps are hurling long sticks with cannon ball sized weights attached to them about. We discover that these are Scottish hammers. Courtesy of some fuzzy announcements, we learn that hammer and caber tossing were originally stages of a Highland job selection process, a sort of pre-interview for the role of bodyguard to the clan chief.

Apparently, it's never too early to start throwing unwieldy branches about. In an enclosure near the MacDonalds, 'Young Highlanders' chuck about four-foot tree trunks. The urchins are rather lackadaisical about this pursuit, so we move on, in search of tree huggers with more conviction. We settle in the corner of the field where half a dozen women in mini-kilts and tank tops are wrestling womanfully with 18-foot cabers, or 'sticks' as they're referred to.

As enormous logs are turfed about a few feet away, Erin draws my attention to an ad in the programme that reads, 'More fun than Osteoporosis. WAY more fun than Alzheimer's. WAY, WAY more fun than Triple Bypass Surgery. Scottish Country Dancing. Good For Everybody.' Three penguins leap about in the picture, presumably elated at having discovered a more entertaining activity than debilitating illness. A few pages further on, an ad declares, 'Celts Beware! 1 in 3,500 Celts may have Alpha-1-Antitrypsin.' In small print below, the ad reads, 'Courtesy of the American Liver Foundation.' At least I know which part of my anatomy is likely to succumb to this Scotcentric ailment. The frolicking penguins were suspiciously quiet about this potential disturbance to dancing. The ad goes on to warn of cirrhosis of the liver, hepatitis, diabetes and/or emphysema, all courtesy of a defective gene from one or both Celtic parents.

In sombre tones Adam says, 'It's not all haggis and Irn Bru.'

We turn the pages and I am pleased to have saved my friends the price of a cup of a tea that they would have to buy in order to 'Hear a true Scottish accent at the Daughters of the British Empire Tea Tent.' On other pages, a motley array of corporate sponsors including Tenth Avenue Liquor, Oregon Hazelnut Marketing Board and Jay's Wide Shoes are thanked for their part in putting on the Games. I examine the dancing penguins' feet in case wide flippers are another trait I should be concerned about.

The programme also gives some helpful phrases for trips across the Atlantic. One is 'Awa' an bile yer heid,' translated as both 'Go away and boil your head' and as 'an expression indicating strong disagreement with an opinion, with strong undertones of dislike for the person concerned.' Useful. I'm glad that the Scottish-Americans of Greater Portland will be so well equipped and ready to befriend the locals during their trips to the Old Country. That's if they make it beyond England and Wales, of course.

One page explains the concept of caber tossing.

I read out to the others, 'From a crouching position, the athlete cradles the base of the caber in his clasped hands. Carefully adjusting his grasp as he rises, he keeps the caber balanced against his shoulder. Running to build up momentum, he plants his feet and lifts the caber so that the base rises at least 19 feet straight up in the air (longer cabers need more lift). The goal of the competitor is to get the caber to pivot or turn on its top and fall over in a straight line away from him, with its base pointing precisely to 12 o'clock.'

As we absorb this information, we watch a burly lady in a knee-length green and red kilt and fetching sleeveless top—or simmit, as we'd call it in Glasgow—slowly hoist a vast tree trunk two feet off the grass and teeter a few steps forward as she tries to keep it vertical. Her back is hunched against the caber. A wavy, brown mullet flows down her back. She breaks into a desperate run and then hurtles the log skywards. It bounces on its end and thuds to the grass.

We are all impressed.

'Ooh, definitely a 1.30,' says Michelle.

Erin comments that Scotland's athletics appear to be ones compatible with near-professional levels of beer consumption. The programme skips over this point. We look at the athletes stomping about the field in front of us. Involuntarily our gazes are drawn to substantial beer guts on the majority of contenders, both male and female.

Next, a peroxide blonde with a yellow mini kilt and distinctly sturdy legs unleashes her caber with a mighty 'heuuurgh.'

'Nice toss!' hollers Adam.

The caber sails through the air. Its base hits the grass and it falls back towards her.

'Oh, baby, it's over,' Adam laments.

And, for us, it is. We are satisfied with having learned the basics of caber tossing, so weave through the crowds milling around the clan tents and booths and spend half an hour searching for the car.

Back in downtown Portland, I slope round the corner to World Cup Coffee on Northwest Glisan Street and get talking to the guy behind the counter. He asks how my weekend is going and I tell him that we went to find my people at the Highland Games.

'Oh, yeah. I've seen them chucking about telephone poles on ESPN,' he tells me.

Why do people know about caber tossing? It seems rather obscure to be so well known. Yesterday I looked online for other unlikely sports of the world. I read about Extreme Ironing, the Unicycle Hockey World Championships and global Rock, Paper, Scissors tournaments. According to a Nebraskan newspaper column, which seems as reliable a source as any for this kind of enquiry, caber tossing is only the world's tenth most ludicrous sport. When it's got Cow Jumping and Wife Carrying to compete with, you can see why it falls so far down the list.

'What was it like?' asks the barista.

I tell him, 'It was like a rainy day in 1745. But with better raffle prizes.' I tell him about Thomas with his chain mail shirt, visor and kilt.

He is clearly embarrassed and says, 'It's the American Way.'

Before I can ask him to elaborate, he's off to serve another customer. It's the American Way to make historical fashion faux pas? To mix and match body armour and rain attire? To get engagingly enthusiastic about their heritage? I don't know. Since he's busy, I ask Google and have the option of choosing from pages entitled the American Way of Life, War, Debt, Spying, Death, Blame, Torture and Idolatry. The rest don't sound like much fun, so I choose 'Life' and am told, 'Decades of wasting energy and large-scale environmental pollution have become two main elements of the American way of life.' I skim on and the Internet tells me that the American Way of Life also 'refers to a nationalist ethos that purports to adhere to principles of "life, liberty and the pursuit of happiness." It has some connection to the concept of American exceptionalism and the American Dream.' Well, that seems about right, the pursuit of happiness bit, anyway. I'm pretty sure you wouldn't stand about a field, wearing deeply uncomfortable millinery if it didn't, at least, make you feel somewhat happier, would you? As I sip my coffee, I wonder, what is the Scottish Way?

I think about my glimpses of the knight and his visor and about the only recognizable bits of my Scotland being a few chocolate bars, the fish and chips, and the pricey Irn Bru at the Californian Scottish Shoppe tent. I'm bemused by this romantic, and enormously popular, take on everything tartan, traditional and from north of Loch Lomond. It's a strangely skewed view of my land. It's as if modern Scotland doesn't exist. If it doesn't come in tartan, wear a cloak or have variations for massed pipes, there seems to be no place for it in Scottish-America. As the Scottish Ambassador, I have more work to do than I had realised.

Where's the Scotland of today with its exhilarating bagpipe-free bands, cutting edge artists, thrilling architecture and rowdy night-life? Where's the Scotland of scintillating cities full of real, living, breathing people?

'Where's my Scotland?' I ask Adam.

'It's cloaked in time,' he tells me.

3. ADDITIONAL BADGERS:
SALEM, PORTLAND AND OREGON CITY, OREGON

Driving towards Salem, we seem to be heading straight into a rain cloud that looms forbiddingly on the horizon. This Salem, an un-witchy one, is the capital of Oregon, home to a population of 140,000, a stately university campus and dozens of imposing government buildings. It also boasts the impressive tally of no less than five prisons and the psychiatric hospital that was the setting for both the book and the film of *One Flew Over the Cuckoo's Nest*.

A few years ago I walked down Salem's Liberty Street and was stopped in my tracks by the sight of an entire shop window full of Scottish-themed Christmas ornaments. I had no idea that so many people peppered trees with plaid-clad pooches on an annual basis. Glittery Scottie dogs and a troop of tall hat-wearing pipers adorned a tinsel tree in the Kilt and Thistle shop window. In one corner Santa Mac-ed it up in a kilt. In the other he had a Scottish Saltire flag stretched across his substantial paunch. I was simultaneously delighted and horrified to find this kind of evidence of home so very far away from home.

Growing up in Glasgow, our Christmas tree—usually removed at twilight from a tree farm in an adjacent chunk of the Highlands—did not groan under the weight of Saltired Santas. There were no packs of sparkly wee dogs adorning its branches. Instead, it had a chaotic melee of decorations painstakingly made by my four siblings and me. Perhaps the most eye-catching of the tree's homemade cargo were bits of chopped up egg carton held loosely together with pipe cleaners and covered in glitter-spattered tissue paper. These creations were what my sister Ciara proudly called 'Christmas bells' and what my dad pointed out—to our horror, every time we had friends round—as 'fairies' bras.' If my mum had chosen the tree it would have been a trim six-footer, neatly tucked into the bay window of the playroom. But, like Saturday night dinners, tree-choosing was my dad's domain and every year the entire clan wrestled man-, woman- and childfully to lug a gargantuan caber of a pine in and out of the Volvo, up the steps and through the front door. Despite the room's far from meagre 16-foot head height, somehow my dad always managed to pick a tree that ended up with its top few feet bent over at a 90-degree angle along the ceiling. 'See! I told you it would fit!' he would say triumphantly to my exasperated, pine needled mother. Then we'd all pile in happily and deck the beast with box after box of un-tartan treasures, enthusiastically glued memories and Ciara's crumpled crimson stock of otherworldly underwear.

Yet, despite this discord between our notions of appropriate tree dressing, the Kilt and Thistle Shop is where I have returned in order to learn about the secrets of tartan and other Scottish sartorial statements and to see if, as I suspect, Scottish-Americans know more about such Scotticisms than I do. Erin, who spent a couple of years in Salem, is being very obliging and supporting me in my quest to attain true Scottish status this morning. I think most of the novelty of my being Scottish has worn off at this stage, but obviously not quite, for here she is. I offer to accompany her to perfect whichever clichéd skills and abilities are expected of those from her part of the world. Perhaps I should first have checked what is expected of people from Wisconsin, America's Dairyland. Not unlike Scotland, stereotypical Wisconsinite activities seem to revolve around the core activities of beer guzzling and the consumption of deep fried items, but I have a niggling suspicion that there may also be polka-dancing involved. Whatever, I owe her.

As Erin and I leave the car park, we pass a sign outside the International United Methodist Church that begs, 'Lord, Give Me the Persistence of a Weed.' I assume they didn't have enough SnapLok letters to spell out 'Lord, Give Me the Persistence of a Telemarketer.'

There is a terrible moment when we realise that the storefront is vacant. Could the search have gone to seed so soon? I display a moment's distinctly un-weedy lack of determination and am on the verge of sloping back to the car. However, we prospect a bit further and discover the Kilt and Thistle Shop has merely moved and is now downstairs at the back of the Reed Opera House shopping arcade, a quirky building from 1870, somewhat perplexingly decorated with 1930s swimwear ads. I halt at the foot of the stairs, barely able to contain my glee at the sight of so much tartan. A female mannequin models a floor-length kilt, ruffled white blouse and black velvet waistcoat. A suit of armour stands to attention by the shop's doorway in a rather forbidding manner. But what really stops me in my tracks is the row of sporrans. I squeal with amazement on spying their display case. Luckily only Erin, the knight and the mannequin can see my cartoon-like surprise. I have only ever really seen my brother Mark's faux leather Boy Scout sporran, having never paid much attention to the few other traditional Scottish man-bags that I've seen dangling over kilts at weddings I attended back home. These belt pouches are different. These sporrans are furry. These sporrans have faces.

'Do you think they're real?' I ask with astonishment.

Erin does. I am amazed anew. I continue to stare and get a wee fright on seeing the beady eyes of a muskrat look back at me. A red fox looks snappy. A badger has tassels. I'd never really thought of badgers as the kind of mammal that makes that much of an effort. I'd half expect those vampy foxes to camp it up a bit when going out on the town, but I had always pictured the badger as more of a leisurewear kind of mammal. This will teach me not to make such hasty judgments in future.

Because I didn't grow up here in this continent, amusing beasties such as raccoons and opossums still have me pointing and exclaiming with delight. I am still not 100% sure of appropriate creature encounter behaviour. I think I've got the basics of bear etiquette down—it's all in the claws, apparently—and just a couple of months ago I found out that I didn't need to be fearful of cougars and mountain lions and pumas, I can just pick one and panic, since it turns out that it's just the same crafty beast with a whole litter of aliases. A cougar over here, of course, is also a pejorative term for a predatory older lady with a penchant for admirers somewhat younger than herself. That's a whole different thing to be afraid of. Despite being at the age when I could qualify as one, I'm afraid I can't offer any advice on how best to evade their pursuit. Our pursuit. It's probably in the claws.

Soon after I moved to the Pacific Northwest, a local tabloid ran the headline, 'Rabid Skunk!' above a photo of a sketchy-looking skunk caught in the kind of bleary-eyed paparazzi-snapped pose usually reserved for the latest freefalling pop disaster and her posse as they cascade out of the emporium du jour. I don't know whether this provoked exaggerated skunk fears on my part, but on the occasions that I've been loping home at night and seen one of the wee stinkers scurrying about the streets, I've pelted off swiftly in the other direction, a look of nearly matching rabid terror in my eyes. Looking at this wee face on the other side of the glass is the closest I've ever been to one of the ominously striped critters. It's an odd experience. If you took a skunk and asked an obliging taxidermist to make you a hot water bottle cover out of it, this is pretty much what it would look like.

Once, when we were quite wee, my sister Orla and I were at a puppet-making class in Glasgow Art Galleries and somehow inadvertently went through the wrong door, finding ourselves in the gallery's taxidermy workshop. Polar bears look disconcerting inside out. These furry faces look disconcerting, too, in a different way. It seems somehow less dignified than lopping their heads off and sticking them up on the wall or stuffing them and placing them in a woodland scene. I stand for some time taking in the row of fine North American creatures, parcelled up into sporrans.

My pace slows as I register the wail of bagpipes filling the synthetically bright, subterranean-level shoppe. The emotion that the pipes provoked in Portland wanes. I am instantly sobered by their sound and have sudden doubts about my ability to complete this quest. I really don't know if I can. It doesn't seem quite such an amusing endeavour now. I had underestimated how much piping I might have to withstand in order to become a proper Scot. Pipes were designed to be heard from a distance, not up close and in surround sound. Maybe the Kilt and Thistle Shop has a stock of fetching tartan earmuffs in my clan colours.

I slink further into the shop, but before I can skulk behind the kilted mannequin, I catch the eye of the smiling woman in the off-white, cable knitted sweater behind the counter. When she hears my accent, Cheryl Duncan immediately calls through to the back and her husband William appears. They start chatting about Scottish-American social goings-on, making the assumption that I know what they are talking about, and are stopped in their tracks by my sheepish admission that I have no idea what my tartan looks like and that I actually had to call my dad on the way here to check which clan I am. Some kind of MacDonald, I knew. My dad informed me that we're MacDonnells, descendants of Somerled, Lord of the Isles, which sounds impressive until you discover that he is the world's most common known genetic ancestor after Genghis Khan.

William is a man who knows his tartans and is happy to show me my colours on an aged monitor similar to the one on which I first played *Donkey Kong* in 1982.

'The Scottish Tartans Authority are sort of the keepers of all tartans,' William says. 'They register all tartans and we use their database, which has about 5,000 tartans. Lots of things have tartan. The state of Washington has a tartan. A lot of states have tartans.'

In fact, there are more states with tartans than states without and many, many things with tartan that might be better without. For instance, there is a Princess Diana Memorial Tartan and even an officially registered Shrek tartan. The Scots took a lot from the Old Country with them when they went west to the New World; the songs and instruments they played, the music and books they loved, the language they spoke, the tartans they wore. An easily identifiable emblem of home, tartan quickly became shorthand for the romanticised land left behind. From the looks of things in the Kilt and Thistle Shop, an awful lot of Oregonians are still eager to purchase assorted samples of such plaid symbolism.

There are dozens of MacDonald tartans. We scroll through various MacDonnells. Past the russet, deep blue and heather purple of the MacDonnells of Keppoch and the black, aged fern and cloudy blue of the MacDonalds of Clanranald, today pronounced by William 'Kipp-OHHHCK' and 'Clan Ran-AAALD.' The Atlantic and a couple of generations have shunted the emphasis from the first to the final syllable. William comes to a stop with the screen showing a slew of different tartans.

'But which one is mine?' I ask, confused.

'The rules of tartan are not too specific. You can wear any of the MacDonnell tartans. You can have any number of items made up in a tartan. You can do a tartan waistcoat or vest for the gentleman who doesn't want to wear a kilt. Or we can do tartan trews, or pants, as we call them here, tartan hats. For ladies we can do skirts, shawls, capes...'

'Did you say capes?' I ask.

'Ehm, yes...' William looks suspicious.

Capes! The mere thought of a tartan cape brings joy to my heart. But I wonder do Scotswomen encounter many cape-wearing occasions? I have never felt the lack of such a garment in my wardrobe until now, but, then again, this whole tartan look is pretty new to me. I feel I should get some guidance before I invest in one. While William is attending to a customer, I make a quick call to my fashion editor friend Jason Salzenstein. Jason doesn't seem to think that my calling to question him on the subject of capes is at all unusual and is swift to dispense advice.

'In my opinion, capes are almost always a bad idea. The only exceptions would be if you're wearing a costume, if you're a giant black man who happens to be the Fashion Director for a major fashion publication, and in the rare case that you want to make a huge fashion statement, in which case you'd need to be tall, thin, and have the attitude to pull it off. This is speaking for men. For women, I think they're fab as long as the woman can pull them off and I'd also say they're more for night time wear rather than day, unless you're in Europe, in which case anything goes.'

'What if I wanted to wear a tartan cape?'

There is a surprised pause.

'Why would you want to wear a tartan cape?'

'Well, it's complicated. Just imagine I did. Can I?'

'Put down the tartan cape. Put it down.'

While William is busy wrapping up swathes of tartan at the till, I make a second call to another fashion editor friend, Pip Christmass.

'I am rather a fan of the cape,' she says. 'Not the floor-sweeping, black velvet, going-to-the-opera variety, which can look a bit gothic and sniggerworthy, but I have two short capes that basically just come down the elbow line and button up at the front. I like the cape's mini-drama.'

'How about if it was a tartan cape? Would that be maxi-drama?'

'A tartan cape?' Pip sounds startled. 'If it's for an 80s party, maybe...' She trails off, sounding far from convinced.

My fashion advisors have shot down my dreams of donning a tartan cape. I should definitely have given my dad their numbers a few years ago before he went on the shopping spree from which he returned with a dashing cloak and fedora, although he definitely has the attitude to pull it off.

I suddenly realise that something important was missing from William's list of tartan items for women. 'Do women not get to wear kilts?' I ask sharply when he returns.

'No,' says William, 'But they do get to wear longer kilted skirts.'

I frown. 'Hostess kilts.'

William nods. He adds hastily, 'Some ladies we have fitted for kilts.' He pauses. 'It's something that not everyone is happy about.' He looks around almost furtively.

The shop is deserted other than one lone browser by the bag-pipe-drenched CDs in the music section.

William lowers his voice. I lean closer to hear what revelations will follow.

He continues, 'There's been some controversy in the pipe band arena about women wearing kilts. In fact, some people think women shouldn't be in the bands at all.'

'Hmmm,' I say, while mulling over the misogynistic politics of the pipe band arena. 'So men get kilts, sporrans and pipe bands? And we get hats, skirts and capes?'

'Well,' William says slowly and diplomatically, 'If you like the look of a sporran, it's possible to use it as a purse. There are some very attractive sporrans that can be worn on the hip.'

I imagine sauntering along the streets of Salem with a decapitated skunk on a string slung fashionably over one shoulder. I will have to check that one with Pip and Jason first. I contemplate which creatures would make suitable traveling companions.

'What can be turned into a sporran?' I enquire of Cheryl.

With enthusiasm, she lists exactly which creatures can be snatched from rural idylls, nipped, tucked and made into a sporran. Badgers seem popular. As do muskrats, arctic foxes and skunks. Cheryl has a tone of regret when she tells me that she and William are unable to import arctic seal sporrans into the US from Canada. I make what I hope looks like a wee sympathetic face. I had no idea what was being gussied up into sartorial statements in my country's name. Oregon, the ninth largest US state, has the nickname of The Beaver State. However, there are no beaver sporrans on show here. They seem to have got away.

William gesticulates at the furry faces. 'These are called mask sporrans. Historically speaking, sporrans were made from the animals found by the regiments. In fact, the regiments are where a lot of

Highland apparel comes from. For instance the Black Watch Regiment wore a bit of bear fur to signify that they'd spent time in North America, and used badgers, which were plentiful in these parts, for sporrans.' He continues, 'Mask or head sporrans are a lot more formal.' William looks down at the row of glassy-eyed faces, 'and prettier.'

Pretty is not the adjective I was thinking of.

'Which are the most popular?' I ask.

'The skunk,' he points at its wee squished face under the glass, 'and the fox.' William pauses and smiles slightly as he looks down. 'It comes as this red fox and as the arctic fox.' The red fox's coat glints and the white fox's fur shines like fresh snow under the fake yellow of the shop lights. It looks pure and vulnerable.

I continue gazing at the sporrans. I have to ask. I ask William if I can see one. He removes a dashing silvery-black muskrat from the wall. I take the sleek rodent. It's the softest creature I have ever picked up. It reminds me of my granny's fox stole that my brothers and I used to terrify our sister Orla with. I pat it and its beady eyes look up at me, gleaming with reflections of the fluorescent strips above. Transformed from a happy, flea-bitten, aquatic rodent to this. This probably wasn't mentioned to young muskrats as a potential career option. I wonder briefly whether there are sporran farms? I once knew a guy who was the reluctant heir to an Alberta chinchilla farm. I should suggest it to him.

I can't see how I'm supposed to open it. There seems only one way. I don't fancy putting my hand in its mouth.

'Do you lift up its, um, head to, um...?'

William nods. I lift up the muskrat's snout gingerly and peer in. It's an unnatural angle. Like its neck is broken. I feel like apologising.

What kind of man thinks it's attractive to wear a reconstituted rat or badger over his bits?

'It's one of the few things in a man's wardrobe that he can have as an accessory,' says William, bringing my attention back to the sporran in my hand.

'The badger is a similar size to the muskrat,' William tells me. 'They use the same frame. The Argyle and Sutherland Regiment has a badger head with six tassels. It's quite an ornate piece of gear. They're quite pretty.'

Once again, I re-evaluate the uses of the badger as a style statement. I glance down and pick up a catalogue with yet more sporrans pictured inside. The leaflet lists 'Exotic Fish Leather Sporrans.'

'Fish leather?' I ask dubiously.

William takes the muskrat from me and places it carefully back up on the wall.

He points at some un-furry sporrans in the next display case and tells me, 'These ones are made with fish leather. It's an extremely colourful leather that takes pigment very well,' he informs me. 'It comes in red, green and blue.'

'But what's fishy about it? Is it really made from fish?'

It seems it is. Is there no creature we Scots won't gussy up and pair with a kilt? A leaflet on 'sea leather wear' explains the 30-day 'chemical and mechanical process' fish skin goes through before a 'flesher' removes 'any remaining yuck.' It really says this. 'Yuck' is apparently an official fish tanning term. Despite having spent a summer working in a fishing village in the Highlands, I was not aware of this technical term. It also tells me that fish leather is the second strongest leather known to man.

'Three strip of certain fish,' the leaflet states confidently, though somewhat ungrammatically, 'half inches wide, braided together, can pull automobile.'

Before setting out for Salem, I regaled Erin with highlights from the Kilt and Thistle Shop's two separate websites, Kilts.com and FeatherBonnets.com. Who wears feather bonnets? Who even says 'feather bonnets?' Back home, black bonnets with what looked like pheasant feathers tucked jauntily in their brims were worn for a short-lived and much-mocked stint by Ryanair's surly check-in staff at Scotland's Prestwick Airport. I am curious as to who might don such headgear now. Looking at the Duncans, impeccably dressed in their kilts and matching fisherman's sweaters, these are definitely the people to explain the intricacies of traditional Scottish attire and complete my knowledge of my country's clothing. I foolishly mention that I feel underdressed.

Within seconds the mannequin in the window is absent from her post and it's me who is wearing the floor-length kilt, puffy white blouse and tight, black velvet waistcoat. They fit me remarkably well. Disconcertingly well. In fact, a middle-aged customer who hadn't noticed my existence until now starts giving me the eye. It is as if I have suddenly stepped onto his tartan radar.

My eyes light up when I see William approach with what looks like a foot high, black feathery nest.

'I figured you'd want to try this on,' he says with a smile. 'It's a feather bonnet. It's made of ostrich feathers. This was the Highland military helmet for almost 100 years. This is what they actually wore into battle.'

Did they think they'd frighten their enemies away by wearing nests on their heads? By modelling feather boa beehive toupees? I try to cram the scary hat on. I get a straggle of ribbons in my eyes.

William corrects me, 'Ribbons in the back. Tails on the side.'

He adjusts my black streamers and surveys his handiwork. I have the pose of an immature seal trying to pull off its very first nose-ball balancing act at the marine park in-crowd initiation ceremony. I try very hard not to laugh. I fail.

'Not very scary,' decides William. 'But with these, six-foot fellas became seven feet tall and very ominous.'

It's more comfortable than you'd think, and as long as I manage to keep the posture my mum wishes I'd maintain in public, my ominous millinery should be fairly safe from cascading I'm flouncing about the store at a brisk martial pace. I suspect that William thinks I'm enjoying myself too much, either because I'm cackling like a demented goose or because I haven't stopped grinning since I tucked a fluffy two-foot sheep under my arm to complete the look.

William cuts in, 'Wait till you march in it and it fills up with water. They really get heavy.'

He says this with the voice of experience. I make a note not to do any marching. Flouncing will have to suffice.

William talks about changing attitudes. He tells me that Scots in Scotland have finally started to realise the importance of our heritage, with it bringing in so much tourism, and now we are grateful to Scottish-America. He sounds slightly hurt that this feeling has been unrequited for so long, slightly defensive as he tells me how good Scottish-America is for Scotland. His love of Scotland feels something of a fragile, hopeful love.

He describes himself as a 'Scotophile.' I am delighted! I had never considered the word! Despite having spent years in Canada, a country where 'Anglophile' and 'Francophile' are constantly bandied about, I never heard or imagined that anyone might say 'Scotophile.' William also says 'The Old Country,' and means it. I honestly had no idea that people actually used the expression.

William continues showing me around the store. He pauses at a solid dark blue kilt with a St Andrew's cross on it. It seems to be the only non-tartan kilt in the store.

'It's the kilt of the Scottish Football Association. Oddly enough,' says William, 'They just don't sell.' He pauses. 'It comes with a white leather sporran.'

'Is the sporran shaped like a soccer ball?' I ask.

William seems surprised, 'Well, no, we try not to go too gimmicky.'

My hat slips sideways as I grip the sheep.

Not going too gimmicky isn't an issue when it comes to the Kilt and Thistle Shop's kids' clothes selection. I look with glee at all these wee outfits. I'd never glance at them if I still lived in Scotland, but now am having trouble restraining myself from snapping them up. The only item of attire I've ever bought my nephew Wee Joe was a lime green, undulating Nessie hat, which he, quite reasonably, refused to wear. Perhaps I would have more luck had I opted for one of William's 'Plaid to the Bone' t-shirts.

He gestures at a mannequin wearing a great swathe of plaid that forms a kilt and a complicated over-the-shoulder, curtain-like section. 'The old Great Kilt, styled after the movie *Braveheart*,' says William. 'It takes a little bit of work to make it happen.'

I would have thought that it should have been the other way round and outfits in *Braveheart* should have been styled after the historic kilt, but apparently history takes the back seat.

There's a small 'British foods' section with some token products such as Lee's Coconut Ice and Bassett's Allsorts. A leaflet with food products offers boxes of 'Violent Crumble,' which I find very tempting; the unintended 'n' making it a far tougher treat to turn down.

'We have quite a few products from the UK,' says William. 'It's most satisfying when a little old lady comes in and finds a candy or food she hasn't had for 20 years.'

But I've been away 20 years and I don't see any foods I associate with home. Also, I don't rank as a 'little old lady' just yet. For starters, I'm far too tall. I suggest more current Scottish products, perhaps some Wham bars or, Scotland's favourites, Tunnock's Teacakes. But modern Scotland is not what sells here and William doesn't have much interest in Scottish treats from more recent decades.

One delicacy we can agree on, however, is tablet. Tablet is one of the things I miss the most about Scotland.

'How do you explain the taste of tablet?' asks William. He tries, but he does not make it sound tasty. My description wouldn't win it many fans either.

Falling somewhere between solid butterscotch sauce and a sugar lobotomy, tablet is hard to describe and even harder to make. People's grannies make tablet. I don't think anyone under the age of 60 is even allowed to buy tablet-making amounts of butter, sugar and sweetened condensed milk. While people's grannies' tablet is the best tablet, there are a few Scottish confectionery companies who rustle up decent batches of fudge's sugarier sibling. I bring it back with me, eking out every last crumb, after every trip home. William and Cheryl apologise for being out of this denture-destroying delight. It seems there is a tablet drought in Oregon.

'A sad problem,' says Cheryl.

William explains that there are only three other people in the Greater Portland area who 'appreciate' tablet.

'I've been here about fifty per cent of the last month,' I say, 'So that takes it up to three and a half.'

William seems pleased by my sum. For a brief moment I feel I am part of an exclusive club. A club, albeit, populated entirely by people destined to be plagued by high dental bills for life.

An urn of hot water and tea bags wait by the door. These people really are Scottish, I think happily as I help myself to a nice cup of Scottish Breakfast Tea. Perhaps the love of tea is passed down genetically through generations. Looking for somewhere to rest my mug, I spy coasters with faded, 1960s-ish colours, pictures of places in Scotland. The coasters feature drab-looking scenes from places so random that I have no idea where most of them are. The only two I've even heard of are Stornoway and Largs. Are these left over from a set of coasters representing every town in Scotland or did someone specifically choose these spots? I try to find a connection. And fail.

Largs looks rainy and miserable in coaster form, just like I remember it from school trips. It is missing, however, the lights of Largs' draughty puggies—the Scots word for arcade games (and, oddly enough, for monkeys and ATM bank machines). The coaster also lacks any reference to Nardini's marshmallow ice cream, a marvel of gelato and the only reason West of Scotland primary school teachers are able to coerce herds of unruly under-12s on buses there in the first place. But this dreich, puggy-free Largs coaster is the first sign I've seen here that Scotland doesn't start somewhere north of Loch Lomond and east of Falkirk. This coaster is the first sign that Southwestern Scotland exists. I'm curious about Scottish-America's concentration on the Highlands and Edinburgh. By the time I've toured the entire store, I find myself feeling a little hurt, a little defensive on my hometown's behalf. Where is Glasgow? Was Scotland's biggest city not part of the Old Country? The book *Scots in the USA* recounts, '... in the US, a Scotland survives that Scots may not recognize, but which has a powerful reality for those who subscribe to its blend of heightened images.' It is strange to come face to face with this—my boisterous hometown wiped off the map.

Erin unfolds a tea towel map of Scotland on which Glasgow is marked by a tiny grey dot and mostly obscure by the words 'The Highlands,' and manages to show mild interest when I point out the Outer Hebrides where my MacDonnell ancestors strutted about and the tiny three-by-one-mile dot of the island of Eriskay where we once spent a month as kids.

Post-tea towel-examination, I ask William where he likes best in Scotland and am gobsmacked by his answer.

'I've never been to Scotland.'

I am stopped short. How can he never have been to Scotland? This is the most Scotland-obsessed man I have ever met. Or is this the most Scottish-heritage-obsessed man I have ever met? For the first time it strikes me that this is a different thing. The bagpipe CD that William has just put on drones away in the background as I look at him, astounded. There's an awful lot more than a syllabic shunt at play here.

'Oddly enough,' William tells me, 'And this was universal on both sides of my family, nobody ever wanted to go back. Both my parents were of Scottish heritage. They were born here, their parents were immigrants.'

He sees me looking baffled and hurries on, 'When my grandfather was in his 70s, my father offered to fly him back and said, 'You haven't seen your brother in 60 years.' They got separated when they were young. And my grandfather's response in typical Scottish dour manner was, 'What would we talk about?' So nobody's ever gone back. Even my dad looks at me and says, 'Why do you do this?' I think we're emblematic of what's going on in the United States at the moment—there's a real renaissance in wanting to know your genealogy and your background and who you are and where you came from.'

William can tell that I've got a Glaswegian accent, but he has never walked down Sauchiehall Street. He can tell me exactly which heather-coated hills and glens my people traipsed about in the Hebrides, but he's never set foot there. He doesn't know how springy the heather is underfoot, how the light comes up over the Minch or the misery of the midging hours. I am flummoxed by this Scottish-American who has made his background into his foreground—and made such an excellent business of it. William knows where his people came from, but seems entirely content to leave it as a one-way trip. He is content to live in Scottish-America.

To cover my astonishment, I ask William to name some famous Scots.

He reels off, 'Sir William Wallace, Robert Burns and Sean Connery. My son's named after Sean Connery,' he says proudly.

'How about Scotswomen?' I probe.

'Ehm, the Royal Family?' I tell him I can't accept that as a blanket answer, but would have made an exception for the Queen Mother who spent much of her childhood at her family home, Glamis Castle in Angus, and for Princess Margaret, who was born there. I would also have accepted Mary Queen of Scots, Old Hollywood star Deborah Kerr, actor Kelly MacDonald, singers Annie Lennox, KT Tunstall, Emeli Sandé, Lulu or Sheena Easton, film director Lynne Ramsay or writer JK Rowling, since she has long adopted Edinburgh as her hometown.

I quiz William to see whether he can name any Scottish music that does not feature a bagpipe.

He thinks for a while, then exclaims, 'The Bay City Rollers and Glass Tiger—their Scottishness got promoted.'

Then he is stumped.

William and Cheryl tell me with regret that the St Andrew's Society dinner is sold out that night. I'm quite relieved—I've had my fill of pipes and tartan for the day. We leave the store, walking past the tea towels with sheep-punctuated maps of my homeland, past the

CDs of tartan-clad lads superimposed onto the backdrop of Eilean Donan Castle, past the pinched faces of fox and muskrat gentleman's accessories, the armour and the sweet tastes of home. Erin and I head off down Liberty Street and on to South Salem's Hacienda Real restaurant. The lights are bright, the Mexican folk art shocking pink and yellow, people all around are speaking Spanish. Tucking into spicy Enchiladas Vallarta, I feel much more at home.

I muse on my theory that Scottish-Americans know more about Scotland than me. It certainly seems they are more expert on the Old Country.

Erin grins, 'But, no matter how much more they know, at the end of the day, you're the one walking out of the shop with the Scottish accent.'

Here I am trotting about feeling like a mere 86% Scot, a know-nothing excuse for a Scot, yet here, among these people to whom Scottish heritage and culture is a way of life, there is no doubt in their minds that I am 100% Scottish. In the rock, paper, scissors game of nationality, accent wins. I feel pleased with our excursion and I feel charmed by the Duncans' devotion to all things Scottish. I may come from the New Country, but it's nice to pay a wee visit to a shrine to the old one.

The next day at the Fresh Pot coffeehouse in Portland, I examine the Kilt and Thistle's website. Under a video of Darth Vader playing the bagpipes, comments such as 'Keep on piping, bro!' and 'I love sporrans, too, hu-rah!' appear. Another exclaims, 'I wish more guys weren't too scared to rock the plaid, it's near impossible to find a hot kilted guy.' Such are the hardships Scotophiles face in Oregon. There are also comments from the Brotherhood of the Kilt and from 'The Scottish *Holigans* Society.' Up top it states, 'Kilt and Thistle rocking some kilts.' My favourite comment reads, 'ah, i love you kilt and thistle with your tartan bounty and rich heritage!' Tartan bounty, hu-rah!

I delve into the 'kilted community' on website X Marks the Scot where members have taglines that include 'Real Admins Wear Kilts,'

'Kilted Gentleman of Tasmania (5 years full time kilted)' and 'Chinese Blood, Kilted Heart. One United.' From the laments of these kilted gentlemen, it appears to be almost as hard to find the perfect alligator sporran, as it is to find a hot kilted guy. But I am distracted from such woes. I keep thinking about those sporran faces. I surreptitiously take out a leaflet I picked up at the Kilt and Thistle and hope that no one sitting either side of me is an animal rights activist. Opening it up, rows of furry wee faces stare glassily at me. Some look fierce. Some look miserable.

Is there any line drawn regarding the kinds of creatures that can be origamied up into sporrans? I remember Mrs Duncan's very definite tone of regret that they can't import arctic seal sporrans from Canada. Unlike its neighbour to the north, the US draws the line at the sporranisation of arctic seals. They don't, however, draw any lines when it comes to taste. I am astounded at the sight of dyed green skunk sporrans and mini-kilts for cans or bottles on the Internet. Women may not get to wear official kilts but your can of Budweiser or bottle of Syrah can. I have a lot to learn. I follow the online sporran trail to Western Florida and Craigie Sporrans of Punta Gorda.

On their website, I survey coyote, Icelandic sheep, Tibetan lamb and 'Angora Goat Ultimate' sporrans. Even after yesterday's sights, my eyes still widen at the snarling bobcat head options. A raccoon 'with open mouth' looks disconcertingly similar to the enormous beastie I tripped over as it was feasting on an aging pumpkin in my yard recently.

Another sporran store offers 'slings,' perfect, they insist, for 'eliminating sporran belts or chains,' for when you want to wear your sporran on one side and for when you need to put a stop to 'pooching,' which turns out to be the term for when a 'sporran hides on the south side of your belly'—something that surely would otherwise decrease the hotness of many a kilted guy.

A couple shuffles into seats to my left as I load yet another sporranerie's wares.

'The last weeks, I've just been decompressing,' she says as she sits down.

'I've been going to sleep with the sun,' answers her enthusiastically dreadlocked companion, nodding understandingly.

I try to angle my screen so they can't see the ranks of massacred woodland creatures that line my laptop screen. I glance at the page that has just downloaded. To my simultaneous delight and consternation, I realise that those accordioned alligators are in fact alligator head sporrans. Complete with teeth. I am speechless, which is just as well, considering the people sitting immediately beside me. Who wants the noggin of an eleven-foot-long swamp predator to keep their car keys in? This takes tartan bounty to, well, a new low. Do people hunt their own and have 'em sporraned up as a sort of Scottish-American take on hunting trophies? I may have to call up the Craigies, put on my best Sarah Palin accent and enquire.

Now the two alongside are talking about mutual friends called Space Monkey and Muse.

'Monkey was evicted the same day as she lost her job. Her boss called her a vampire.'

The guy with the dreadlocks whistles. 'I'm not sure about her energy.'

I glance surreptitiously at the purple and silver clad woman to my left and see her nod her knotty head knowingly, 'Yeah, her energy is just tarnished.'

I put 'Scotland sporran maker' into the search box and find some Scots quietly rustling up examples of tartan taxidermy in Scotland. One has a badger full mask sporran on his site, complete with front feet. It looks like it's giving itself a wee frightened hug. It looks small and meek. I'd like to give it a hug myself. Elsewhere, I find a disconcerting nest of three mink heads that reminds me of the stuffed, two-headed lamb at the Drover's Inn in Inverarnan on Loch Lomond, plus a roadkill-esque muskrat and a couple of squinty-eyed grey foxes. I learn that the silver edge bits on a sporran are called 'cantles.'

Back on the Craigie website, I see that as well as sporrans made from the heads of swamp-dwelling carnivores, the Craigie people in Florida have a lot of badger options. They have two pages of them, the second entitled 'Additional Badgers,' which, for some reason I find terribly amusing. I'm not sure why I find this superfluity of den-dwelling mammals so entertaining, but I've found various Floridian things funny recently. Only last month I was reporting from down there and found myself stuck on a minibus down the Florida Keys with five hung-over drag queens and an off duty conch shell. That was pretty amusing too. Now I'm smirking and getting looks like I'm the weirdo from Space Monkey and Muse's companions.

I leave Fresh Pot and go out onto Hawthorne Boulevard, where a sausage dog lollops by, wearing a fetching Royal Stuart tartan scarf. Suddenly I see tartan everywhere. I screech to a halt beside a window full of yet more tartan attire. It's crammed full of garments for those wanting to perfect the club wear/fetish wear crossover look. My gaze falls on some mini-kilts. I am going to need some tartan attire if I'm going to fit in this world, I reason, and the traditional floor-length options are not really me, despite what the customers of the Kilt and Thistle might think.

I duck in and find myself amid racks of tartan mini-skirts with more safety pins than seem strictly necessary. I'm quite relieved when I see they're only available in small and miniscule sizes. I am neither. Feeling almost as out of place here as I did in the world of hostess kilts and velour vests and feeling that I now have to try something on in order to pretend I'm entirely comfortable in this environment, I scoop up a couple of random items with tartan bits and find the changing rooms. As I attempt to work out where all the zips and catches go, I wonder if Arthur Herman's book *How the Scots Invented the Modern World* mentions our contributions to fetish fashion. I'm frowning at my reflection in the mirror when I hear rustles and thumps from the cubicle next door.

'Well?'

'I love it!'

'But can you sit down?' There is a pause. Then a lot of squeaking. 'Maybe I could just stand all night?' comes the dubious answer.

I struggle out of the tight tartan-adorned shirt that I had hoped would reflect my rich heritage, narrowly avoiding stabbing myself with its thistly plethora of pins.

On the bus back downtown, two hippie teens who have inked dinosaurs over all available limbs belt out an operatic version of 'The Lion Sleeps Tonight.' They both wear hats that curl around unruly mops of hair like snail shells, and shorts that cascade over loose leggings. The bus passengers momentarily transfer their attention from their belligerent duet to a guy who gets on the bus wearing lime green, frantically patterned three-quarter length pants, teased 1980s hair and clown shoes. It's like the bus that fashion forgot. I could have got away with wearing pretty much anything from the fetish shop, although I might have had to stand for the duration of the journey.

It's a few hours later and Erin and I coast along a high bank above the Willamette River. We spot a whitewashed two-storey building ahead. Erin parks alongside mud-spattered, two-tone pick-up trucks with wheel flaps that ask us to 'Keep Oregon Green.'

The Highland Stillhouse in Oregon City—a former mill town, founded in 1829 by a Scot called John McLoughlin—is the perfect pub. Downstairs is a warm bar with low, wood-beamed ceilings. Upstairs, a cosy fireplace glows and locals mingle over pints of Twisted Thistle and Kelpie Seaweed Ale. A four-page-long whisky menu lists over 200 whiskies sourced from Speyside to Japan. Outside on the patio, a cannon sits, seemingly poised to fire out over the dying, century-old paper mill and Willamette Falls in the gorge below.

A jovial bearded man in his 50s is working the tables like a master socialiser. It turns out to be Mick Secor, our host and a local cardiologist. This latter occupation comes as something of a surprise after glancing at a bar food menu featuring many of the foods I grew up on, including authentic Scottish delicacies such as battered and deep fried Scotch eggs.

Mick proudly shows us features of the pub; blue and white stained glass panels with St Andrew's crosses on them, the mahogany bar made out of old four poster beds from Sheffield, rusting, lethal-looking farm implements hung on walls.

'They're peat shovels,' Mick explains. 'We brought them back on the plane. That was tricky to explain at customs.'

The Stillhouse feels like a suitably historic pub for a historic town, but this olde pub that could have been transported from the Highlands only opened in 2006. Mick and his wife Tammy have no Scottish heritage, yet they've got this place just right. It feels like the Highlands I spent my summers in. Okay, I'm drinking Yakima Chardonnay from Washington State, but otherwise I could be in a really great bar in Oban or somewhere along the brim of Loch Lomond.

At a photo of whisky barrels that are aging for him and Tammy on the island of Islay, Mick stops and says affectionately, 'These are our girls.'

He and Tammy have been going to Scotland every year for almost 20 years. Their enthusiasm for Scotland affects my heart in a much better way than those Scotch eggs.

Mick presents us with Highland Stillhouse t-shirts, adorned with black Scottie dogs.

'Just because you're Scottish,' he says as he hands them over.

Being Scottish is great! After a free t-shirt and a few encounters with Mick and Tammy's older 'girls,' being born Scottish is really beginning to seem like a winning hand in the lottery of nations. I enthuse about how magnificent it is to be Scottish. Erin, tonight's designated driver, rolls her eyes.

Driving north up the War Veterans Memorial Freeway, we get a flat tyre. We pull off the freeway and into a parking lot. An unsmiling man in overalls comes over to survey the damage.

'If you'd been two guys I would have left you to it,' he says gruffly.

He helps get the spare out and while Erin slaves over the jack, he tells me about his time in the Navy and his life in Alaska and Colorado. Portland has become way too liberal for his liking.

'I've been here 16 years, but it's got out of hand,' he says. 'All these gays, these East Coast lefties. I don't like it, but I'm stuck here now.' He pauses. 'I like the Scots, though. Scotland is the one place I have always wanted to go. I know I'd like Scotland.'

I ask him why.

'I've never met a Scottish person I didn't like.'

'There's a lot for me to live up to then,' I joke.

'Every Scottish person I've ever met,' he declares, fixing me with a steely stare, 'I have liked.'

'Oh well, I'll have to try to live up to...'

'As I said,' he interrupts with a stern tone, 'I have never met a Scottish person I didn't like.'

I was already included.

'How do you do that?' Erin asks as we trundle over the struts of the Steel Bridge and back into downtown Portland.

'How do I do what?'

'It always comes back to how everyone loves the Scots.'

I tell her, 'Well, it's an irresistible combination: our "romantic Highland past", our distinctive culinary repertoire and our ability to make a fashion statement out of a decapitated badger. How could anyone not love that?'

4. THE SCOTTISH WAY:
CHICAGO, ILLINOIS

Lights flicker on and off as the train hurtles away from Chicago O'Hare Airport. Then we're out of the tunnel. Bright blue cloudless sky stretches overhead. The carriage quickly fills with people wearing t-shirts that declare 'Cubs,' 'Go Cubs!' and, on one guy in the corner, 'Cubs Suck.'

An hour later, I'm in a Cuban place in Bucktown, suffering menu indecision. Several dinner options have comments printed after their names. I'm torn between Havana-stuffed crab (fabulous), Sanibel Island octopus (spectacular) and Red Snapper Bahia-style (spicy and outstanding!) 'Spicy and outstanding!' is hard to pass up. Lights flash maniacally around the windows and over-the-top big cat prints adorn all non-transparent surfaces, from the chair seats to the heating vent pipes above. I am not at all surprised when my drink comes adorned with a bouquet of cherries and an accordion of orange slices.

When I walked in, the owner was surprised I didn't want to sit outside.

'But it's hot out!' I pleaded weakly.

It's late September, the time of year when back home in Glasgow I'd be fishing out the coats and thinking of padding up for winter. Here it's still hot and sticky at 7 pm.

The café is bold, bright, loud and cheerfully trashy. It paints Cuba as spicy and outstanding and makes me want to go there to experience such colour and chaos. I think back to how Scotland is portrayed by its bars and restaurants on this side of the Atlantic. Judging the

country by a swift pint stop a few days ago, Portland's Rose and Thistle pub—run by a Glaswegian who left in the 70s, Scotland is dimly
lit and surly. But if you go by Oregon City's Highland Stillhouse, it's
lively, welcoming and like the best Highland holiday you ever had.
The owners' Scotlands stand revealed.

While I wrestle with the profusion of cherries that bobs between
me and my drink, I think about the fact that I still don't know what the
official Scottish Way is. But I've found someone who does—someone
who can initiate me into the secrets of my nation's guiding ethos.
Gus Noble, from Duns in the Scottish Borders, is a former diplomat,
a part-time member of a 'rock and roll band' and the president of
the Illinois St Andrew's Society. He is also president of Chicago's
Scottish Home for the Elderly, the world's only retirement home for
Scots—other than the ones in Scotland, I have to assume. According to the website for the Scottish Home, the institution is run 'the
Scottish Way.' So, if anyone knows the Way, it's Gus. I'm expecting
insight, knowledge, revelation. I'm expecting a lot from the tartan
zenmaster if he returns my call.

As I wait for my superlative Red Snapper, I delve into the new edi-
tion of *The Scottish Banner*, the 'world's largest international Scottish
paper.' I love that the random news items page is called 'Scot Pourri.'
There is a sparsely populated 'Lights... Cameras... Kilts' section and
'This Month in Scottish History,' which seems rather partial to royal
murders, beheadings, executions and deaths. *The Banner* has a few
vital pieces of information about Scotland that I wasn't aware of,
including the facts that, 'If you unravelled Scotland's coastline it
would stretch from Edinburgh to Timbuktu and back again,' that there
are 857 offshore islands and that the most remote pub in Britain is
St Kilda's Puff Inn. There are photos of people who have FSA Scot
and GTS after their names—Fellows of the Society of Antiquaries of
Scotland and Guild of Tartan Scholars. The paper also informs me
that the most popular names for children born in Scotland today
are Sophie, Emma and Ellie, Jack, Lewis and Callum, and reports the
death of Scotland's and Britain's oldest person.

Annie Knight, who died at 111, attributed her long life to eating porridge every morning. This potentially vital ingredient of longevity seems un-fabulous, un-spectacular and unlikely to inspire anyone to decide to visit Scotland. In addition to her diligent porridge consumption, Annie Knight never drank or smoked, adds *The Banner*. I frown at my cherry-obscured rum. I am reading an article called 'Feel the Need for (Harris) Tweed' when a not especially outstanding snapper arrives. I pick my way through the fish as I read ads for the dance spectacle *Scotland the Brave* and for Mid Atlantic Scottish Deerhounds, 'the Royal Dogs of Scotland.' More ads offer Scottish joke books with categories that include 'Scotsmen Scotswomen,' 'Kilts and Bagpipes and Stuff' and 'Marriage.' A Highland Bagpipe Clock that plays tunes on the hour, including 'Scotland the Brave,' 'Highland Laddie' and the 'Skye Boat Song,' is tempting.

The next day the phone rings in the hotel room. It's Gus and he's happy to pick me up the following morning and drive me out to the Scottish Home, which is also the site of the world's only Scottish-American Hall of Fame and the only museum dedicated to Scottish-American culture.

By the coffee machine in the restaurant downstairs, I talk to a Hair Designer from Vegas. His hair rises in a four-inch-high, determinedly chestnut pompadour and he is wearing an inadvisably tight, sequin-studded sweatshirt. The Hair Designer is late 50s-ish and portly.

He asks where I'm from and then tells me, in a confidential tone, 'I've done a lot of hair for both British and Scottish people.'

Possibly the swiftest way anyone can incense a Scot, other than shouting 'Freedom!' or quoting any other part of *Braveheart* at us, is by using 'British' when meaning 'English' or by saying 'English' when meaning 'British.' Great Britain is an island. A big island. The ninth biggest island in the world, in fact. This island has a lot of sheep on it, many of the world's best Indian restaurants and staggering numbers of teen binge drinkers. Scotland, home of many of those sheep, an impressive proportion of the Indian restaurants and gallons of those teen binge drinkers, is on that island. So is Wales. So is England. Geographically speaking, Scotland plus England plus Wales equals Great Britain. Politically speaking, when 'Britain' is used as shorthand for the United Kingdom, Northern Ireland is added to the sum of Britain's parts. I'm thinking of printing out a wee card that explains this calculation and carrying it alongside my allergy card. Until then, I will have to make do with scowling at Nevadan hair designers, several *Daily Telegraph* journalists and some deliberately provocative Irish cousins.

Well, at least, I reason, as my frown begins to recede, our hairdos are covered from both national angles and I need not fear that my countrypeople will be roaming the streets of Vegas with unruly locks. I feel myself calming and feeling more generous towards my fellow guest.

'Oh, hey, Scotland…' calls the Hair Designer as he leaves the breakfast room.

I look at him exquiringly.

'Freedom!' he bellows, his paunch twinkling under the orange hotel lights.

Dominic, a Filipino-American in Chicago for business, tells me at the buffet about how his people congregate in communities in the US and asks why the Scots don't do this.

Why don't we? Is it the Scottish Way to skulk off alone? To get absorbed into a new country? It seems we did congregate back when the first significant hordes of us set off in this direction back in the 1650s. But by now, descendants of early Scottish-Americans are well absorbed. Perhaps our more modern-day departures feel less permanent—home doesn't feel quite so far away—so we have less need to cluster together in nationalistic clumps? The US Census states that Lonaconing in Maryland is the US city with the highest percentage of Scottish ancestry. But there are different, far more precise criteria that can be used to locate concentrations of Scotland-born Scots. Based on my studies of how swiftly supplies of Irn Bru, black pudding and Tunnock's Teacakes dwindle, I can tell you that San Francisco, New York, Toronto and Vancouver stand out as top North American hotspots for collections of more recently arrived Scots or, at least, for collections of well-fed Scots.

Personally, other than the difficulties involved in procuring black pudding, I've quite liked being the only kelpie on the block for most of my two decades away from Scotland. The novelty of being the lone Scot has definitely won me many free drinks, a higher share of accent attention and the opportunity to answer questions about my homeland without anyone pointing out that I just reinvented various crucial aspects of Scottish history. I fear the flow of complimentary beverages might ebb and the corrections might flow if there was a whole posse of Scots present.

Dominic is looking at me expectantly. Once again, I have to answer for my people.

'We did congregate in the beginning, but the neighbours complained about the noise of all those bagpipes.'

'I was not aware of that,' Dominic says with interest and I feel a small pang of guilt as I imagine this report spreading throughout the close-knit Filipino community of Illinois.

I have a whole day before me to get excited about my visit to the Scottish Home, so I head downtown. Chicago is a city where people on the street catch your eye and smile. As on all previous visits, I love the spacious grandeur and elegance of the city. I am as awestruck as ever by Michigan Avenue's imposing skyscrapers.

Along the brim of Lake Michigan, a seemingly infinite number of security guards patrol on Segway motorised scooters. Perhaps it just looks like they're omnipresent because of all the reflective surfaces around Millennium Park. Whatever angle I look at the gleaming mirrored 'Cloud Gate' sculpture, or 'The Bean,' as it's known locally, one of them zips into view. I walk off in the direction of the lake, past a dozen cheerleaders in blue tracksuits who are practising a routine on the grass.

'Pump, pump it up! We got to pump, pump, pump, pump, pump, pump, pump it up,' they bark, punching the air with upbeat pompoms. Why or what they need to pump up is unclear, but I enjoy their inflated enthusiasm and grin at several security guards as they zip past.

It's fantastically hot, without a cloud in the sky. With The Bean, the tangled steel tentacles of Frank Gehry's amphitheatre and the slithering silver of the BP Bridge, everything is reflective and the heat feels like it is amplified.

'Hot!' I protest eloquently to a succession of zipping patrol people as I trek south along the lake to visit the Shedd Aquarium, looking for fish from my part of the world.

The first aquarium I ever visited was Mallaig's Marine World in the West Highlands. Marine World had had most of its fish donated by local fishermen and boasted approximately the same décor and fish-meets-petrol odour as the twin rigger prawn trawlers that had landed aquarium specimens. I remember the aquarium had turbots, limpets and a handy printout with translations of all tank and pool inhabitants' names in Italian. Although I spent the whole summer in the fishing port, I never met a single Italian tourist. To this day I can still point out rombo chiodato and patella. Marine World was pretty exciting when you'd never seen an aquarium before. The Shedd is on an entirely different scale.

I am distracted from my recollections of Italian ichthyology by a scuba diver feeding a rescued turtle with a 'buoyancy problem,' one of 32,600 creatures that live in the Shedd's swishy digs. The diver is speaking through a mike while swimming, informing a rapt audience of fascinating facts about her charges.

'Hchhhh... rescued... chhhhh.... speedboat. Buoyan-chhhh problem,' she informs us as she flippers in slow motion through cables and excited amphibians.

We all turn to look at the hapless turtle. She does indeed have a noticeable buoyancy problem. As she swims happily about the circular tank, head-butting the diver in an effort to speed up the feeding process, her back end is a good foot closer to the surface than her voracious wee mouth. I am too entertained by the turtle to seek out the fish of my homeland and remain glued to the glass until I have to leave for my next booking.

I hop on a ferry to Navy Pier and head to the Chicago River. It's time to experience another watery wonder of Chicago. This morning Gus told me if I didn't do anything else in Chicago, I had to go on the Chicago Architecture Foundation river cruise.

As I stand in line with the hordes waiting by Michigan Avenue Bridge, Docent Rebecca smiles her way along the line, asking people where they're from. She stops when she hears I'm from Scotland and proudly shows me her name badge.

'I'm a good Presbyterian girl.'

I say, 'Great!'

It seems more polite than telling Rebecca that I'm one of the 57.6% of Scots that the last census found not to be Presbyterians.

Rebecca tells me that she's from Virginia. 'There are a lot of people in my part of the world from Scotland,' she beams at me significantly.

'Great!' I beam back at her.

'I nearly cut off my finger one time,' she recounts, 'and I knew I'd need a book to read in the waiting room. So I took a book about the Scots in my part of the country and I learned a whole lot of things.'

This seems an admirably practical approach to digit-threatening injuries. We are a pragmatic people.

I claim a white plastic lawn chair on the lower deck of the boat. I am disappointed that the couple in front is arguing in a language I can't identify, substantially cutting down on eavesdropping opportunities. This does not cut down, however, amusement provided by the woman's jacket. I wonder if she knows that, alongside the old luggage label prints on her quilted back, her outfit also proclaims, 'Peacock's Improved Double Dissection.'

We pass the white and terracotta Wrigley Building, built in 1921, and the Gothic tower of the Tribune building. The First Lady chugs past the vast empire of catalogue-shopping baron Montgomery Ward, built in 1908 and once the largest concrete structure in the world. At the fork of the river's North and South branches, a delicious smell of chocolate wafts from the Blommer's factory. This city looks good and it smells even better. Chicago really has this whole River City heritage lark down. I wish Glasgow worked its waterfront as successfully.

The Windy City stacks up some impressive statistics. In 1885, the world's first skyscraper, the nine-storey Home Insurance Building, rose. By 1973, the 110-storey Sears Tower (or the Willis Tower, as it's now officially called) was completed. It nested at the top of the list of the world's tallest structures for the next 25 years. A quarter of a mile high, it has 103 elevators, its own zip code and three more minutes of sun a day at the top. Chicago can also boast a good number of impressive inventions; roller skates in 1884, 1899's discreet zipper, 1902's revealing window envelope. However, the city's achievements display a noticeable slouch as the decades march on. Twinkies sponge cakes upped America's calorific intake in 1930, Raymond Maloney kickstarted the gaming industry with the production of Ballyhoo pinball machines here in the mid-1930s, spray paint made its first splash in the late 1940s, and in 1955, one of the city's most successful innovations, the first McDonald's franchise, fired up its grills.

When I was growing up in Scotland, we didn't have McDonald's. Or rather, we did, but they tended to be wee tearooms run by little old ladies called Mrs McDonald or restaurants long in the hands of a family called MacDonald. These restaurants, and the other such places in which we idled away after-school afternoons, rarely put burgers in buns or boasted of supersized servings, preferring to provide their patrons with healthy choices such as a chocolate bar tucked in a bread roll or a pizza recently fished out of a deep-fat fryer.

Perhaps the place I miss the most, though, I think as I walk along majestic Chicago streets, is the Grosvenor Café. The diminutive

Grosvenor, the domain of the Zanotti family since 1929, did a distinctly Glasgwegian take on bumping up the portion size in a direction that would make even the healthiest heart quiver. The Zanottis not only deep-fried their pizzas, they then popped a tasty fried egg on top of each one. Fried dough with a fried egg! They filled soft but somehow simultaneously chewy Morton's bread rolls with buttery, fried potato scones. Carbs with carbs inside! They obscured substantial sugar doughnuts with unwieldy dollops of vanilla ice cream and called this magnificent creation the Ben Lawers after the 3,983-foot-high mountain that towers over the north side of Loch Tay. The Zanottis were dairy and deep fryer geniuses and Glasgow loved them for it. Chicago might be the birthplace of the Big Mac, but Glasgow can claim chicken tikka masala and the Zanottis' artery-inhibiting inventions for its culinary crown.

My wee brother Brian and I used to spend Saturday afternoons at the Grosvenor, devouring another house speciality, the tuna croissant. It was pretty exciting because it didn't just have tuna, it had onions, too. In the Mulholland household, sandwiches were straightforward and self-explanatory affairs. We were strictly a one-ingredient-per-sandwich family. If you asked for a ham sandwich, you got two slices of buttered bread with one slice of ham in between. If you had a cheese sandwich, it was expected that there would be one layer of uneven, but unadulterated hunks of red Scottish cheddar digging into the soft bread either side. Garnishes were no-gos. You didn't get fancy extras such as tomato, lettuce or onion. This bonus item croissant hinted at a whole world of multi-ingredient sandwich possibilities to come. My first week in the US, I encountered Subway's approximately 700 sandwich fillings and practically fainted with indecision. I think my first sub had 699 of those 700 options. I could barely hoist the beast off the counter. It was an incredible sight. I wrote long letters to Brian telling him of this land of plenty with its lobster bakes, infinite sandwich fillings and people who didn't just pay for the price of their meal—they actually paid extra on top as a thank you. Brian and I were amazed at such abundance.

All this thought of food has made me peckish, so I pop in to a store. There's nothing even remotely resembling a Ben Lawers or a multi-ingredient croissant. My hand is hovering over the packets of nuts when two women standing beside me start to discuss how one of them was recently hospitalised after choking on a pistachio. I opt for wasabi peas instead. I manage two. These horseradish-coated hot peas are outstandingly spicy. I definitely prefer the Zanottis' vinegar-sodden versions. Tears stream from my eyes as I stagger along Michigan Avenue, hoping people will merely think I am profoundly moved by the beauty of this city.

'Hot!' I protest to a concerned passer-by, gesticulating frantically at the wasabi pea culprits.

It's early evening, and Manuel, a local lawyer friend, has met me at the Duke of Perth, one of Chicago's two Scottish bars. It's famed for its weekly All You Can Eat Fish and Chips. On our way to the beer garden, we pass a once mighty stag's head on the wall. The addition of a Strathclyde Police cap makes it look decidedly less dramatic and somehow strangely like actor Robert Carlyle. Staff t-shirts mimic an old milk marketing campaign and query, 'Got Scotch?' Outside, everyone is tearing into overloaded plates of thickly battered fish and chips. The drinks list has single malt flights and ales, including those from 'Englandshire, a small county to the south of Scotland.' Our Southern neighbour finally put in her place. Menu highlights include the Cajun-Scottish fusion of Lochinver Fish Po-boy, the Ghillie's Meatloaf, Haggis Wings with hot or BBQ sauce, a nod to Scotland's national rugby stadium in the form of a Murrayfield macaroni, plus a 'wee mac' for any urchins. There is also the rather unappealing concept of a Scotch Egg Burger—a squished and battered egg and sausage combination that is right at home here in the cradle of the McDonald's empire.

The menu also offers Hebridean Leek Pie. I hadn't realised leeks were a major crop on Scotland's outer isles. The summer my family spent on Eriskay, a wee wind-whipped dot of an island at the southern tail of the Outer Hebrides, it seemed to me that the main Hebridean crops were rain, whisky and seaweed. I don't believe I consumed a single leek that summer. Meanwhile, the rain won no fans, my dad was in favour of the whisky and my mum was enthusiastic enough about the seaweed to add chocolate and boil it up into a discon-certingly putty-like dessert that we all made valiant, but ultimately unsuccessful, efforts to consume.

    I was seven when we went to Eriskay and my strongest memory of the island, other than how long it took to chew each lovingly made tentacle of dessert, is what happened immediately after I promised my parents that I wouldn't stray off the planks that lead the way through the island's patches of bog. Of course, the minute I was out of sight of the house, I tested the waters, as it were, to see what would happen if I didn't walk on the official path. What happened was that I sunk impressively quickly. The peaty muck rose to my middle before I managed to grab and cling onto the plank that had been placed at that spot expressly to prevent such scenarios. But I wasn't too worried. My parents would soon save me. Help would come. My mum had given us all whistles to blow if we needed her whilst we explored. I blew and blew. And blew. I was getting quite exasperated when a shadow finally fell. I looked up expecting to see a concerned parent bursting with worry and sympathy, and was extremely surprised to see a petite three-foot-high pony looming above me. I was delighted that my whistle had summoned such an unlikely saviour! This would be a splendid story to tell the others! It was just like in the Scottish fairy tales I read where kindly animals came to the rescue of children who had inconveniently scampered into the path of misfortune. I held my hand up to pat the helpful creature to thank it for its assistance. The wee scunner promptly bit me and cantered off, whinnying in an evil manner. Then I remembered Scots writer Mollie Hunter's tales of the kelpie—the evil Highland water sprite that takes the form of a horse to lure foolish humans to their doom. The whinny sounded again, hooves were coming closer. Sheer terror gave me the strength to clamber onto the plank, leaving one welly boot behind. I dashed the hundred yards home.

My parents seemed remarkably unconcerned about my narrow escape from the demonic horse, no matter how many times I increased the pony's girth and dental dimensions. In fact, it seemed to rather amuse them. Their amusement only got worse when the stupid wee beast cantered meekly up to the house looking for carrots, thistles or whatever it is that satanic three-foot ponies eat when they're not feasting on the blood of seven-year-olds.

As a result, the Hebrides do not make me think of leeks.

Back outside the Duke of Perth, Manuel asks, 'Is the thistle your national symbol?' He has a look of wonder.

'It is,' I say proudly, thinking about the noble plant that has been Scotland's national emblem since the 1200s.

'In New Mexico, thistles are weeds.'

Before I have managed to recover from this botanical slight, our server lollops up to the table and interrupts with, 'You wan' more feesh?'

Talking loudly to cover the sounds of my spluttering, Manuel tells me, 'I really identify with the Scots.'

'Other than our choice of a prickly and persistent garden pest as an emblem?' I ask. Manuel ignores this point.

'I'm gay and Latino, so I know what it's like to be a minority. That was why I went there. I felt at home—a minority visiting a minority. Well, that and I loved all the bagpipes.'

In the taxi on the way back to the hotel, the driver exclaims, 'You're from Scotland! Awesome!'

'Yes, um, thank you.'

'Man, you've got the accent that everybody loves. And you've got that cool castle. And, bagpipes, man, bagpipes!'

'Er, thank you.'

'Freedom!' says the taxi driver.

I experience a moment's pure hatred for Mel Gibson.

Next morning, I'm sitting outside in the sun when a Mini pulls up. It's Gus. He looks dapper in a dark suit. He looks like a man who knows a thing or two. As we thread our way through residential streets, Gus tells me that Chicago's Society is the largest St Andrew's Society in the world and, true to its original undertaking, is 'still celebrating our Scottish heritage and relieving the distressed.'

Life in the New World was often far from easy for early Scots emigrants as they struggled to adapt. The Society, the oldest charity in Illinois, started in 1845. It went far beyond being a mere social group.

Gus says, 'The Society was there for Scots who fell on hard times, to provide necessities such as coal, shoes, roofs and even graves. The Society bought a plot and vowed to make sure no Scot would be buried in a paupers' field.'

'Who do you consider a Scot?' I ask.

'We like to say that people can be Scots by blood, Scots by heritage or Scots by inclination,' he says.

This decision to celebrate one specific part of ancestry over another or others—to make that a main identity when few today are of entirely one background—is interesting. For so many North Americans it is a choice and, depending on which estimate you take, between 10 and 80 million Americans can claim Scottish ancestry—if they feel so inclined. It's an incredible diaspora for a country with a population of 5.2 million.

The Chicago Scots are definitely a more progressive bunch than many St Andrew's Societies in the US, in terms of being inclusive. Not only are they delighted to include anyone Scots-minded, but, radically, they also include women. In fact, this was the first St Andrew's Society to welcome women. New York's venerable version, founded in 1756, long remained mired in the misogynistic era of its beginnings and wouldn't allow women to join.

'We're not grey beard stroking, whisky drinking types,' says Gus with a smile.

After half an hour's drive, we arrive at the Scottish Home. It's in leafy woodland in Riverside, Illinois. There's an old man basking in a patch of sun at the front door. Gus greets him and introduces me to Scotty from Ayrshire. Scotty says something that could be a shard of poetry. I'm not quite sure. I understand the smile, though, and feel welcome. A faded photograph hangs on the wall and says 'First Scotch Old People's Home.'

Opened in 1901 with 16 residents, today's building was rebuilt in 1917 after a fire that killed four elderly Scots and the Home's Scottish Terriers. Within two weeks of the tragedy, the city's Scots had donated enough funds to completely rebuild the Home. Today, it houses up to 85 residents.

'A quarter to a third of them have Scottish heritage,' says Gus.

'That leaves a lot of people who are Scots by marriage or inclination,' I calculate.

The upper floor of the home is called the Highlands. An arrow points to a further away wing, the Shetlands.

'Where are the Lowlands?' I ask sharply.

'We decided against the Lowlands,' says Gus apologetically. 'You know how it is.'

I sigh. the Lowlands are once again deemed unsuitable to appear before the diaspora. Part of the Home's ethos is to 'nourish the Scottish identity,' other than that of that undesirable Lowland bit, of course.

'How do you nourish the identity?'

'With piping, whisky, golf, Robbie Burns and all those other iconic things that are part of our identity,' Gus answers. 'And we give educational scholarships to pipers and dancers. We make Scottish culture a part of the environment that people live in. They choose to live in that environment.'

Gus has also chosen to live in that environment.

'After moving over here, the first thing I did was buy a kilt,' he says. 'Last year I was the MC of an event called Men in Kilts and I thought, what has happened to me?'

He looks slightly sheepish, but accepting of his fate.

It's time. I have to ask. 'So what is the Scottish Way?'

Gus pauses and then says, 'The board of the home was grappling with something that was originally built to be full of Scots, but, today, if we're going to be inclusive, we can't insist on Scots only. We needed to decide whether we exist to take care of needy Scots or to take care of the needy in the Scottish Way. That seems more important. The Scottish Way is a quality of care. We wanted to make the Home a home, not an institution.' He continues, 'The Scottish Way is a respect for independence. Don't come here to die, come here to live. The Scottish Way is about treating everyone with dignity and respect. That's the Scottish Way.'

Gus greets each resident by name, whether they're sprightly and bright-eyed or seemingly beyond the reach of such pleasantries. We walk along the tartan carpet, past the Wee Bonnie Shop, on our way to The Highlands for a coffee. I definitely see dignity and respect. I see happy old folks. I also see a lot of tartan. The tartan volume goes up significantly as we walk through the Scottish museum. It has a jumble of items, from Highland quaich drinking bowls and the possessions of early migrants, to a City of Glasgow Tartan tie, a Midlothian Scottish Pipe Band LP to and a copy of a *Braveheart* video signed by director Randall Wallace.

We move on to the 100 brass plaques that line the panelled hallway of the world's only Scottish-American Hall of Fame.

In the book *Video Night in Kathmandu* Pico Iyer talks of trying to 'measure the country by the shadow it casts.' Although Iyer was talking about the shadow cast by the US, the 'Best Small Country in the World,' as the Scottish Government slogan used to tag Scotland, casts quite a shadow, even if we don't always get credited for it. I admire evidence of great Scottish-Americans from the US's founding fathers to 20th-century stars such as Pulitzer Prize-winning lawyer and poet, Archibald MacLeish. Telephone inventor Alexander Graham Bell from Edinburgh is here. Naturalist John Muir from Dunbar is here. There's steel tycoon and philanthropist Andrew Carnegie of

Carnegie libraries fame, and frontiersmen Daniel Boone, Kit Carson and Davy Crockett. A majority of the US's founding fathers are up on these walls—10 signatories of the Declaration of Independence and nine US presidents were Scottish or of Scottish descent. There's Sam Houston, the 'Father of Texas' and William McLure, the 'Father of American Geology.' The US, like most countries, has distinctly dad-centric forebears.

As a child, I sat opposite Brian at the dinner table. While our more academically inclined siblings conversed with my parents on subjects such as an obscure philosophical twist in Huysmans' *À Rebours* or the deteriorating political situation in Uganda, Brian and I would occupy ourselves with intellectual pursuits such as making faces at each other over our plates or writing notes to each other with stalks of asparagus. At the point when I was on the verge of descending into inappropriate giggles, I'd bite my lip and try to focus on reading the titles of the books on the shelves behind Brian's head. One book always caught my eye. It was called *Our Illustrious Forebears*. Both Brian and I were puzzled and disappointed when we finally took the book off the shelf, crowded over it and found not one single illustration of a bear.

Gus invites me to tonight's party for the British Consul—a real Consul, not a wannabe, honorary one like in Oregon. Despite Gus's earlier protests that the Society is not the preserve of 'grey beard stroking, whisky drinking' folks, I am also given an invitation to a whisky tasting that shows a bunch of 1920s-era women holding a placard that states, 'Lips that touch liquor will never touch ours.' Underneath someone has added 'Unless we're served first.' Only a couple of the ladies have grey beards. It seems it is also the Scottish Way to be extremely hospitable. I am impressed. I would not be socially needy if I was a Scottish-Chicagoan. I am sorry to have to leave Chicago tonight.

As we drive back downtown, Gus starts telling me about last year's Highland Games.

'Have you heard of the Seventeen-year Cicadas?' asks Gus.

I wrack my memory for some bagpipe-drenched Celtic band, until I remember seeing a terrifying news report about the chaos caused by billions of long-dormant creepy crawlies emerging to breed.

'It was 96 degrees. They were everywhere,' Gus continues. 'The air was thick with bugs. I usually do a meet and greet, this time I was going about with a walkie-talkie, calling for paramedics. People were passing out all over the place. You'd think a band sounded strangely off-key and then see half the pipers had bugs on their face.'

I hope for similarly B-movie-esque tales from the St Andrew's Society's other events, but the Feast of the Haggis on St Andrew's Day, the Burns Supper, the Scottish Home Picnic, the annual Scottish-North American Global Leadership Conference and the Kilted Golf Classic all sound entirely charming and far less likely to inspire plaid pandemonium.

We get back to talking about the Scottish-American Hall of Fame.

'I would have liked to induct Johnny Cash.'

The former diplomat has a real tone of regret.

'Donald Trump's mother was from the Isle of Skye,' I say.

'We don't want him,' says Gus, less diplomatically.

Peering up through the mini's sunroof as we drive along downtown's North Wacker Drive, skyscrapers loom above, glass gleaming in the afternoon sun. We cross the Chicago River and I tell Gus that I feel quite humbled by discovering how well liked the Scots are.

Gus says, 'It's funny, isn't it? On the one hand, people think of us as liking to drink and have a good time. On the other hand, we do also have a reputation as dour. Groundskeeper Willie in *The Simpsons* doesn't help.'

'Lucky we've got Scrooge McDuck and Shrek to balance that grumpy Scots image out.'

If we take Robert Burns' advice and try to 'see ourselves as others see us,' we're in trouble. The American TV-watching public is most familiar with a flock of fictional Scots. Unofficial Scottish ambassadors are rarely real live Scots. Other than a handful of high-profile actors, probably the best-known Scots these days are imaginary—along with Groundsman Willie, Shrek and Scrooge McDuck, we've got Professor McGonagall from *Harry Potter*. It's quite the crew of miserly misanthropes. Yet, still, the Scots are loved.

The only seat left on the Blue Line from Clark and Lake Station is one facing backwards. I watch the city recede and think about the Scottish Way. It's like Jedi force, but tartan. It seems a pretty powerful thing to wield. The train trundles away from downtown.

'Soliciting and gambling is prohibited on CTA vehicles,' declares a reproachful, recorded female voice as we leave Western Station.

I do a quick scan of the carriage. One guy's on the phone, probably chancing his shirt on an outside chance at the dog track, otherwise everyone has a zombie gaze.

'Smoking, littering and eating is prohibited on CTA vehicles,' the voice admonishes as we leave California Station.

I'm curious what else will be ruled out. O'Hare Airport is still ten train stops away. The flat, almost belligerent tone sounds like she won't put up with too much of our nonsense between now and then.

'Priority seating is intended for the elderly and those with disabilities. Your cooperation will be appreciated.'

We will be model citizens by Irving Park. I begin to wonder whether I mistakenly got on the train to repentance, instead of the one destined to drop me at O'Hare with just enough time to bolt onto my flight back to Seattle.

'Keep your belongings off the seat next to you so others may sit down,' are our instructions as we leave Belmont.

I'm getting pretty tired of being told what to do. I put my bag down defiantly on the empty seat beside me and then spend the rest of the journey feeling guilty.

'Please be considerate while talking on your cell phone or listening to other electronic devices, so as not to disturb other customers,' she requests as we leave Addison.

At least she said 'please' this time. As if this was her cue, a brunette in aviator shades that obscure half her face picks up her phone and starts speaking loudly in Polish. She flips between two calls, ricocheting from Polish to English. She sounds cross in both languages.

It's hard to hear the next announcement over the Polish tirade. A lot of people seem to be reminded of calls they have to make at this stage. The broad-shouldered guy with the Southern accent across from me whips out his phone and competes with the Pole for aural control of the carriage. The carriage is suddenly overflowing with noise. I can hardly hear the final announcement over the hubbub.

I'm not sure, it's really quite noisy in here now, but I think I hear, 'Please treat your fellow passengers with dignity and respect.' There is a pause and then I'm sure I hear that tinny, slightly pushy voice inform us, 'It's the Scottish Way.'

5. HARK, THE PIES ARE CALLING:
MEMPHIS, TENNESSEE

Back in Seattle, I weigh up my Scottish-American education so far. I feel I've got a handle on the Scottish Way, on Highland dress and on which urban wildlife best suits sporranisation, but my excursion to Portland Highland Games left me with more questions than answers. Should I add a mini-kilt to my wardrobe or opt for a cloak and visor ensemble? To what other mysterious ailments are we Scots suscep-tible? Is a cup of tea the going rate for a Scottish accent? I need answers and there seems to be nothing else for it; I need to go to another Highland Games. The thought fills me with no small amount of dread. I'm not sure I'm ready for another onslaught of bagpipes and perplexing Celtic shamrockery, but I have to know.

Rummaging online, I stumble upon Scottish shenanigans in Kalama-zoo, Michigan, and am intrigued. Obviously, Kalamazoo is appealing because it has an amusing name. I have not learned from a hazardous trip to Truth or Consequences, New Mexico or a tedious excursion to Boring, Oregon. The website increases my excitement when I read, 'Hark, the pies are calling!' My excitement is short-lived. I read the page again and realise that it is 'pipes' that are calling, not 'pies.' I am disappointed. Personally I react better to the call of pies. Still, the event has potential. After all, the website does also inform me that Kalamazoo County Fairgrounds offers not only 'great facilities,' but 'protection from Mother McNature' as well. That's always a winning combination.

Colorado Scottish Festival and Rocky Mountain Highland Games offers 'a Bit of *Brigadoon* in your Own Back Yard.' Tempting. Liberty, New Jersey is the home of Bonnie Brae Scottish Festival, which is enticing because it offers the utterly intriguing option of a Highland games in a residential treatment centre for troubled adolescent boys. Perhaps they hold the restorative powers of the bagpipe in higher esteem than I do. Delving deeper, I read of Wakeeney, Kansas' Gatherin' Fire Festival of Beltane. Of Northampton, Massachusetts' Glasgowlands. Of Fischer, Texas' Days of the Scots. Of a hundred more Scottish festivals scattered across Canada and the US. It seems that when you look for a bit o' *Brigadoon*, you find it and then some. I am amazed and somewhat humbled by this profusion of celebrations of Scottishness.

A few mouse scurries later, I find what I'm looking for, and snap up a flight to Tennessee. It's the prospect of both a Dourest Scot tournament and a Bonniest Knees competition that makes a trip to Clanjamfry, Memphis' Scottish festival, irresistible. I am sure to learn many secrets about both the Scottish psyche and ideals of beauty. Plus I read somewhere that it's customary for the woman who wins the Haggis Hurl to blind judge the Bonniest Knees. This sounds like a sure-fire recipe for hilarity. Or for disaster. Whichever. I'm in.

At Chicago O'Hare, the incoming flight offloads an impressive number of cowboy hats. Once they've bobbed off into the airport, the United Airlines agent unrolls a scrap of red carpet. It's approximately three feet by five. She places a sign beside this suddenly elite patch of flooring that reads 'First class boarding' and stands back to admire her handiwork with a contented air. With just a change of carpeting she has created class distinction. Such is the power of cheap flooring. The rest of the passengers look on as half a dozen business-suited men leap up and scurry over the carpet and through a doorway.

On board, I am seated beside a precisely dressed older lady who introduces herself as Eugenie. She has the look of one who has attended many charity luncheons in her days. Early in the 90-minute flight, Eugenie asks if I will be meeting my husband in Memphis and seems thrown when I laugh and tell her I do not have a husband to meet. She seems entirely perplexed by my heading to the South without either a life companion in tow or one meeting me off the plane. From her tales, it sounds as though she's used to having at least one such character on hand with another waiting in the wings. She appears to have gone through a number of husbands and tells me about the latest one's courtship in great detail, although by the time we fly over Northern Arkansas I begin to have my suspicions that she still has hankerings for his predecessor.

As Eugenie is mulling over the troubling concept of a woman travelling through life without an appropriate chaperone and clearly no intentions of acquiring one, I look out the window at Tennessee, hazy below us. It's 20 years since I was last in this state. My first summer in the US, my brother Mark and I survived an overnight Greyhound bus trip from New York to Bristol, East Tennessee, to pay our respects to the world's only three-storey-high guitar-shaped building. Now I'm back on my way to Tennessee for just as unlikely a reason. I'm suddenly excited about the prospect of a Southern take on Scottishness. And by the thought of the vats of barbecue I intend to devour in the Pork Barbecue Capital of the World.

For want of anything more scintillating to say, I tell Jama, the Somalian taxi driver who whisks me away from the airport, that it's my first time in Memphis.

He snorts with disdain and tells me, 'I am not a fan of this city. In my next life I will not come back to Memphis. I don't like Elvis.'

It's nice to meet a man already considering accommodation options for the life after this one. Eugenie might approve. Lacking a ready answer to this revelation, I make an attempt at an understanding smile. I catch a glimpse of myself in the mirror: I look like I have just eaten a mouthful of parboiled squirrel.

We pass billboards for cheque cashing businesses, phone networks and drive time radio shows, directions to Little Rock and Nashville, and shacks with cagey-looking signs such as 'Tammy's XXX Roadside Emporium' across furtive, low-browed frontages. Cars and trucks with Tennessee and Mississippi plates whoosh by alongside. As we coast along the Coretta Scott King Memorial Highway I spy a billboard for 'Elvis Presley's Graceland' and find myself grinning. Let the Elvis begin! Although I am not about to admit it to Jama, I do like Elvis.

Jama breaks into my contemplation of the King, 'They speak what in Scotland, Dutch?'

I launch into a poor explanation of what Scots speak and where Scotland is.

Jama interrupts, 'The movie! The movie with the Australian man!' he exclaims with more excitement than he has displayed at any previous stage of our ten miles together.

I sigh. 'Yes. *Braveheart*.'

He begins to warm to the subject. '*Braveheart*! Yes, yes! And this is true? The ending? The quarters?'

Unbeknownst to Jama, the ending of *Braveheart* is something of a sore subject for me. When the film came out, I went to see it with my sister Orla. As we stood in line for tickets, it began to become clear to me that she was about to give away crucial plot details. 'No, don't give away the ending!' I blurted. She stopped and looked horrified. 'You don't know who is going to win? You don't know whether Scotland or England won the Battle of Stirling Bridge?' I didn't. In my defence, during my 12 years of schooling in Glasgow, we never studied Scottish history. And the task of spending extra time learning such trivial details was something I left to my more studious sibling, while I learned off more important facts, such as star signs of all members of Duran Duran and lyrics of the entire Eurythmics back catalogue.

American National Public Radio once did a show called 'This Is the End: Best Movie Death Scenes' and alongside a number of James Cagney movies, the Wicked Witch of the West's downfall in *The Wizard of Oz* and the repeated demises of Buffy the Vampire Slayer, stands *Braveheart*. Illustrious company. While I assume that *Braveheart*'s gory hanging, drawing and quartering finale was the only one with any historical accuracy, I'm really not the person to ask.

Facts such as this are the kinds of thing I would normally check with Orla. She is a reliable alternative when there isn't a convenient 32-volume encyclopaedia to hand. In fact, were she to disagree with any encyclopaedic details presented, I would put my money on Orla. Whenever one wants to know how many changes of dictatorship an ancient Persian kingdom went through in the fourth century, what dialect is more prevalent in North Central Angola or the swiftest route through the Apennines if travelling with half a dozen mediumly burdened elephants and a phalanx of warriors, Orla is the woman to ask. However, she is in Germany and I suspect she might not appreciate my enquiry at 2 am, Berlin-time, so have to come up with the answer myself.

'Um, yeah. I think.'

Jama is grinning. 'That is a bad ending for a man. You think so?' he asks gleefully.

I do think so and nod emphatically. Jama beams. He may not like Elvis, but he certainly likes disembowellings.

We're now on Elvis Presley Boulevard. With some relief, I spy the sign for my glamorous accommodations for the night, the Scottish Inn.

Jama is still musing on Mel Gibson's gruesome finale, perhaps a bad time to ask him whether he thinks it's safe for me to walk about on my own in this area. He looks alarmed.

'During the day, maybe,' he says dubiously. 'If there are a lot of people about, but only if they are the right kind of people.'

We pull up outside the motel's main entrance. The building stretches round in a lethargic, two-storey, beige 'L' to a seemingly forgotten, patchy-grassed construction site. A scatter of cars and some monster Harley Davidson bikes are parked outside a few motel doors. I look out of the taxi window at a vast red sun setting over the litter-strewn highway and see a few lone, jumpy-looking tourists skulking up the highway with Elvis-adorned plastic bags. Jama might have his doubts about them. Surrounding streets are called Bluebird Road, Singing Trees Drive, Old Hickory Road, Twinkletown Road, Dove Flight Lane, Pidgeon Perch. It sounds like this stretch of boulevard might once have been a nice place to live.

In the motel lobby, the smell of mothballs is so intense it takes the knees from under me. I stumble, eyes watering, to the desk. A short, tired woman sighs and asks me if I have a reservation. I tell her that I do. Her expression indicates that she had feared as much.

A skinny, blonde woman in tight jeans and cowboy boots flounces into the lobby behind me. She half leans, half sprawls on the counter, one booted foot propped nonchalantly behind her. She asks the desk clerk if she has a room, managing to cram an impressive number of syllables into each vowel. The woman merely holds up a weary hand and doesn't answer.

When faced with this real, exhausted person behind the desk whose bed I can see crammed in what looks like a windowless cupboard behind the filing cabinets, the fact that I chose this motel because of its name doesn't seem amusing any more. However I feel I have to ask why it's called the Scottish Inn.

I brave the query, but, for some reason that I'm not entirely sure of, I decide the query will sound somehow more valid and less frivolous if she doesn't know I'm Scottish. In the hopes that she won't place my accent, I slur the corners of my words as much as possible and end up sounding like the Swedish Chef from *The Muppets* half way through consuming the Cookie Monster.

She sighs audibly and doesn't look up from the screen. 'The partners. One is Scottish. One is Indian. I'm Indian. That's how I got my job and that's all I care about.'

'Ain't that the truth?' brays the woman beside me. 'That's all it comes down to.'

The receptionist gives her a wan smile and I am left out of the club.

She hands me my room key card and a menu for Marlowe's Restaurant and Ribs in case I want a 'pick up.' I look down at the menu and note that they offer, as well as the generous offer of pick up and delivery to the restaurant in a pink limo, 'refreshing adult beverages.' I am partial to such beverages.

My room is bigger than my apartment at home, which, admittedly, is not difficult. In another unexpected deviation from my own personal living situation, this room is adorned with a frieze of clarinets, trumpets, saxophones and violins. Sure, I contemplated this motif for my home at one stage, but felt it was lacking in percussion.

The Scottish Inn is not a place you'd choose specifically for its view. Beyond the forgotten construction site to the south lies a drab stretch of mortgage loans huts, car dealers' lots and fast food prefabs. The pool is in a corner of the car park and has, as online reviews advised, a spectacularly grubby highway view. Having a swim there would be similar to settling down in a bikini in the midst of the refuse-strewn, straggly-grassed meridian. I find this strangely appealing. It's hot and sticky and I'd love to swim, but I accept that it wouldn't be the best decision I've ever made, though, without doubt, it wouldn't be my all time worst. After all I did once think that starting a company making hand-painted snowglobes would provide a quick canter to financial success.

The urge for exercise vanquished, I locate the phone.

'Hello, I'd like to arrange to get picked up by the Pink Limo.'

There is silence. I think the phone has gone dead and, for some reason, I shake it. There is a slight creak at the other end. It's the sound made when someone moves the phone into a more comfortable position and nestles down on the couch for a good long chat.

'Hello? Um... '

'Ma'am...' comes a voice and then there's silence once again.

'Hello, I'd like to arrange to get picked up by the Pink Limo.'

There's nothing.

'I'm at the Scottish Inn.'

'Ma'am,' she repeats. A decade passes. 'You're going to need to slow down.'

In between her asking me to repeat where I'm staying and what time of pick up I would like, I have unpacked my bag, re-arranged the furniture, juggled my room's meagre allocation of coffee sachets and sketched out a few alternative percussion-inclusive decorative borders. Life is definitely on a different speed setting in Tennessee.

'Just one person?'

'Just one.'

What feels like an eternity passes, but it's just a Tennessee pause. It gives the impression that she's really giving serious consideration to my request and dispensing wisdom.

Eventually she says, 'Ow-kaayyyyy.'

I feel strangely grateful for her acquiescence. I decide that in an effort to sound all knowing and munificent I will pause, Tennessee-style, after all future questions.

After popping back into the lobby to inhale another few lungfuls of mothball-saturated air, I bound into the back of a very long, very aged, very pink Cadillac. My ride swoops out onto Elvis Presley Boulevard and cruises east. We detour down Lonely Street (yes, really), swoop down Teddy Bear Lane and back out of the trailer park beside Heartbreak Hotel (where I have it on good authority that the desk clerks are indeed dressed in black.)

I scramble out at Marlowe's Restaurant and Ribs beside a bright piggy-pink converted caravan trailer with a snout and curly tail. To my delight, the restaurant foyer contains a treasure trove of barbecue trophies and a 2D cardboard Elvis during his gold lamé phase. I am relieved to note that the gift shop stays open till 2 am, in case I develop any late night needs for some Don't Be Cruel Hot Sauce or an All Shook Up Sugar Shaker. The menu features bucketloads of Elvis-esque adult beverages, including Blue Hawaiians, Blue Suede Shoes and Burning Loves.

'What can I get you, sweetheart?' asks the server.

I briefly consider an Elvis Burger and a tall glass of Burning Love, but then find the concept too disconcerting and instead order iced tea and a pulled pork plate instead.

'You like it sweet?'

I stare at her like a fool, perplexed momentarily and then realise she's talking about the tea.

I overcompensate for my Tennessee-length pause and gush, 'Oh, yes, I do!' forgetting that I'm in the South, where they take sweet to new levels of molar melting fervour.

When the tea arrives, I realise the error of my enthusiasm with one small gulp. Gasp, it's sweet! As is the pulled pork… and the coleslaw… and the bread rolls. At this rate, I will have no teeth left by Sunday. Luckily I'm planning to devour plates of slow cooked pulled pork all weekend and it doesn't require much chewing.

As I'm bouncing up and down in my plastic banquette seat from the sugar rush, I look up and fluttering above me, to the right of the Stars and Stripes, there hangs a Scottish flag. I look to see if the majority of countries are represented, but no, only five flags have been chosen to adorn Marlowe's ceiling: American, Canadian, Japanese, Welsh and Scottish. And I am the only one sitting in the Scottish corner. I don't think my 'table for one' really gave them the time to file me away in the appropriate ethnic corner. Anyway, if they were seating by accent I'd be in the demented Swedish puppet section tonight.

Are these the countries most obsessed with El P? I know there are allegations that Elvis is Scottish and Welsh, but Japan and Canada have been surprisingly quiet on Kingly claims. When Scottish fans aren't visiting the obscure corner of Aberdeenshire his ancestors are alleged to have come from, they're talking fondly of the 60 minutes he spent on Scottish soil at Prestwick Airport in 1960 on his way home from doing national service in Germany. And there's more! According to *The London Times*, he also once sang 'Auld Lang Syne.' The Welsh don't have a leg to stand on. The man is ours.

A photo collage covers my table. In one large sepia-hued shot, a teen Elvis smoulders at the lens. In another he's wrapped around a stunning woman. Even with his tongue sticking out foolishly, he manages to look breathtakingly, heartbreakingly beautiful.

I am distracted from my musing by a lanky server with a t-shirt that enquires, 'You're riding in that Long Pink Limousine?' He says something to me and winks. Mere hours into my Memphis visit, I fail entirely to catch what he has just drawled. He repeats it. I shake my head and feel foolish once again. I begin to colour and am enormously relieved to get it on the fourth try.

I have just been informed, 'Ma'am, you are too cute.'

I am now quite red, although from feeling exceedingly dumb, rather than from being charmed by his attentions.

However, he seems pleased with the effect his compliment is having, and adds, 'You are. You are one beautiful lady.'

If the iced tea doesn't do for my teeth, the syrupy sweet compliments just might.

The limo takes me back up the boulevard, past Elvis's jets and other assorted Elvis-related signs and paraphernalia. Suddenly I see a runway's worth of coloured lights glittering from trees between the highway and a spot lit house. I catch my breath—it's Graceland.

Back at the motel, the fronds of a green neon palm tree flash on and off over the pool and, in the brief lulls between the thunderous trundling of 18-wheeler trucks, it's almost possible to imagine having a hasty wee dip.

To distract myself from counting cigarette burn holes in the bed covers in my non-smoking room, I try pretending the noise of the trucks whooshing by on the highway is the sound of the ocean, like Emmylou Harris does in one of my favourite songs, 'Boulder to Birmingham.' I try that at home, too, in my downtown eyrie, but the drunks cavorting along the street below my window rather ruin that impression. It makes it seem more like the ocean at one of those beach parties where there are hordes of intoxicated skinny dippers chucking cans about and lighting beach fires without a permit. And I rarely got invited to those kinds of soirees; so thinking about that merely stirs up a vortex of teen slights. So, all in all, it's not quite the contemplative recipe that Emmylou probably intended. Anyway, for tonight, hearing trucks as trucks, and all the crickets, Harleys and strange noises of the boulevard is excitement enough.

The next morning, the Graceland shuttle beetles back and forwards the 100 yards from the ticket building, across Elvis Presley Boulevard, through the famous, music-note-adorned gates of Graceland, to the home itself. The considerable proportion of middle-aged Middle America with whom I am about to be force-fed through the famous house is dutifully wearing the headphones we've been given. I'm still fumbling with my tangle of wires when I hear percolate out of dozens of headsets, a chorus of tinny, ever so slightly out-of-synch Elvises break into 'Welcome to My World.'

I'm here to pay my respects to Elvis' Scottish heritage. Although EP himself doesn't seem to have given too much thought to his ancestry, the same can't be said for his Scottish fans. Beanie bears with Scottish flags across their paunches hunker down at the grave of Elvis' dad, Vernon Presley and there's a St Andrew's Cross created entirely from blue and white roses in the meditation garden, sent by the Glasgow Elvis In-Touch fan club. It's tastefully subdued compared to some of the other floral statements on display nearby. I'm not sure which country is responsible for the wilted white carnation jumpsuit, crumpled on the grass. I blame the Welsh.

Outside, strata of graffiti on Graceland's walls declare, 'Mary Pat Will Always Love Elvis,' 'All shook up without you' and 'Oh, Big Boy...'

Downtown Memphis is a half and half kind of place. Actually, three quarters and a quarter is more accurate. The majority of buildings is run down and ramshackle, while a select few are all slicked up for the tourists. I read that Blue Suede car service is 'fit for a king.' A poster tells passers by that the book *Elvis and You* will be a guide to the pleasures of being an Elvis fan, for those unsure quite how to enjoy such a thing. A coffee shop warns me to 'Be Nice or Leave.' I decide not to risk a visit and move on to Automatic Slim's Tonga Club. 'Soul Man' plays as I peer above the menu and survey the scenery. Around me tables are filled with groups of people in business wear. Towering platters of onion fritters form tasty table centrepieces. It seems like any other city at lunchtime. Well, it does until I start eavesdropping on the conversation at the next table.

One of the two soberly suited men has just uttered the arresting words, 'Ah shoot 'em. Ah hunt an' kill 'em.'

His companion chimes in with matching zeal, 'I go out there and I just want to kill things. Last weekend I shot two double doubles.'

I pause, onion fritter halfway to my mouth. The first hotshot is now talking about having moved away from Memphis once for a few months.

'I wouldn't want to live there.'

'Where?' asks the other guy.

'Anywhere that's not Memphis!' exclaims his companion. 'Why live anywhere that you couldn't drive half an hour to go duck hunting?'

Guy number two grunts his agreement and they both go back to cramming onion rings into their mouths.

Round the corner on Beale Street, the famed birthplace of the blues, neon signs vie for attention along a couple of brightly lit blocks. One, declaring 'Pig—Pork with attitude' has a mean, mean pig in shades, glaring and baring muscles. BB King's Company Store blares blues out into the midday heat. Outside Tater Red's a skull with a top hat and glowing neon red eyes grins fiendishly. The Handy Bar, named for blues legend WC Handy, offers 'Big Ass Beers to go.' Signs state sternly, 'No loitering. Beale Street cleared at 3 am.' Then it says again, 'No loitering,' just in case we missed the red letters up top. I loiter, distracted by the sign on the bar next door. It reads 'Biggest Ass Beers.'

On the same block sits Schwab's General Store. The stock is indeed general. I fail to find any cohesive theme. Chipped ceramic kittens, cowboy hats and posters jostle alongside souvenir mugs and eclectic knick-knacks. I find a number of perplexing boxes of powder at the back of the cavernous space. Handwritten scrawls describe their purposes. 'Destroy Everything,' 'Fast Luck,' 'Helping Hand,' 'Keep Away Enemies,' 'I Can, You Can't,' 'Seven African Powers.' I'm torn between 'Destroy Everything' and 'I Can, You Can't,' but end up leaving with a guitar-shaped fly swatter and a ten pack of tasty Tootsie Rolls. I also leave with the knowledge that someday I'll regret not stocking up on whatever magic dust it takes to destroy everything.

Since the main events of the Scottish festival aren't scheduled till tomorrow, I clamber over the vast, uneven cobblestone blocks that arrived as ballast in English cotton merchants' ships and now slope down to the murky Mississippi, and buy a riverboat ticket. The 90-minute tour chugs slowly out into an eddy of the muddy river and parks its load of wilting tourists beside an unwieldy-looking bridge. It's far from scenic. As we writhe and blister in the midday heat, we are subjected to a monotone commentary from a cynical guide called Randy. We learn that Memphis was once the Cotton Capital of the World and the Hardwood Capital of the World. We are informed that it was also the Mule Capital of the World, although our guide doesn't go into specifics of how this was measured. It's a very pro-Memphis, pro-male, pro-duck-hunting take on history and life.

Once we've churned back to the banks, I climb up the steep cobbles again and back to the heart of downtown. I am disappointed that Downto'n Wigs is shut and the Peanut Shoppe, which sells both 'peanuts and other nuts,' is closed for prayer time. In a bar window I spy a poster for tomorrow's festivities. In it a cool-looking Scottie dog is wearing aviator shades and a tartan biker bandana. I am still grinning when I slope in a side door of Memphis' grand old Peabody Hotel.

The opulent 1869 hotel is crammed. People strain to peer over people's shoulders throughout the lobby, as close to the fountain as they can get without getting their feet wet. Yet more eager viewers lean over the ornate railings of the wide mezzanine balcony above. There is an air of anticipation and excitement. I manage to squeeze into a sliver of space on the mezzanine, right above the ground floor elevator. At five on the dot, a liveried gentleman marches into sight, accompanied by a woman in a gold evening dress and sash. The man taps sharply on the edge of the marble fountain, and its inhabitants, five North American Mallard ducks, obediently paddle over to the step, hop over the edge and march down an awaiting red carpet to the elevator. Red carpets are for very important poultry too, I see.

Since 1933 ducks have waddled out of the Duck Palace on the roof each morning at 11, into the elevator, onto the red carpet on the ground floor and into the fountain. At five they reverse their ritual journey. The tradition started when an inebriated general manager and his friend returned from a hunting trip and filled the fountain with some leftover live duck decoys. These days, the Peabody has a full time Duckmaster. On special occasions he is even joined by a Celebrity Duckmaster. As I peer over the mezzanine railing I get a flying duck's eye view of today's special guest and manage to read her sash. It's Miss Tennessee.

She stands smiling beside the Duckmaster and doesn't flinch when five wet ducks walk by her obviously pricey frock. I wonder did they teach her this in pageant school: techniques for grace when upstaged by close to half a dozen ducks?

On my way back to my hotel I think about beauty. Miss Tennessee certainly looked most decorative with a troupe of ducks at her toes. True, she looked as if she was mildly disconcerted, but still beautiful. Bonnie, even. But what constitutes a bonnie knee? Bonniest Knees competitions are seemingly a mainstay of Highland Games and Scottish gatherings across the US, but knees are not particularly bonnie or attractive parts of the anatomy. Back in the hotel, I examine the Internet. I don't even find sites for people with knee fetishes. Every other unlikely part of the anatomy, yes. Knees, no. Knees just do not rate.

I give up and listen to a local radio station. My attention is caught by lyrics about hot buck-teethed women. Even buckteeth are hot. In country music, anyway. I drift off to sleep with toothsome lyrics two-stepping round my head.

The next morning I'm sidling through the sweltering, deserted streets of the Pinchgut District, the old Irish area that the Irish couldn't afford to move out of when the city's yellow fever epidemic struck in 1873, past Memphis' silver pyramid convention centre and to the bus station. Around sixty people mill around, cramming into shady corners out of the sun. I go in to ask when my bus is due. I spy a young guy at the security desk. His cap informs me that he is a 'Fruit of Islam.' We get chatting and AJ, the Fruit of Islam, is surprised that I'm taking public transport in the first place. It's obviously not a usual tourist choice. I ramble on about it being a great way to meet people and really feel like you're somewhere else.

He whistles. 'That's deep.'

In much the same way that I fail to admit to commissioning editors when they ask me to write road trip stories, I don't mention to AJ that I also take public transport because I've never bothered to learn to drive. Admitting this fact usually makes Americans incredulous. They can barely believe it and exclaim and point and bring their friends over to meet me. It makes me feel like a talking dog.

'You all alone?' AJ asks with wonder.

I confirm that I am.

There is a long, amazed pause before AJ says, 'You a long way from home.' He shakes his head with wonder once again and adds, 'You are one interesting lady.'

We chat for twenty minutes until the number 53 arrives to take me deep into the Memphis suburbs. The driver looks concerned at letting me out in this still, leafy neighbourhood when I seem to have no idea where I am and makes sure I know where the bus stop is for my return journey. But I do know where I am. I have spotted Scottish flags up ahead, waving lazily in the slight breeze, and I know my people are nearby. I head eagerly towards a white wooden church, nestled among shady, centuries-old oaks.

Clanjamfry, Memphis' Scottish festival, describes itself as 'a festival celebrating our Scottish heritage.' My Scots dictionary translates a clanjamfrie or clamjamfrie as 'a word used to refer to a group of people, especially if one considers them a rabble.' It adds that it can also be used to sum up 'a varied assortment of things; a mixed bag.' I'm going to assume the festival organisers intend the latter meaning.

Two men man the Memphis Scottish Society stand. I look at the leaflets and books amidst the scatter of Scottish flags on the table. We chat and they seem excited by my having a 'real' Scottish accent. The older guy offers me a paper fan that states, 'Madainn Mhath, y'all.' I ask him what it means. They look incredulous.

'It means "good morning,"' says the more substantial of the two. He looks at his friend.

His friend adds, 'Y'all. It means "good morning, y'all."'

The larger gentleman is now flirting with me jokily but persistently, so I make my excuses and move on, narrowly avoiding a collision with a trio of passers by in kilts and red t-shirts declaring, '17th Annual Elvis-a-go-go Tournament.'

I scour the programme, but there is no sign of any Dourest Scots competition. I am relieved to see, however, that the Bonniest Knees are set to be revealed at two this afternoon.

Over near the church steps awaits a selection of Clanjamfry festival wares. Previous years' posters are displayed on the table.

My favourite one reads, 'Bagpipes, check. Kilts, check. Shortbread, check. Presbyterians, check.' Then there's a picture of a roll of Scotch brand tape. Underneath, it reads, 'Tape, No.'

I get talking to an older Southern lady called Ethel. She asks whether I took part in this morning's 5-mile run. I smile, shake my head and tell her that I am a lethargic Scot.

She confides, 'Oh, my daddy was one hundred per cent Scottish, so I know what you mean.'

'Were you at the gala last night?' she asks. 'They were serving whisky,' she adds. Her disapproval is evident. There is a pause before she adds, 'I was very disappointed.'

I tut supportively and add, 'I'm not much of a whisky drinker myself.'

'Whisky!' She hrumphs and frowns. 'I like wine,' she confides with a deliciously cheeky grin. 'In fact, I need to go home right now to have myself a glass.'

I sneak a look at the time. It's 10.30 am.

'Did you like our church?' she asks as she gathers her belongings together.

I tell her I haven't been in many Presbyterian churches. I can almost feel her sharp intake of breath.

'You're not Presbyterian?' she looks shocked and stops what she's doing. 'I thought all Scots were Presbyterian!'

'Well, no, a lot of us are Catholic, too,' I tell her.

'I think I will go home for that glass of wine now,' she says.

She looks a bit shaky. I wonder whether I should say that I was only kidding.

A plate of red beans and rice is the only thing I'm not allergic to at the food stand, but I'm not really in the mood for beans for breakfast. I dig out the Tootsie rolls I bought at Schwab's instead and tuck into them as I saunter about the church grounds. One table is laden with tartan Christmas ornaments. Snowmen wear tammy hats and sport bagpipes, alongside some glittery, geographically freeloading leprechauns. At the Arkansas Game and Fish Commission stall, four cross birds of prey glower and screech. The golden eagle keeps lunging off its perch, much to the consternation of both the red-tailed hawk and a guy in his twenties wearing a Confederate flag t-shirt that declares, 'These Colors Don't Run. Never Have. Never Will.' On the dance stage, a girl of about seven is competing at some form of Highland dancing. Contestant 101 smiles as she bows, smiles as she dances and beams as she scampers off stage. I have rarely seen so much delight contained in one child.

I follow a sign that directs me to the 'Children's Court.' A few children brandish fishing nets in 'Nessie Nettin' attempts and a couple traipse through an archway to 'Scotland Yard,' but 'Kick the English' is where the action is. It's the only one with an impatient queue. Small children and their parents line up to enthusiastically kick footballs at three cut-out figures in English football jerseys. It feels like I've stumbled on a neighbourhood street party that someone thought would be more entertaining if they opted for a loose Scottish theme. A phone rings and I grin on hearing the ring tone. It's a pipe band.

An elderly shepherd wearing an oxygen tank is masterminding a sheepherding demo. Every so often the collie bounds out of the herding area and races round through all the stalls. Not being up on collie whistling, it's unclear to me whether this is in response to a command or because it wants to check out which clans are most generous with their shortbread—a time-honoured sign of hospitality.

For the sheer hell of it, I go to talk to my ancestral enemies, the Campbells. Even someone with as hazy a grasp of official Scottishness as I knows that the Campbells are the historical baddies. The man and woman behind the stall frown at me as I attempt to chat.

I'm about to give up and walk away when the woman asks, 'So... where you actually from?'

I tell her that I'm from Glasgow and her face breaks into a smile and she says, 'Oh, I thought you was just putting on the accent, I didn't know it was real!'

She offers me some shortbread.

I am excited when I meet one charming older gentleman with a Korean War Vet baseball cap. Unlike everyone else I've met today, Clyde H Campbell has actually been to Scotland. In fact he spent over three months in the country. Admittedly, it turns out, not by choice. He spent three months in hospital there after a head-on collision on the Loch Lomond road, but he still seems eager to return to his ancestral homeland.

I also meet a blonde woman in an 18th-century milkmaid-type-get-up. She has the most *Dukes of Hazzard* accent I have yet heard in my time in Tennessee. I am delighted. I didn't think accents like this were real. She asks me where I'm from.

'Glasgow.'

'Golly, really? I am so pleased to meet you.'

She quite clearly is and grabs both my hands to hold onto them as she beams at me and invites me to 'mosey on down to Kittrell, Tennessee' for their upcoming Celtic Fest.

'Your accent!' she says with delight. 'It's real! I've only heard Scottish accents on TV!'

Kittrell's Celtic Fest Family is 'an all-inclusive celebration of Celtic Nations.' The leaflet informs me, 'The Seven Celtic Nations from which our lineage hearkens are Scotland, Ireland, Cornwall, Isle of Man, Brittany, Wales, and Galicia.' As soon as I've chosen whether to buy a carved stone that declares, 'I heart Irish Dancers' or 'Kiss My Ass' in Irish, I'm going to work on finding opportunities to use the phrase 'my lineage hearkens.'

The milkmaid's festival looks great. I really like the fact that festival-goers can have their picture taken with Mary Queen of Scots, though the lure of 'axe throwing' and a 'haggis hurl' is pretty compelling, too. 'Fun for the entire family,' the leaflet proclaims. Axe throwing, whisky drinking and photo opportunities with Mary Queen of Scots—my family would love it.

She tells me that she's very pleased that they've changed the location of the festival this year. The new spot is behind the firehouse.

'It's nice and flat. Last year it was on a hill.'

I make some polite noises about hills being good and suitably Scottish.

'Oh, no. It weren't so good.' She sees me look confused and adds, 'Well, you see, it's their knees.'

I still look politely puzzled.

'A lot of these folks can't get up the hill. Bad knees,' she adds confidentially.

'A lot of these folks?' I gesture at the clans behind me, wondering if we Scots are not only likely to succumb to liver decline and girthy flippers, as was revealed at Portland Highland Games, but should expect joint failure in later life. 'Surely they should be used to hills, being Highlanders?' I ask.

She leans over. 'Oh, it's been bred out of them,' she tells me in confidential tones. She looks around to make sure she can't be overheard. 'These ones can't do hills.'

I wander away, sorry not to be able to mosey on down to Kittrell.

There's still an hour to go till the dramatic knee unveiling and it seems as good a time as any to learn about Scotch whisky. Now that Ethel's vamoosed home for her morning flagon of wine, I am without a drinking partner. I join Ruby and Joanie, two teachers from Germantown, Tennessee, and we start on an Isle of Jura, which is what the guy pouring the shots describes as 'beginners' whisky.' I think he uses adjectives like 'sweet,' 'smooth' and 'light,' but it's hard to tell over the sound of my spluttering. I ask if there's anything in the pre-beginners category and only get a raised eyebrow. Ruby and Joanie tell me they spend their evenings seeking out bars far away from their students. By the time we've worked our way to Glenmorangie, we're onto the advanced whiskies and the more risqué stories from the Greater Memphis School Board area, and everything seems vastly more entertaining.

More Scottie dogs dart about than I am used to seeing. They seem to like the bagpipes and wag their tails whenever the Wolf River Pipe Band members so much as tune up.

The more flirtatious of the 'Good morning, y'all' guys sees me as I try to skulk by and hustles me into a front row seat in the History Tent. I am alarmed to find myself equipped with a sheaf of lyrics to Jacobite love songs. I manage a tuneless drone to 'Over the Sea to Skye.' This is torture. I'm having flashbacks to being forced to attend Orla's Fiddle Orchestra concerts. Six burly Tennesseans in white peasant smocks and kilts smile encouragingly. I realise that this is only song number two of something like fifteen. I thrust the songbook at an unsuspecting bystander and flee.

I need to hide for the duration of approximately a dozen 18th-century love songs. On the far side of the church grounds, there's a live music stage—the future site of bonnie knees. I lurk down the front, in prime position for the knee revealing. A four-piece is on stage. One of the guys announces that the next song is called 'Old Hag You've Killed Me.' The border collie races past the stage again and back to his sheep pen.

'Oh, look, that little dog, he's found his goats,' says the woman in the hostess kilt on stage.

There's a pause, while the three guys in the band look at her.

The lead singer says, 'His goats? I think they're sheep.'

'Well, they don't have hardly no fur on them,' she answers defensively.

Four dozen teenage Wind Dancers sit down all around me and open their lunch containers in one choreographed swoop. Their lunch coolers are of a size that in Scotland would suffice for a week's holiday in a caravan by the seaside. They tuck into their vast feasts with uncontained zeal. I wonder what the collective noun for Wind Dancers might be. A storm? A bluster? A gust? The Wind Dancers whoop and cheer while some teen poster boys of the Celtic folk rock world take the stage. Behind me I hear a few swells of laughter. I peer behind me, but engulfed in a sea of Wind Dancers I see nothing amusing.

I hear the sound of more laughter behind me and check the time. Any time now the bonniest knees should be revealed on stage. I direct my attention back to the front again. Another gale of laughter blows over my shoulder from the church steps. I strain to look, but a Wind Dancer has perched his lanky adolescent frame on top of his lunch chest and towers above me. I think about struggling to my feet, but my breakfast of whisky and Tootsie Rolls seems to have afflicted my own knees. I make a quarter hearted effort to stand, but am distracted by earnest lyrics about hearts and the Highlands.

'Yeah!' holler the Wind Dancers en masse.

You really just need to say 'Highlands' every so often to get this crowd going.

The band continues with various impressive statements of conviction about which lochs they would swim and which mountains they would climb for love.

Whistles and whoops ring out. Applause resounds.

One teen dancer yells, 'Highlands, yeah!'

There is yet more clapping. There is a good deal more langing, then they move smoothly into a jazzy number about longships, pillaging and failed attempts to escape destruction.

In one sudden squall, the Wind Dancers depart, the band brings their set to a close and the next act is promptly announced. What? What about the knees? I rush down to the front and plead for information. There was a change of schedule, a smiling person informs me. They were moved to the church steps. I dash up, but I know it's no good. I heard the mirth. I heard the hilarity. I hover about the steps for half an hour, narrowly avoiding being swept into another round of Jacobite love songs. Damn those Wind Dancers! A hot breeze blows through the church grounds. There's still the Kirkin' O' the Tartans to come—a seemingly obligatory part of all Scottish-American Highland Games because we're all Presbyterians—but having consumed the sum total of five whiskies and some chewy sweets today, I decide to go in search of more substantial sustenance downtown. En route I have my first encounter with Memphis' Blue Suede Brigade, the city's downtown ambassadors. Signs have warned me that I can 'ask them anything' but 'just don't step on their shoes.'

After giving me directions to the famed Rendezvous restaurant, Tim, the Blue Suede Brigadier, asks, 'You travel alone?'

I tell him I do.

Tim, resplendent in a pith helmet, blue suede sash and matching shoes, laments, 'I wish you were staying longer. I'd take you round and show you the town.'

I seem to be a hit with these Memphis boys. Tim also informs me that I am 'one beautiful lady.' I get his compliments on the third attempt. I am pleased with my progress.

Inside the 'world-famous' Rendezvous I slink onto a barstool. A few seats away two women gnaw vast bones. One holds a phone in one hand and gesticulates expansively with the other.

With a voice so husky it too could have been hickory-smoked and charcoaled in a pit for weeks, she spits into the phone, 'I ain't gonna marry you. Hell, I ain't ever gonna marry you.'

She slams down the phone, picks up a rib and continues a conversation about football with her friend.

'You're about to settle in over a slab of Rendezvous ribs,' declares the menu, 'About as far as a pig can go in this world. And we picked out the good ones for you.' I am distracted from descriptions of pig possibilities by a server jokingly threatening to break the bartender's arm. At least, I think he's joking.

The manager sees me writing, looms over and says, 'We don't allow diary-keeping in here.'

I think he's joking too. Where is the offhand service the Rendezvous is famed for? They also don't allow cutlery, it seems, but after my first bite of rib I don't care. Cutlery would just slow me down. I finally understand the concept of 'finger licking good,' something that had evaded me for all my years in North America until this moment, and finish the entire slab in approximately 11 seconds. On a TV in the corner the Memphis Grizzlies play Central Florida. Every so often a staff member comes over and asks me what's happening in the game. Despite the fact that my answers reveal that I obviously have no idea which team is the Grizzlies, the enquiries continue.

'Uh, the blue guys just... um...'

I'm just walking towards the exit, congratulating myself on not having had to get anyone to repeat a compliment for at least an hour when one of the guys working a different section of the restaurant dashes over and says something incomprehensible. He gestures to my head and I peer upward assuming I must have barbecue sauce slathered across my forehead. I feel almost proud when I get what he says on only the second repeat. He's just told me, 'I like that hat on you.' Memphians appear to have swallowed Dale Carnegie's *How To Make Friends and Influence People* whole.

It's almost six, so the Peabody ducks have done their stuff and the tour buses have departed till tomorrow morning. I reckon it's safe to pop in for a drink.

Just in case anyone was torn between guzzling more sugar or imbibing something with a higher proof, the kind folks at the Peabody have thoughtfully combined the two: Drinking options here include a truckload of desserts in their lesser-known, alcoholic form. I consider downing a glassful of Girl Scout Cookie, Chocolate Cake, Pineapple Upside Down Cake or Cherry Cheesecake. They also have a Scotch drink called, of course, a Presbyterian, described as 'a summer delight with Old Charter, ginger ale and club soda.' I wonder briefly about the alcoholic components of a Catholic. Martinis include the obligatory Elvis references, but I opt to pass on the Blue Suede Shoes and all the delights of the liquid dessert trolley and order a Bonnie Doon Riesling for its name, of course, and for its 'hints of mango, peaches and a variety of wild flowers.' All those tastes of home I've been missing.

An incredibly aged woman is moving slowly from one table to another, straightening chairs and checking everything is orderly. I inch my chair forward to give her room to pass, narrowly avoiding jamming my hand between seat and table.

She creaks over to me and softly pats my shoulder, saying, 'Careful, baby, don't you hurt your hand.'

I am touched by her gentle thoughtfulness.

Elvis once said, 'Somebody asked what I missed about Memphis, and I said, "Everything."' I know what he means. I'm going to miss it, too. I'll miss the baffling compliments and all the terms of endearment from complete strangers. Baby. Honey. Sweetheart. All these strangers who have made me feel so at home. From the tea to the barbecue to the people, Memphis is one sweet, sweet city. I may not have glimpsed any knees, but I glimpsed the Scottish side of Elvis and I learned what my dad could have told me a few decades ago—whisky doesn't make the best breakfast. As my new Presbyterian friend Ethel knows, mornings are for drinking wine.

6. THE GREAT SCOTTIE:
SAVANNAH AND WARM SPRINGS, GEORGIA

It's heading towards midnight and my Scottish friend Arran and I are driving through northeastern Georgia to Savannah. We're a day early for the Scottish Terrier Club of Greater Atlanta's annual Fala Day, held in Warm Springs, 240 miles from here. I'm excited about the prospect of Savannah, the 'gently mannered city by the sea … aloof from the coast' that Margaret Mitchell described in *Gone With the Wind*.

We turn off Highway 16 and see no sign of the sea. Where's the sea? Is there a view of it, perhaps, from behind that boarded-up building? Or guarded by that fiercely tattooed guy over there? Or blocked by the dejected mound of rubbish bags heaped in front of the closed-down Western Union office?

The sea is decidedly aloof and we do not catch even a glimpse of it as we edge through a tousled neighbourhood with dark, straggling streets and unkempt houses. We pass two heavily fenced liquor stores with malingerers outside and large signs stating, 'We Accept Food Stamps' adorning their dishevelled exteriors.

Arran frowns at me. 'Are you sure this was the right exit?' he asks as we inch past a hunched, barred convenience store. Forms loiter in the shadows outside the squat one-storey building.

'Yes! Ehm, well…'

I peer out through the night at unlit houses crowding round us.

Hmmm, I muse. Margaret Mitchell probably didn't have to go through quite as many streetside Police Drug Check Points. She probably spent less time loitering outside the KwikStop, too.

The evidence continues to stack up and I, official map-reader for this Halloween weekend trip, admit that I may not have been paying very much attention when I gesticulated at what I thought was the appropriate exit for Historic Downtown Savannah.

After a few increasingly rapid loops of the same dishevelled blocks, we attempt to re-find the highway. A barrage of highway numbers looms before us.

'Which one?' asks Arran, as we idle on a quiet corner.

I look at car lights cruising towards us with what seems like menace.

'Any one,' I decide, and we career back into the realm of highway lighting and streets that have yet to be equipped with narcotics search points.

Twenty minutes later, we check into the Thunderbird Motel. I have been relieved of map-reading and route deciding duties. Despite my protests that we didn't actually get stopped at any drug checkpoints, Arran dismisses my suggestion that we just wander around in the hopes of stumbling upon somewhere to eat. Instead, he attempts to coax the disinterested desk clerk into recommending a specific eatery nearby. At this prompt, another guest, up till this point slumped in a chair in the disconcertingly decorated sky blue, lime and oxblood red lobby, splutters to unsteady feet and elbows her way into the conversation before the yawning front desk rep has had time to finish sighing with exasperation at our existence.

'You like chicken?' the guest asks, excitedly. Her otherwise pasty white cheeks are tinged with dabs of magenta, courtesy of what I suspect may either be post-closing time zeal or a head-on collision with an army of fuchsia bingo daubers. Her lilac blouse flaps with fervour as she talks.

Before I've even confirmed my partiality to poultry, she continues, jabbing at the map that Arran is trying to coerce the receptionist to glance at.

'Here! Here! Here!' she says emphatically, stabbing various geographically unrelated points of downtown Savannah with one insistent finger. The thin map is no equal for the brunt of her enthusiasm and soon buckles out of Arran's hands and onto the counter. The guest spreads it out before her and stabs it once again.

'Here! Mmm, chicken! So much chicken! More dead chicken than you ever seen in your life. Twenty-one courses…'

There is a pause while our sweating advisor looks upwards at the not-so-recently painted ceiling and smiles. She looks back at me.

'… of chicken. Twenty-one courses of chicken,' she crows to make sure we have fully appreciated the bounty of birds that we can consume.

'Thank you. That sounds perfect,' I stutter.

'Mmm-hmmm,' she says happily as she stalks out of the lobby.

The door flutters gently closed behind her.

The brightly lit lobby is suddenly silent. Arran and I look at each other.

Arran, a staunch vegetarian, looks aghast at the profusion of poultry the woman has proffered. Even I, a committed carnivore, blanch slightly at the concept of devouring what has to be a substantial proportion of the population of a medium-sized chicken farm, although I'm curious as to whether there's a chicken dessert course or if something egg-based has been substituted.

The desk clerk, momentarily distracted from the state of her chipped and chewed nails, says, 'I guess you're having chicken.'

Arran follows me meekly out into the street. Outside on the sidewalk, a wheelchair zips by.

Its grizzled occupant says to me as he passes, 'How you doin', ma'am?'

I grin and reply, 'Smashing. You?'

He drawls back at me, 'Oh, me, I'm doin' fine, yeah, getting on down the line. Bless you, my child.'

I've just arrived and Savannah has already introduced itself as a city of characters or at least of people skilled at bestowing impromptu rhyming haikus on recently arrived visitors.

We wander around and eventually find a place where drug checks are not compulsory and chicken options don't run to double digits.

By the next morning, even before I've seen the 24 squares, lush with Spanish moss, for which Savannah is famed, I have fallen for the city. As always, there is something I cannot resist about America's South—those eccentric characters, that slow drawling accent, that leisurely pace, the irresistible artery-attacking food—but Savannah seems to take Southern charm a few unlikely sidesteps further.

We trek past obligatory sights of the US's first planned city, taking them in but not stopping. We pass the notorious Mercer House and all the gorgeous Victorian and Renaissance Revival mansions that preside over those precisely planned squares—demurely set back from the action, but with every window's focus sharply honed on goings-on around the squares' fountains, obelisks and shady oaks. We walk along River Street's waterfront, squeezing past hordes of tourists stocking up on pralines, plastic beakers of brightly coloured cocktails and 'I Got River-Faced On Shit Street' t-shirts. We make our way past Savannah College of Art and Design and continue on. We don't even stop at the lavish Gryphon Tea Room with its supply of ornate sweet treats and tables of even more ornate Savannah society ladies. We have a mission—a mission with a deadline. It's Halloween and we are hunting for costumes for tonight.

Savannah seems like the kind of city that will really go to town on a night like this, so we need to make sure that we fit in. Arran soon picks up a simple Venetian eye mask, declares his shopping spree a success and prepares to go off to drink tea at the Gryphon. Considering where we are, it might be appropriate for me to opt for a voodoo-do, perhaps something good and evil as homage to John Berendt's literary portrait of the city, *Midnight in the Garden of Good and Evil*, but I have already decided what I'm dressing as tonight and the ingredients of my costume take a little longer to locate. As the Scottish Ambassador, I have to represent my homeland and, in preparation for tomorrow's Scottie dog festival, I have decided it would be hilarious to do so by spending my first Halloween in Savannah in the guise of a Scottish terrier. Having never actually patted a Scottie dog, I reckon that a night as a Scottish terrier is sure to get me in tune with the wee beasties before tomorrow's festivities. Despite having no components of a canine costume with me, I am convinced that I just need a few wee bits and pieces to rustle a perfect pooch outfit into place.

Arran is dubious, but I remain stubbornly determined in the same way that, as a nine-year-old, I remained sure of my ability to concoct a brilliant dragon costume out of an orange rug, a few egg trays and some wilting stalks of celery. Despite then being forced to wander round the streets of Glasgow's West End looking like a corrugated carrot, when it comes to making costumes, my enthusiasm-to-ability ratio remains resolutely out of kilter. Pity any child ever misfortunate enough to come under my costume control.

The first indication that today's transformation might not be quite as straightforward as I anticipated is when I fail to easily find anything I need to pose as a passable terrier.

'Maybe you should get a dog magazine to help with costume details,' suggests Arran, before he departs for tea.

In the convenience store, the magazine selection is extensive. It ranges from *Southern Lady* to the brown paper bag-obscured *Best of Black Tail*, but there is nothing terrier-specific and something about the XXX-stamped paper bag makes me suspect that *Black Tail* is not designed to compete with *Dog Fancy Monthly*.

Eventually, however, I find substitute costume items and sashay happily back to the motel. To my amazement, even after seeing the bounty of things I found in the College of Art store, Arran sounds unsure about whether he wants to be seen with me tonight. I am incredulous. I have pipe cleaners! I have several sheets of black fuzzy felt! I know roughly what dogs look like! His doubt merely makes me proclaim that I will be the finest Scottish terrier that Savannah has ever seen. The city's 136,000 citizens will surely talk about this look for years to come. Although, I concede reluctantly, it is possible that I will face fierce competition from packs of other artfully executed creatures racing around Liberty Street tonight.

Back at the Thunderbird, Arran pops on his stylish black and gold mask and his costume is complete. He settles down for a snooze while I wrestle with obstinate fronds of black felt. I hook wayward wires around my ears for my terrier beard. I cut soft spiky ears and pipe cleaner them into place. I chop craggy eyebrows and thread them onto wires. I look utterly moronic. My eyebrows stubbornly refuse to cooperate. I manhandle the second eyebrow into place as my ill-fitting beard and moustache tickle my nose. I sneeze and an eyebrow falls off. Finally, doubt strikes.

I am dismayed to realise that I have forgotten several vital bits of my Scottish terrier costume. A black hat would have been nice. Terrier-shaped cookies could have been useful ingredients with which to win new friends. Some glue could have persuaded my brows to become more biddable. While any of those things would have been nice optional extras for my outfit, I have forgotten something much more important. I have forgotten to acquire any alcohol. I am going to have to take to the streets of Savannah, dressed as an unconvincing Scottish Terrier, entirely sober.

When concocting this outfit idea, I neglected to consider that I regularly succumb to major bouts of stage fright, even when not dressed as an amateur animal. Aged seven, I froze before my one bar triangle solo when I won the prestigious role of third camel on the left in the Notre Dame Primary School take on *Joseph and the Technicolour Dreamcoat*. I retired from the stage and all such high stress activities immediately afterwards. No amount of coaxing from my mum could get me to wield a triangle or come in close proximity to hoofed ruminants for the rest of my childhood. I should know better than to attempt to appear in public as any kind of beast, triangle poised in hoof or paw or not. I wish I'd opted for a nonchalant tartan mask or that I'd decided to head out tonight unrecognisable under the rugged pelt of a carrot. As doubts gnaw, I would give a lot to look less idiotic than I currently do. A wee dram to help the nerves would really have been helpful at this stage.

Arran wakes from a nap, wanders into my room and guffaws, 'You look like a cross between a Playboy Bunny and an angry garden gnome.'

This is not helpful. He does not seem to understand that his job now is to convince me to venture out into the streets of Savannah looking like this and instead appears to think that his main duties are pointing and dissolving into helpless laughter. I frown and the other eyebrow disappears down the back of an armchair.

I lay the finished masterpiece out on the bed to survey my handiwork. Dammit, Arran was right! The exaggerated eyebrows and shaggy beard do look weirdly like a wildly inappropriate miniature bra and bikini Playboy bunny outfit for a malevolent gnome.

It will be okay, I tell myself. This is Savannah. People will be dressed far more improbably and outrageously than me. Nobody will notice one patchy Scottie gnome-dog skulking about the place.

Nobody on Savannah's streets is dressed up. People look curiously at me as I pass. Arran finds this immensely amusing. Dinner at a Thai place on Broughton Street is swift and embarrassing. Arran is not allowed dessert. On the way to our next booking, we pass a traffic crossing that has been adapted to say, 'Press Button (For Everything To Be Okay).' I press the button, but everything is not okay. I still look like I was on the losing side of a wrestling match between a pot of glue and a drunk black sheep.

A zombie staggers down the street ahead of us. I troop eagerly behind him in my felt face pelt as the citizens of Savannah look and shake their heads.

Our post-dinner ghost tour of the city is conveniently dark and helpfully full of other weirdoes. Pre-tour, in the 1835 Sorrel Weed House, Savannah's most haunted address, I am dismayed to hear that the lights are broken in the House's lugubrious, lone bathroom. My need is urgent enough that, even under these conditions, I still go. I manage to feel my way along the wall and lock the door in the dark, but when I'm ready to re-emerge, the lock absolutely refuses to unlock. No matter how I rattle and push, it refuses to budge. It is really, truly and terrifyingly stuck. I am locked in, in a haunted house. It is deafeningly quiet. I can no longer even hear a murmur of conversation from other tour participants in the parlour at the end of the hall. The silence is oppressive. Lights suddenly snake across the wall and I yelp in a terrified terrier-like manner, whimpering even once I have worked out that they are merely car headlights from the street. I shake and pull the door so ferociously that it eventually bursts the lock open. I am still twitching and shaking as I scuttle back to join the group, tail very much between my legs.

After the bathroom incident, the tour fails to faze me. Murders, hangings, betrayals do not make as much of an impact as two minutes in a toilet in the dark in a house famed for its shadowy former residents and disembodied voices. My imagination is piqued, though, by reports of 'haunted bagpipes' that play in Madison Square between 4 and 6 some mornings. The square was the site of the last stand of a Highlander fighting in the Civil War and it seems that he returns to the site regularly.

The last time I scoured Savannah's drink listings looking for Scottish pubs, I was delighted to discover no less than two bars that both claimed to be the 'only Scottish pub in Savannah.' Now Molly MacPherson's Scottish Pub and Grill's claim is indeed true, as the Caledonian has closed down.

We leave the haunted houses and graveyards behind and walk down deserted streets to the bar. We see road signs to South Carolina and pass the Rail Pub with its hand-scrawled sign advertising 'Helium Karaoke Tonite' and '$1 Hot Dawgs.' In Molly's windows, posters of a kilted Frankenstein, a tartan zombie and a werewolf with a broadsword announce tonight's Halloween party. I'm looking forward to getting this exercise in public humiliation over, so I straighten my ears, take a deep breath and walk in.

Inside, it's a relief to find that I am not the only one in costume. There are a couple of South Carolina quarters, an Amelia Earhardt, a Gladiator and three gay Hillbillies leaning on the bar. Other than the goggled Amelia, however, most of the other female bar patrons are decked out in professional 'sexy' costumes, from police women in pelmet-length uniforms to scantily attired fire fighters. Beside us, a sexy pirate is screeching drunkenly at a sexy nurse and a sexy Snow White. There are also several ethnic stereotypes at Mrs MacPherson's tonight. There is a sexy Roman in a raunchy, abbreviated toga, a couple of guys dressed as 'Italian firemen' and what I presume is a sexy Canadian in a plaid mini skirt, fleecy boots and a beaver tail cap.

'Are you Canadian?' I ask her at the bar, pushing one persistently flopping terrier ear out of my eye.

'Everything is open to interpretation,' she says cryptically and goes back to hitting on a South Carolina quarter.

I read the nametag on the outfit beside me. I am standing beside a 'Sexy Latina Nurse.' It seems her sexiness is not open to interpretation. Two unsexy male surgeons interpret this correctly and pay her a lot of attention. From the lack of Georgians swarming round me, I suspect that terriers fall into the 'Not Sexy' costume category. Even after I attach a handwritten tag that declares me to be a 'Sexy Scottish Terrier,' I still have no admirers. Maybe I should have picked up a copy of *Best of Black Tail*, after all.

When we were kids, we always made our own costumes, hence the carrot debacle and my subsequent unsuccessful attempts to amaze the world with my uncanny impersonation of Evil Edna, the wicked television set from British cartoon series *Willo the Wisp*, and a mortifying mission to pass as a packet of salt and vinegar crisps. In Molly MacPherson's, unless anyone here is a professional tailor, I am the only one who has done anything other than pop down to the nearest costume shop or pilfer from the staff changing room at Savannah General Hospital.

Earlier, I saw that the bar's website listed its interests as including Gaelic, and pretty much every Scottish instrument; 'Harps, Flute, Bodhrans, Citterns, Guitars, Mandolins, Fiddle, and of course.... BAG-PIPES.' Bagpipes got capital letters and three exclamation marks. The website also professed love of 'all *Highlander* movies, *Monty Python,* Travel Channel on Scotland, Food Network' and, rather generously, 'any Scottish authors.' The website names as its heroes William Wallace and Molly MacPherson, the owners' Scottish great-grandmother, a pub owner in Nova Scotia in the 1890s.

While I'm reading about Mrs MacPherson, Arran is puzzling over the menu.

'Do you think of tuna when you think of Stirling?' he asks unexpectedly.

'Well, I don't think of either tuna or of Stirling all that often.'

'There's Stirling Tuna on the menu.'

This seems even more of a stretch than a Braveheart Burger or Chicago's Hebridean Leek Pies.

'But Stirling's nowhere near the sea. Maybe they meant Stirling lamb... or Stirling venison... or Stirling, um, hedgehog,' I venture.

'Maybe they swim up the Firth of Forth, thinking that Alloa sounds like a nice place for a holiday?' Arran suggests.

'A holiday in Alloa? Surely even tuna wouldn't be that foolish?'

All sorts of incredible things have been spotted in the Firth of Forth: sharks, killer whales, porpoises, lobster, oysters, a torpedo, every major supermarket brand of shopping trolley and the Queen and Prince Philip, but not, to my knowledge, tuna.

The menu proves to be a fascinating source of information about Scotland. I tuck in my beard, hold my ears out of the way and we pore over the whisky refresher page. It tells us that West Highland whiskies are 'peaty and smokey' and that North Highland versions are 'full bodied, sweeter, mellow with substance and smoke.' When I lived in the Highlands, I met more than a few Highlanders who qualified as sweet, mellow with substance and who usually had a Benson & Hedges cigarette in hand, so this seems reasonable. Molly's menu says the Lowlanders on its liquor shelves are 'dry and spirity,' which also seems like a good take on people from my part of Scotland. I make a note to myself to avoid folks from Islay, though, since Molly's menu describes those from the famed whisky isle as 'pungent.'

At Club One, the club made famous in *Midnight in the Garden of Good and Evil* as the stomping grounds of performer the Lady Chablis, it turns out that Scottish terriers are sexy! Even at a Halloween party run by famed drag queens and frequented by people far more courageously attired than me, my guise gets way more attention than at Molly's. Perhaps this is to do with the fact that I've now discarded the gnome bra and bikini parts of my outfit and am now just one-third of the terrier I once was. Perhaps the Scottish accent is working for me once again. Perhaps it's to do with how much alcohol the club's patrons are in the process of gulping down. Whatever the reason, those Georgians sure like straightening my ears. A hefty Kirstie Alley, a huge man who is dressed as either the devil or a toucan, a hastily assembled Dr Spock and a Georgian Sarah Palin are particularly enthusiastic about both drinking and straightening my ears.

I feel my left ear being tucked down, turn round and see the Georgian Sarah Palin and her Trekkie friend. Posters for this place declare that Club One offers the best conversation in town. Once these two join us, the conversation is indeed among the best we've encountered since we got to Savannah.

Georgian Palin says, 'We're friendly in Georgia. It's the way we're raised.'

Spock agrees, 'We're raised to be friendly and especially to people from other countries. Everyone from everywhere else hates our government so much, we have to be extra friendly to make up for it.'

Georgian Palin reaches over and straightens my lopsided ears in a friendly manner.

'What kind of animals do you have in Scotland?' asks Spock.

'Scottie dogs!' shouts pretend Palin.

She and Spock find this hilarious.

'Ehm... hedgehogs...' I offer, trying to buy time while I think of other creatures with which to amaze our new friends.

'Yeah, I know what they are. Okay, hedgehogs.' Spock is keeping score. He counts hedgehogs on one finger and looks expectantly for us to continue.

'Squirrels,' adds Arran.

'What are they?' asks Spock.

'Squirrels,' Arran repeats.

Spock looks blank.

'You must get squirrels here,' insists Arran.

I add helpfully, 'Squirrels...' This just makes it worse. My accent is stronger than Arran's.

'Skwiddles? What? Are they, like, from *Star Trek*?' asks Spock, amazed.

'Um, no. They're small, furry creatures with bushy tails,' tries Arran.

'I don't believe it. For real?' asks Spock.

'A bit like a chipmunk,' Arran adds. 'They eat nuts.'

'A-mazing,' Spock marvels.

Arran and I exchange perplexed looks and give up.

A passer-by pats my ears on his way to the bar, giving me a nonchalant, yet somewhat jaunty air.

After a couple more cocktails, Spock and Sarah Palin decide they will join us for tomorrow's terrier excursion, but only if they can remain in costume and if they can be assured of copious drinks during the day. The idea of a drunken fake Palin deep in the woods of rural, staunchly Republican Georgia seems simultaneously hysterical and like a terrible idea.

Sometime around two, Spock suddenly blurts to Arran, 'It's not going to happen. I will never see one of those Scottish chipmunk things. It's just too sad.'

He then storms off. Arran, Sarah Palin and I search for him on all three floors of the club, but Spock is nowhere to be seen. A tad inconveniently, Spock was the one who knew the name and address of the hotel they were staying at.

Sarah Palin slurs, 'I think it's near a huddle house.'

'What is a huddle house?' Arran wonders.

'It's a huddle house,' insists the Georgian Sarah Palin. 'HUDDLE house,' she says louder.

The three of us trek through Historic Savannah, Sarah Palin alternating apologies and murmurs about mysterious huddle houses every step of the way. We eventually drop a very bleary Georgian Palin outside The Huddle House, which turns out to be a drive-thru pancake emporium in a suburb on Savannah's hem.

'No skwiddles. No Scottish dogs. Sleep,' says Sarah Palin as she cascades out of the cab.

As we cross the Ogeechee River the next morning, I see a grey, ridged shape at the side of the road. Could that possibly have been an armadillo? I have never seen an armadillo and I'm not sure I entirely believe they're real. I say nothing until we approach the next lumpen, squishy shape slumped alongside the highway and point it out to Arran.

'An armadillo?' Arran is equally incredulous. 'Amazing!'

We scan the roadsides for other astounding sights. A strange bush with orange blotches paints bright blurts of colour along the highway beside a sign that entreats us to 'Keep Georgia Peachy Clean!' We pass through Lizella Unincorporated where it seems the majority of inhabitants would like everyone to 'Vote for Lee for Sherriff.' A bumper sticker declares, 'Gun Control Means Using Both Hands.'

We stop for breakfast at a truck stop in Pulaski. Sitting on a red vinyl banquette, I tuck into bacon and eggs while Arran looks dejectedly at the pile of gloop that steams before him. Rural Georgia is not a great place to be a vegetarian.

While rural Georgia might not be the world's best destination for vegetarians, it is the perfect place if you want to stock up on gun and hunting magazines or when you want a decent choice of baseball caps that feature both stags and Confederate flags. I opt to pass on the magazines, hats and snowglobes in which a Confederate flag flies over a featureless grey figure that could be a fallen soldier, a Firth of Forth tuna or a roadkilled armadillo.

Back in the car, I get out my magnetic *Backroads Bingo* to pass the time and scan the roadsides to see if I can fill in the board's squares for an 'individual cabin motel,' some 'retired military equipment' or an 'abandoned dairy treat stand.' If there was a version for the Scottish road trips of my youth it would feature squares for items such as 'obligatory rainwear,' 'oversized vehicle encounter on single track road,' 'road sign to site of battle that Scotland lost,' 'contentious wind farm,' 'hotel serving high tea of scampi and chips' and a selection of 'scenic outlooks obscured by impenetrable drizzle.'

On rare, but thrilling, occasions, my dad would take me for a drive to some adjacent part of the Highlands. My favourite destination was Killin because it had both an impressive waterfall and a hotel from which to peer through the drizzle in the approximate direction of where it sounded like the river was, plus it was far enough away from Glasgow to allow time to wheedle my dad into treating me to scampi for dinner.

Driving in Scotland, there are vast swathes of moor, mountain and forest, inhabited only by sheep, deer and squirrels, with only a very occasional scampi emporium. It's different in this part of Georgia. I don't see anywhere likely to serve breaded fish bits, but there are signs of human life everywhere. Round one bend, we encounter Bob's

Magic Mart. The next reveals The Waterin' Hole and Extreme Wildlife Taxidermy. I lose count of the signs for churches after a succession that includes the Church of Christ, the House of Christ and Providence Primitive Baptist Church. Tarnished mailboxes slant along US80. We pass the Piggly Wiggly in Knoxville, population 999, which was the birthplace of John Pemberton, inventor of Coca-Cola.

Arran has put on the audiobook of *Midnight in the Garden of Good and Evil.* Somewhere past Sand Hill Lake, the narrator confides that the half hour before midnight is the time one is supposed to do good. The half hour afterwards, it seems, is for doing evil. That explains quite a lot about the change in mood and some of the antics at that club last night.

We drive on through the russet leaves that blaze throughout Upson County. Faded cabins with dented tin roofs sag beside the road. Deer lawn ornaments are still and watchful, ankle-deep in leaves, beside a tired green pickup truck. Branches cascade in frenzies of scarlet and crimson above gold and grey bark. The grass is high, yellow and parched as we speed on. We turn between more red dirt-lined backroads that lead towards Americus and Columbus. Burnt orange leaves continue to drift softly down and yawning tree shadows almost stretch right across the slow, muddy Flint River as we reach Taylor County. Rusting lawn chairs sit at the roadside. A sign above a carefully painted cabin reads 'Bubba's Acres, 1905.' Hay bales nestle in a field by a pond. An old Subaru rolls to a halt and a hand stretches out to open and check a mailbox.

The pillars of plantation-style mansions are poised along long verandas in tiny Talbotton, where I mark 'church supper placard' and 'collapsed barn' off the bingo board. Arran reports an unconfirmed 'lawn appliance' sighting near the Circle Feed N Corn.

We pass two Scottish Inns but don't stop. Instead we race on through the fall foliage towards the Alabama border. The deep, crinkled orange leaves perfectly match the rusty earth as we approach our destination, the town of Warm Springs.

After a few wrong turns that allow me to cross 'individual cabin motel' off the board, we are suddenly in no doubt as to where we're going. We hear the Scottie dog festival before we see it. An incredible volume of shrill barks ricochet between gnarled pine trees clustered around Warm Spring's Little White House, Franklin Delano Roosevelt's holiday home and memorial museum.

The polio-sufferer FDR first visited the area in 1924 to swim in the 88-degree springs. He loved the place so much that he built a cottage here in 1932. But the people here today are not particularly interested in the pools, the polio exhibits or the legacy of the New Deal. They're not really even all that interested in the president. The big name being commemorated today—by around 300 Scottie enthusiasts and their hundreds of canine companions—is FDR's beloved black Scottish Terrier, Fala. It seems the perfect place to learn about my homeland's most famous breed of canine.

Fala Day, 'a tribute to FDR's faithful companion,' is well under way. We join a crowd of people clad entirely in Scottie dog attire. Some have sewn Scottie patches onto every item of clothing. Other model hats with black felt ears. Others simply wear sweatshirts featuring Scotties, heads cocked, on the front. There are wee short-legged black dogs everywhere—on leads, in arms, in pens, in buggies.

A white haired man in a light blue blazer with black and white Scotties embroidered on his lapels, and a black Scottie clutched under one arm, drawls to me as we pass, 'They're darling dogs, ain't they?'

'Everyone knows who Fala is!' says a voice over a loudspeaker as we dart over to take seats for the speeches.

Several dogs yap as an elegant woman of about 80 in a cerise turtleneck and a natty mint green jacket walks stiffly to the podium.

Through a rhapsody of barks and yaps, she says, 'Thank you, I'd like to tell you how we all started this. Actually, it was the brainchild of my departed husband who is over the Rainbow Bridge now. I certainly think he is sitting there with Fala in his lap. He was such, such a Scottie lover.'

Her accent is pure *Gone With the Wind*. She could read me my rights at any drug checkpoint and I'd be thrilled. I am transfixed as the speaker laments the unacceptable rates of bladder cancer in Scottie dogs.

'My husband thought,' she continues, 'if we have a specialty show in the spring, we should have something for pet owners in the fall. They love Scotties as much as the breeders do. He was a history buff. When we moved here, he found out we were within twenty minutes of the Little White House and he came racing down. I did not see him again for a long while.' She smiles at the memory. 'He used to come here every day when he found out that this was the home place of Fala.' Her tone lowers and becomes reverential as she adds, 'Fala was, of course, the Great Scottie.'

The people beside me nod knowingly. A woman in a cream cardigan covered in terrier badges, says quietly and respectfully, 'Oh, Fala.'

The lady continues, 'Fala has been an immense, an immense tribute to our breed. We had two more Scotties in the Big White House with Mr Bush, with GW. And I wonder how Mr Roosevelt would have felt about that. Aft-ah all those years, Scotties back in the White House.'

There is a ripple of applause.

'Our breed was called the Diehard and how... better... to... describe... the Scottie. Fala Day started off so small. I am so thrilled to see all you Scottie lovers here all these years later. Please, some loud applause would be very kind.'

There is applause and a couple of whistles. Several Scotties bark at this cue and their owners try to calm them.

There are stands with Scottie information, and Scottie-themed toys, t-shirts and treats around the car park. At one, I spy a book about the former First Dog. It informs me that Roosevelt was given the puppy as a Christmas present in 1940 and named him Murray the Outlaw of Falahill, after a notorious Scottish ancestor. The famed presidential pet was known as Fala for short, and trotted after his master everywhere. He was even made an honorary private in the

US Army and travelled with the president by air, rail and sea. He attended meetings and conferences around the world with FDR. He was adored by his master and by the masses. Fala got so much mail, Roosevelt had to hire him a secretary.

Fala was in attendance at FDR's funeral in 1945, but, according to Eleanor Roosevelt's 1958 autobiography, *On My Own*, her husband's little dog never accepted that his master was gone. The faithful wee beastie died in 1952, seven years after his master. He is buried alongside the Roosevelts in Hyde Park, upstate New York.

The bond between Scotties and their humans is a strong one and it goes both ways, I realise, while talking to Scott and Gina Smith. Gina is wearing aviator shades and a burgundy sweatshirt decorated with plush tartan Scottie shapes and the words 'Scotties Gone Wild' quilted across her midriff.

'We are Scotties gone wild!' proclaims her husband, resplendent in a furry black hat with nose, eyes and ears, and a sweatshirt that declares, 'Arooo! Scotties Rule!'

He casts a critical eye over Arran's and my lack of Scottie clothing and adds, 'You're a little underdressed.'

The Smiths have three of their beloved brood with them today, Dottie, Linus and Lucy.

'No bias, but we expect you to aroo along for our babies,' says Scott.

'We waited so long to do this. Our lifestyle didn't permit us to have dogs until our daughter left home,' explains Gina. 'You see, our daughter was a cheerleader.'

'Oh,' I say, in a manner that I hope conveys understanding.

Scott says, 'Scotties are not dogs you can leave on their own.'

'Do you show them?'

'No, we just show them off!' Scott and Gina say in unison, and burst into peals of delighted laughter at this obviously synchronised and practised joke.

I hadn't realised that dogs and daughters were mutually exclusive. I wonder what kinds of outfits the Smiths wore on their daughter's game days. I sincerely hope Scott wore themed headgear with pom-poms and/or pyramids of teenagers for his daughter's performances. Teenagers love that kind of thing.

My parents managed to have five of us and a cross ginger tabby called Muffin at approximately the same time. Scott and Gina would be horrified to hear that they very rarely ventured out of the house dressed in cat-related headgear and, on the few unavoidable occasions that I was coerced into appearing as Left Wing for the school hockey team, I don't recollect my parents even showing up at the field. I suspect my parents and the tabby were quite happy to have the house free of warring teens for a few hours.

There are enclaves of Scotties in makeshift kennels and runs under the pines. I get talking to an older lady named Kay. She has carefully stitched dozens of wee black and white Scottie patches all over her jeans, white t-shirt and cardigan.

Gesturing at the dog pen, she tells me, 'This is McCallan and this is Laguvulin.'

I admit, 'I've never patted a Scottie.'

'That's terrible!' She looks at me with consternation. 'Well, now's your chance.'

I hold my hand out tentatively to the white beastie in the pen and give him a wee pat. His coat is sleek and soft.

'There! I have patted my first Scottie!'

'No, you haven't,' corrects Kay. 'Laguvulin is a Westie. A West Highland White Terrier. That's different. Pet McCallan he's a Scottie.'

I give the black one a pat. McCallan is just as soft and docile. To my delight, he rolls over.

'He likes you!' crows Kay, pleased. 'Everyone agrees that a Scottie is unconditional love at the end of a leash.'

McCallan rolls about with his toes in the air. I didn't even have to resort to slipping him one of my secret stash of Snausage dog treats.

Originally used as fox and vermin hunters in the Highlands and the Hebrides, the first Scottie put its shaggy paws on US soil in 1883.

The breed is one of five types of terrier to have come from Scotland. Now, the feisty Scottie is the best known of the pack, although the wiry-coated, long-snouted terrier is lower down the popularity scale than the taller, round-faced West Highland White—the Westie, which ranks as the 37th most popular dog in the US, according to the American Kennel Club. The Scottie only makes number 52. The most popular Scottish dog of all is the Shetland Sheepdog, a top 20 US family favourite at number 19.

'The Scottie,' Kay tells me, 'can be black, wheaten or brindled black and brown. Only five to ten per cent of Scotties are the straw to white wheaten variety, so the little white dogs you see are usually Westies.'

Kay also reveals that FDR and GW weren't the only famous Scottie owners; Shirley Temple, Julie Andrews, Liza Minnelli, Bette Davis, Zsa Zsa Gabor, Humphrey Bogart, Dustin Hoffman, Charles Lindbergh, Rudyard Kipling and Queen Victoria have all had the hardy wee beasties scurrying about their feet.

It's time for the contests. A local TV presenter with a comb-over introduces the judges and tells the audience that judge Marion actually knew Fala and had something to do with the making of Franklin Roosevelt's leg braces. The crowd oohs, aahs and gasps.

'Why did the dog need braces?' asks an elderly lady nearby.

A procession of black Scotties are led out.

'What's this?' asks one elderly judge halfway through the first contest.

'It's the Fala Look-alike Contest,' a co-judge whispers loudly in his ear.

'Who?'

As another line of slow and stocky beasties plod into sight for the Oldest Scottie

Contest, the announcer coos, 'This is Molly, she's a rescue and two weeks shy of 12.'

This seems to be quite an age for a Scottie.

'Prove it!' shouts a voice to my right.

There is a stunned silence.

'Shame!' tuts a lady behind me, loudly, as Molly limps slowly across the tarmac.

There are gasps of amazement as one creaky old 15-year-old beast labours onto the asphalt.

The sock race is hilarious. Much like snails, Scotties don't seem inclined to race. And they travel at approximately the same speed. A dozen of the silly looking wee creatures amble along on their short wee legs, shedding socks for all thirty feet of the far from strenuous course. The winner is the canine that manages to keep one sock on.

The rescue parade is the one that really gets the crowd going. There are tears all around me as about 20 black Scotties, one Westie and one three-legged whippet-esque mutt in a tartan coat scuttle across the tarmac.

The furthest travelled competition is announced and a woman from New Hampshire who is parading about in black velvet bellbottoms, a black velvet tunic, tartan minikilt and white neck ruff beats various four-legged contestants from around the US. Having travelled a greater distance, I can't believe I didn't think of this. This would have been a far more appropriate half hour to do good with my last night's outfit.

'You should go straighten her ears,' scowls Arran.

Next up is the Aroo contest where the best howl wins.

'First up we have Virginia and Isobel,' says the announcer.

Isobel waddles up, sniffs the microphone and looks like she's considering whether to gnaw it. The announcer snatches it away from her. Isobel loses interest and does not deign to aroo for the crowd. MacDuff takes her place.

'MacDuff, are you going to say something, MacDuff?'

MacDuff maintains a dignified silence.

'Aroo?' says MacDuff's owner hopefully.

MacDuff's human aroos enthusiastically. The dog manages a half-hearted squeak. Next, Kincaid and McKenzie come up for a duet. Georgia gets extra applause—a favourite round these parts just because of her name. Any mention of their state and the Georgians go wild.

'Okay, here's Rocker.'

Rockers trots into view, his haunches neatly tucked into a Royal Stuart kiltcoat.

'Go, Rocker!' shout a boisterous duo behind me. 'Yay, Rocker!'

'Owooo, ow, owooo,' yelps Rocker's owner.

Rocker barks a few times, then throws his shaggy head back and howls.

'Aroo! Aroooooo!' echoes through the pines.

The crowd erupts. People are clapping, cheering, jumping on their feet hollering, 'Go, Rocker!' Rocker bays along with the crowd. He knows the glory is his. Rocker is a champion aroo-er. Snausages rain at his furry wee feet.

Then an elderly lady weaves behind the microphone to read 'Rainbow Bridge' and a sombre mood settles on the crowd.

'Just this side of heaven is a place called Rainbow Bridge. When an animal dies that has been especially close to someone here, that pet goes to Rainbow Bridge,' she reads in a wavering voice. 'They all run and play together, but the day comes when one suddenly stops and looks into the distance. His bright eyes are intent. His eager body quivers.'

The crowd is rapt. Even the dogs seem stilled.

'You have been spotted, and when you and your special friend finally meet, you cling together in joyous reunion, never to be parted again. ... and you look once more into the trusting eyes of your pet, so long gone from your life but never absent from your heart. Then you cross Rainbow Bridge together....'

Wind rustles through the pine trees. A lone dog barks.

'Now,' says the announcer, with a grave pause, 'The reading of those waiting at the Rainbow Bridge.'

Two women approach the podium. One says, 'We are both going to read the list because it's rather extensive this year.'

'Angus MacDuff. Stuart and Ginger. Hamish of Shadyside.'

Yaps and yelps punctuate the litany of names.

'Winston, Wilson, Sherman, Sherlock.'

Bladder cancer seems to have been a culprit in many of the deaths. I make a note to add this to my Scottish Ambassadorial duties.

'Ceilidh, Queenie, Maggie, Stuart of the North, another Maggie, last year's oldest Scottie, Mackie, Stevie Nicks, Big Boy Casey, Missy McTavish, Mavis, our third Maggie, Fraser Glenrothes McWelton, Snickers and Moby, Cameron McIntosh, Duncan the Highlander, Maggie again, Duffy and Megan, all rescues, Bonnie Lass...'

The list goes on and on. Over a hundred names are read out. Bereaved Scottie owners are comforted as their lost beasties' names are called out.

The costume contest lifts the mood and is another crowd-pleaser. There are a couple of very cute bees, several dogs in kilts and one in a tuxedo. There are two ladybirds and half a dozen pumpkins. One bearded mutt is paraded through in a specially built miniature caravan trailer—an exact match for his humans' Scottie-adorned trailer parked nearby. Miss Piggy keeps trying to attack a frightened frog, much to the distress of the frog's owner, a tidy, bearded man with hand-painted Scottie portraits on his denim shirt. A stocky black creature tries to shake a Varsity hot dog hat from where it's been tied onto her rump. The Smiths and their Scotties Gone Wild friends pull a Depression-era wagon laden with docile Scotties dressed in soft hats and jeans. Old Dottie sits at the back of the wagon alongside a kennelmate dressed as a mule. The elderly Scottie patiently models a long blue nightgown, grey wig and glasses and does not appear to mind. Arran and I aroo politely.

Then it happens. The next contestants are Tinkerbell and Peter Pan. They are four months old and they are irresistible.

I've never been a dog person. There has never been a moment when I've been tempted to get a canine companion. Growing up, the only dog fan in my family was my brother Brian.

Brian was always attempting to adopt mutts. He campaigned from the age of three for a dog and when, more than a decade later, our parents finally caved in, he got Ricky. Among the myriad breeds that clashed in Ricky, there could well have been some Scottie. If so, any contribution to intelligence was watered down by his other ancestors, surely a motley collection of whatever are the dumbest breeds of dog ever to exist. Ricky was a lovely creature but one of the least intelligent canines ever to trot about the planet and Brian adored him.

But when I see Peter Pan and Tinkerbell, I fall in love. I imagine two wee Scotties scampering about my home and like that picture. Like so many people here today who have Scottish heritage, I love these wee beasties more because they're Scottish. They provide a link to home, despite the fact that if I was to be true to my Scottish upbringing, I should be on the hunt for yet another bad tempered tabby. This trip, this looking for Scotland in Scottish-America, has changed me. It's opened up Scotland in a different way. It's taught me about the country and it's taught me things I didn't know about myself. It's inflicted a shocking amount of bagpipe music on me and it could be on the verge of changing me from a cat lady to a Scottie lover. My head is birling as I watch Peter Pan and Tinkerbell being carried out of the car park.

An hour later, Arran and I are in Warm Springs' Paradise Grill, sitting beside an award-winning pumpkin, the size of a small asteroid. The pumpkin is impressive—it would make a perfect carriage for a Scottie Cinderella, I note for future Scottie costume shenanigans. It's obviously an in-demand seat, but makes a disconcerting tablemate. I eat a tasty burger while Arran makes a valiant effort to work through another plate of steaming gloop.

'Let's take backroads back to Atlanta,' I suggest.

Arran didn't learn his lesson en route to Savannah and foolishly agrees.

We fill up the bingo board faster this time. Discarded kitchen appliance, check. Abandoned dairy treat stand, check. At the gas station in Sharpsburg, a pickup disgorges several men carrying 18-inch-long knives. Terrifying backwoods locals, check. We pass a wood carving that may have been intended to look like Elvis. Or Susan Boyle. Or ET.

We finally get a winning line on *Backroads Bingo*, but I don't think a winning line is enough. I didn't see it coming, but for me, for a full house, it's going to take something more, I think it might take a Scottish Terrier.

7. THE HELLHOLE OF THE PACIFIC:
ABERDEEN, WASHINGTON

After a couple of weeks, I feel it's time to continue my Scottish quest again. But where to go next? Where will I find more crucial pieces of Scotland on this side of the Atlantic? A quick glance through Michelin's *Road Atlas of North America* reveals a Scotch Plains, a Scotchtown, two Scotias and no less than five Scotlands. Further scanning shows that six Glasgows, one Glasgow Village, one Edinboro, five Edinburgs, one Edinburgh and seven Aberdeens grace America's pages. There are no Coatbridges or Auchinlecks. There are some places no one wanted to remember.

I wonder what crucial kernel of these cities' spirits or settings inspired their inhabitants to name them after their hometowns. Would I discover any striking similarities with the Scottish versions if I went to Paisley, Florida or Edinburgh, Indiana? Would I learn something important about Scottishness? Or would I discover nothing alike, just a name, the only bit of home emigrants could take with them?

I contemplate Glasgows in Montana and Kentucky, Scotlands in Texas, Connecticut and Virginia. Aberdeen, Maryland is home to a nude square dancing festival, Moon Over Maryland. I can live without making a pilgrimage to that one. I am particularly taken with Aberdeen, South Dakota. Their Convention and Visitors Bureau website encourages me to 'Follow the Yellow Brick Road… through the Land of Oohs and Oz!' I find no detail on specifics of either 'oohs' or 'oz,' but don't need much further convincing that it should be placed high on my list of must-visit Scottish name twins.

I scan the map, weighing up various namesake cities—newer, younger models of Old World towns—and am all set to depart for Glasgow, Montana and Aberdeen, South Dakota when it occurs to me that mid-November might not reveal either of these towns at their finest. Current temperatures would likely freeze the oohs and oz right off. I look for Scot spots where a visit doesn't come with complimentary hypothermia. I frown at the pages again. I spy an Aberdeen in Washington State, and my course is decided.

The Scottish Aberdeen merely has two tame nicknames: The Granite City and The Silver City. Its progeny, Aberdeen, Washington is way ahead. For a town of only 16,000, it has a bristle of aliases: The Gateway to the Olympic Peninsula, The Birthplace of Grunge, the old nickname The Port of Missing Men, and, my personal favourite, The Hellhole of the Pacific.

Grays Harbor County, where Aberdeen stands, is three hours drive from Seattle on the southwest corner of the Olympic Peninsula. It's a mix of rainforest, striking coastline, mountains that Rudyard Kipling compared to the Himalayas, dying lumber towns and quaint small settlements. Aberdeen is the largest city round here and its mayor is called Dorothy. I decide it would be amusing to give her a pop quiz testing her knowledge of all things Aberdeen. Having recently done a series of interviews with US politicians, covering matters of national importance such as whether they prefer Eggs Benedict or Eggs Florentine, I'm ready for another hard-hitting interview. After all, wasn't I the one who got the Senator from Utah to reveal his favourite brunch spot? The one to cajole Houston's City Controller into spilling the beans on Space City's top barbeque joint? The one to squeeze out how the Mayor of Plattsburgh liked his hot dogs? I e-mail Mayor Dorothy and eagerly await her reply. She manages to restrain herself from getting back to me at all.

I survey public transport to Aberdeen. From where I happen to be working on a magazine assignment in northwestern Washington

State, it involves catching practically an entire fleet of several buses, including two Greyhounds. I quail at the thought. Fighting back memories of the tripped-out hippy sprite who danced up and down the aisle, singing and spouting poetry, during the entirety of my last Greyhound bus trip, and the hefty, odorous gentleman with what seemed to be his life's possessions in a bin bag in the next seat, I buy a ticket to Aberdeen, Washington.

Early the next morning I am standing shivering at the Greyhound Station in Bellingham, Washington, when I hear a bus driver protest with weary heard-this-one-before tones, to an indignant bus passenger, 'Just because a person smells, that's not a reason to not let them ride.'

I grimace.

A small, smiling woman approaches me and asks if I'm going to Seattle. She tells me that she is a Quechua Indian from Machu Picchu. She has never heard of Scotland, but asks if it's near England, so she either has some suspicions of my homeland's whereabouts or is definitely the kind of woman you'd want on your team when playing high stakes *Pin the Tail on the Donkey*.

'Is Scotland a Cat Lick country?' she asks.

I tell her there are more Protestants than Catholics and that we have significant numbers of Muslims, Sikhs and...

'But you are Cat Lick?' she queries, looking at me piercingly.

I hesitate. As she professed ignorance of Scotland's existence mere minutes ago, I have to assume that she is unaware that people from Glasgow are frequently assailed with the religion question. Even over here, on the hem of the Pacific, the Celtic or Rangers football-related religion question occasionally rears its ugly head. Usually from the kind of people who happily guzzle drinks called things like Belfast Car Bomb, with no comprehension of the politics behind their 40% proof.

'Cat Lick?' she insists. 'Cat Lick?'

It's a refreshing change from being assumed to be Presbyterian, so I admit that, yes; I was brought up Cat Lick. This is obviously the right answer. She gives me a beatific smile, tells me, 'I will bless you,' steals my place in the queue and clambers on board.

The driver scowls at everybody, firmly locks the heavy-duty plastic protector between his cab and us, his assumed-to-be-unruly-un-til-proven-otherwise cargo, and we slide away from the bus bay. I am enormously relieved to have no one pungent adjacent to me. Perhaps the odoriferous would-be passenger was headed north or the potential passenger censor had an especially sensitive snout. I am awash with gratitude at my fellow passengers' attention to their personal hygiene.

'This is a friendly warning,' announces our driver, Bob, sternly. 'No smoking. No alcohol.'

The mike sputters off. Bob fumbles it back on.

'I said, NO alcohol,' he growls.

You can hear the capital letters. It's 10.36 am.

Perhaps after years of taking Greyhounds the woman in the seat behind me is immune to offence or perhaps she is hard of hearing. She doesn't appear to register that the man across the aisle to our right is taking catcalling to a new extreme, staring at her, desperately attempting to attract her attention by beseeching 'Psh-shw-shw-shw.' He sounds as if he is trying to lure a wilful feline to its doom. We pull out of Bellingham, The Gateway to Alaska. Catwoman digs what feels like her knees, elbows and possibly a pickaxe into the back of my seat and sighs with content. Her admirer gives up, glares out the window and starts humming aggressively.

I check my phone. There is still no word from Mayor Dorothy. Pah, I think, I bet Mayor Mike of Aberdeen, South Dakota, would have played ball. We chug down the I5 towards Seattle. It's 10.46. I could do with a drink.

Clouds wisp through the trees in the pass in a picturesque sort of way. The rain has finally relented and we lumber through Whatcom

County, past Lake Samish. Misty hills are reflected in the water in hazy soft morning light. No one's dancing. No one's overly pungent. No one's catcalling. I'm well on my way. I begin to have hope for my trip. I begin to allow myself to think that it might not be pouring in Aberdeen. I begin to relax when I am jolted back to my senses. Catwoman has settled her knees even more comfortably into the back of my shoddy bus seat, applying an enthusiastic Heimlich manoeuvre to my lower spine. We turn a corner. The skies frown ahead. Torrential rain and grey murk swallow us once again.

In Seattle Greyhound Station, dishevelled and disgruntled passengers slump in moulded, once orange, plastic chairs. A tumult of arcade machines chirp and whistle off to one side. From the numbers of people waiting, it looks like I'll need to perfect professional glowering skills and attain truly shocking levels of pungency or I'll have no chance of getting a double seat to myself on the next leg of the journey. Fearing an even worse fate—getting left behind in this grim station—I race to make the most of the station stop.

The restaurant that lurks in the lower level of the station building has blocky concrete pillars separating tables. The ceiling is low and the floor is cobbled. It reminds me of a place my brother Mark and I once ended up in Saltillo in Coahuila, Mexico, where beds were whitewashed adobe rectangles built onto the floor. These grand accommodations set us back $8 a night. Having arrived by bus after sunset, we spent an evening delighting in our surrounding's rudimentary, rural charm and soaking up the village atmosphere, thrilled with our off the beaten track discovery. We left the next morning and only found out years later that Saltillo is, in fact, a metropolis with a population of 634,000 people and a huge automotive industry, known as the Detroit of Mexico. The bus station just happened to deposit us in a poor suburb on the outskirts of the city. Sometimes we see what we want to see.

Mark and I spent a month exploring random corners of the US and Mexico by bus. We saw more of the place than we'd ever seen of

Scotland. Apart from when I occasionally disowned him for playing guitar on board during overnight bus journeys and when he disowned me for forgetting to take the battery out of the insanely loud and easily set off New Orleans commemorative laughing bag souvenir on bumpy bus journeys, we got on pretty well. If ever looking for ways to get to know an older sibling better, I can tell you that being stuck in places such as Tulsa, Oklahoma and Bristol, Tennessee for the eternity that yawns until the next bus appears is quite a bonding experience. Despite several pits of stops, we still never learned to question our itinerary when drivers said things like 'You sure y'all want to get off here?' and 'You might want to just get back on the bus now, this station is about all the good bits this place got.' We usually thought the warnings were hilarious until about ten minutes after the bus had left town and we realised the next way out was nine hours ahead.

Mark is three years older than I am and six foot four. He was very easy to spot, towering above the crowds in Mexico. At the time we travelled round together, Mark was in his early 20s and had managed to perfect the precise combination of dishevelled long hair and neglected beard that would provoke counter attendants in Tennessee to call to their co-workers, 'Come see! There's a hippy in the place!' and to be pointed out by a small child in California as 'Jesus.' Fast-forward to today, my older brother is a rather debonair composer and guitarist who flits about the world with his delightful diplomat spouse. No one has told him that he looks like Jesus in years, possibly because Jesus was generally not found in quite such frequent proximity to rows of absinthe shots and because the Son of God didn't usually travel under a diplomatic passport. Another reason the American public is usually able to differentiate between my brother and the Messiah is because Jesus tended not to make impromptu appearances on stages with musical outfits called The Ould Bog Warriors From Hell, Impure Thoughts or Lord Mouse and the Kalypso Katz. Otherwise, they're near identical.

Back in the Seattle eatery, the colour scheme yodels an enthusiastic 'México!' Red and yellow arches overhead match bright plastic mustard and ketchup dispensers on each table. The décor is part homage to the 50s, part homage to Christmas. The menu and staff are Vietnamese. I love it, from the year-round fibre optic Christmas tree to the plastic plates branded with the name of some other, presumably long-closed, Vietnamese pho house. I barely have time to down a speedy plate of pork fried rice and be surprised by the number of empty wine bottles in the bin in the ladies' 'restrooms' before it's time to grab a place in the bus queue and get back on board.

I find two seats together on my next bus. I try glowering but I know it's in vain. There are just too many way more pungent passengers to compete with. I don't stand a chance of traveling solo. I look out at the people still straggling on board. A gangly man in his late 30s with dreadlocks and a voluminous, stained mustard sweatshirt weaves his way alongside the bus, talking to himself. My heart sinks slightly as he waves at an imaginary friend. I know I'm looking at my travelling companion to Olympia.

At least it will be an interesting trip, I think, as he crumples, somewhat elegantly, into the seat beside me. He immediately starts hunting through an array of plastic bags. Half a dozen magazines, five different brands of water, chips and several cans of Red Bull are rummaged out. He offers me a pot of sour cream, half a Hershey's chocolate bar, a hunk of plastic-wrapped sponge cake, all the water varieties, with the exception of the Evian, and a choice of magazines, except *Interview*. He tells me a convoluted story that implies that a friend paid him for drugs with the pot of sour cream and he felt it was impolite to say no. Although sour cream is a 'repulsive concept,' he's taking it with him on a 24-hour bus trip to San Francisco, surely ensuring a lifetime's aversion to the product for all on board.

'It would have been rude to leave it behind,' he insists.

He babbles incessantly, trailing off and mumbling at the ends of sentences. Stories rise up to great heights and then he loses them, looking confused as to their destination.

Eventually, after my thanking him politely but refusing all offers of gifts, he turns to me, fixes me with a serious look and says, 'You have to take something. It's a friendship gesture. I insist. Gâteau?'

'Um...' I muster.

He looks down at his stash, weighs up a magazine and his drink selection, and gives me a Red Bull and a stern look. I accept meekly and take the can. Our friendship is sealed. He gives me his hand-written card and I attempt to read his scrawl.

'McT? Is your name McT?'

'MC T. I am an MC, darling. Master of Ceremonies,' he tells me grandly.

I tell him that I've re-named him 'McT,' an honorary Scot for the journey.

'I shall be McT for you,' he allows graciously.

For the next ninety minutes we talk, often in French, much to the aggressive incomprehension of the Texan with the meagre teen 'tache and white cowboy hat across the aisle. He leans over to listen.

Interrupting, he drawls, 'I have not one idea what the heck you two were just saying. What were you saying in foreign?'

There is a split second where I am excruciatingly aware of the possibly explosive combination of a precocious, strung out, gay black man and a pasty white, blustery cowboy, but McT swiftly dismisses him with an unlikely summary and returns, twitching and sweating, to his monologue. Reaching into one of the bags, he extracts a scrappy off-white paper folder, spilling with loose papers, and reads me extracts from his anarchist manifesto. He sings me reggae tunes that he insists are the works of 70s star David Essex. He gives me fashion advice.

'Never say ochre; it is bohemian beige.'

'There is cool. There is chic. Some things are cool. Some are chic. Never mix the two.' He pauses and adds, 'Not even in jest.'

It is a sombre moment.

'Scotland,' he pauses to consider, 'is chic.'

'My favourite president,' he announces, 'was Mitterand.'

'You have a favourite president?' I ask, surprised.

'Of course I have a favourite president.' McT is outraged at my question. 'I have a favourite president and it is Mitterand,' he states firmly, 'Mitterand rocked it.'

McT lived in Paris, he tells me, until he 'fromaged out.' I begin to worry that he may be about to do more than fromage out. He shakes and twitches and tries to pick what he calls his 'thug chic' sweatshirt away from his clammy skin. The same thought obviously strikes him.

He leans over and says, 'I think I might be about to have a psychotic episode.'

I am concerned for my new friend. He manages not to have any episodes between Seattle and Olympia. We reach the state capital and say our goodbyes.

Too addled to remember my full name, he professes as I get up to leave the bus, 'I shall be your McT and you shall be my Lady A.'

Watching the bus lurch away from the station, I feel very sorry for both McT and the rest of the passengers bound for San Francisco.

The rest of the trip to Aberdeen turns out to be restfully uneventful. It's late Friday afternoon and the Grays Harbor Transit bus from Olympia to Hoquiam is modern and clean, half full with people quiet after their weeks' work. We pass squat, windowless bars and tiny dots of settlements: Mud Bay, McCleary, Satsop. Road signs direct drivers to the '8 West to Ocean Beaches,' to the '101 to the Olympic Peninsula.' The ribbon of a highway squeezes between the firs, pines and cedars that hem the road. Light misty rain blurs treetops on further ridges. I worry again about how McT's doing, doubting that he's found another receptive audience for the monologues he seems incapable of stemming.

A road sign foretells unspecified 'Tourist Activities Next Left.' I scan eagerly, but see no break in the wall of trees. In McCleary hand-painted signs urge residents to 'Vote Yes For Schools.' A United Methodist Church is perched amid neat, wooden Victorian houses: one- and two-storey homes in cornflower blues, apricots and creams. A flashing sign tells us that we are passing through the 'Home of the Wildcats.' It's technology à la what we thought the future would look like, back in 1983, and so manages to look hopelessly dated. A gormless 3D black pig perches inexplicably on top of the police station. A cluster of guys in sweatshirts neck bottles of Bud along-side big bikes outside Rounders Bar. We drive on past a two-room schoolhouse, past a cemetery with fresh flowers decking practically every grave, past a small trailer park and a few mobile homes on their own scrappy patches of grass, car parts and discarded appliances strewn across their muddy acreages.

We leave behind Elma McCleary Road and then pass signs to the separate settlements of Elma and McCleary. The 76 Express Mart and Deli offers the touchingly romantic, but rather belated Valentine's Special of '8 piece Chicken Jojos, 9.99. Pre-order 8.99.' I've no idea what a chicken jojo is, but hope that my partner knows me well enough to know that I would be decidedly underwhelmed to find any number of them delivered as a Valentine's gift.

Elma is the 'Home of the Eagles,' and looks to be a one-bar town. A young guy in a navy baseball cap and close-fitting t-shirt peers under the hood of a faded bottle green pick-up in his driveway. Stores advertise chainsaws and trimmers. Souped up 1970s Chevrolets sit outside washed-out houses.

The bus speeds through Satsop. The fire station is the size of a two-car garage. Everything seems miniature. Six Shetland ponies graze in a field and two lockers are tucked neatly in the corner of a field, a sign declaring them to be 'Satsop Mini Storage.' One-bedroom prefabs are dolloped in the middle of lots, their half-pint, half-hearted lawns straggling to the edge of the highway.

Approaching Montesano, mailboxes announce residents 'John and Gladys' and 'The Styners.' A poster tells of an upcoming Montes-ano Banjo Band concert. Another announces a game coming up for

Montesano High School Girls Varsity Fastpitch Team. A fleet of yellow school buses shuttles off in the direction we have just come. Despite all my time in the US, I still find yellow school buses a pleasingly American sight, far more exciting than the mud-spattered orange double deckers that we clambered aboard with our hockey sticks each school morning of my childhood.

As I watch a snub-snouted yellow bus disappear, it suddenly strikes me that mine was, actually, one of the better school commutes on offer, possibly more interesting than the one the school children of Montesano experience daily. Now that I think about it, we had an incredible school run; I just didn't notice. As the number 59 hurtled towards Sauchiehall Street, I didn't notice how the rows of light sandstone tenements stood proudly along Hyndland Road—bay windows stacked four high, up to an apex of starlings; how the sun glinted on the Gothic revival spires and towers of Glasgow University, the fourth-oldest university in the English-speaking world; how the bronze statue of cartoon character Lobey Dosser and his faithful two-legged horse El Fideldo leaned cheekily towards Woodlands Road; how majestic the grand Victorian townhouses looked, perched along the brim of Park Crescent; how the Edwardian baroque Mitchell Library held court over the M8 to Edinburgh; how the twin cus-tard-coloured fins of the old Beresford hotel's Art Deco façade rose at precise right angles above the morning traffic; or how the Art Nou-veau curlicues of the Charles Rennie Mackintosh-designed Glasgow School of Art angled elegantly upwards to the school's eaves. No, I didn't notice any of this. I shuffled through my Walkman, immersed in homemade tapes of the week's Top 30 hits, recorded complete with me singing along, my wee brother Brian asking obscure questions and my mum calling us downstairs for dinner.

While I pine for a Glasgow morning and a long gone Strathclyde Passenger Transport route, I still think that this rural Washington State commute looks pretty exciting. The US is still so enjoyably foreign to me, even after all these years. Cranberry farms! Awesome deals on chicken jojos! Men with substantial gun racks and even more substantial mullets! I'm glad I haven't got entirely used to it, although I do now take for granted things such as the existence of qualifications in latte art, dinner portions I can feast on for a week and the fact that people would like me to have a nice day. But I've never quite let go of that feeling of how alien and thrilling this North American life of mine is.

My excitement rises with every exclamation-marked billboard we pass, each one promising coastal wonders ahead: 'A New Beach Town!' 'The Sun Is Setting On This Opportunity! Buy Now!' 'Beachfront Resort!' 'Ocean Shores Casino!' 'New Hotel!' 'Tsunami Evacuation Route.' There's no exuberant punctuation for that last one, just a terrified figure scrambling up a steep slope while simultaneously cowering underneath an enormous wave.

The scenery switches from Small Town to Smoky Industrial. A sign looms on the right, 'Welcome to Aberdeen! Come as you are.' I have. I've made it. I'm here.

That first summer in the US, when I travelled around the country with Mark, people looked up from glowing televisions to ask whether Scotland had electricity. I don't think they believed us when we told them that television was invented by a Scot, John Logie Baird, in 1925. In two different states, we were asked if there were schools in Scotland, and we got sceptical smiles when we mentioned that Scotland's oldest school, The High School of Glasgow, opened in 1124, more than half a millennium earlier than the most ancient such institution in the US. As we marked up thousands of miles on the blacktop—a surface invented by John Loudon McAdam in Scotland in the late 1700s—we were complimented several times on the excellent English we spoke. I often wondered if people were joking, but the earnest and interested expressions implied not. I have hopes that people in Aberdeen will have more awareness of the city and country their home is named after, or will, at least, ask me if we have phones so I can tell that Edinburgh's Alexander Graham Bell invented that clever contraption as well. As the Scottish Ambassador, it's the least I can do.

Aberdeen's historic downtown is a sad affair—one of those American towns with its heart slowly dying. Faded turn-of-the-century buildings that must have housed fine department stores and once been all a-bustle have sparse window displays or 'Lease' signs. I walk down Wishkah Street where decorative metal surrounds have been placed round skulking, uncertain trees along the sidewalk. In homage to Kurt Cobain, who was born here, one commemorates the band Nirvana. It's the result of a local group's petitioning and fundraising. The group is also responsible for a stock of commemorative Cobain items available online, featuring Kurt's 'Come As You Are' lyrics on the town's welcome sign. I'm torn between a barbecue apron, a 'classic thong' or an unintentionally abbreviated badge that states, 'ome as you ar.' It could sit alongside my Washington State snowglobe with the upside down lobster.

Cobain is a big selling point here. Stained red letters on a fast food shack's marquee offer 'The New Kurt Cobain Book' in between 'Oyster Fritters' and 'Clam Chowder.' The troubled singer's time here earned Aberdeen the title of The Birthplace of Grunge. This minor-keyed musical genre sensibly moved to Olympia and then onto Seattle as soon as it saved up the bus fare. I don't blame it. After a block's walk through this damp port on the edge of the rainforest I began to suspect that grunge is the direct descendent of drizzle, drabness and depression.

Called Wishkah by its first settlers, Aberdeen wasn't actually named after the Scottish city of Aberdeen. It turns out that it was named after the adjacent Aberdeen Salmon Cannery, itself named by the James B Stewarts, Scottish immigrants who arrived in 1875. By 1900, things at the mouth of the Wishkah River had got rowdy and Aberdeen was one of the roughest towns on the West Coast, earning it its 'Hellhole of the Pacific' accolade. Primarily a mill and fishing town, Aberdeen's is a hard luck story. It was hit hard by the

Great Depression in the 1930s, by running out of big trees in the 1950s and by running out of fish in the 1970s and 80s. A brief spark of hope about nuclear energy came to nothing. When Spotted Owls inconveniently landed on the Endangered Species list, many forests that provided a livelihood to the town's population were closed to logging. The sawmill, as well as the nearby Cosmopolis Pulp Mill, closed. Now Aberdeen's got its hopes pinned on tourism and a new biodiesel plant. I've got to admire this pummelled boxer of a town that refuses to admit defeat.

Aberdeen has appealing things to visit, from turn of the century timber barons' mansions in the Broadway Hill area, Aberdeen Museum of History and a historical shipyard that is home to The Lady Washington, to riverfront parks, watershed trails and fish hatcheries, but this bleak day doesn't show off the town at its best.

A restaurant I'd found online turns out to be a dingy looking 'dance bar' by the docks. Wandering the damp streets looking for somewhere more salubrious, I decide to check out another place I'd seen mentioned in a guidebook, Mac's Tavern. It's the only even vaguely Scottish-sounding place in Aberdeen. This surprises me. In so many American towns, even the most tenuous link, fact or fiction, is excuse enough to launch tourist-luring attempts. Riverside, Iowa proclaims itself the future birthplace of Captain Kirk on account of a *Star Trek* storyline that lands the captain's first moments here in 2233, and the small farming community has changed the name of its annual Riverfest to Trekfest. Dilley, Texas introduces itself as 'The Self-Proclaimed Watermelon Capital of Texas' on account of its juicy crop. McPherson, Kansas, has no discernible Scottish population but holds a Highland Games based entirely on its 'Mc.' Hot Springs, New Mexico went even further. It accepted a dare from the game show of the same name to rename the town Truth or Consequences. I want to tell the Aberdonians that Aberdeen is missing a fine marketing opportunity, but the streets are empty and there's no one to tell.

The light has all but gone, and drizzle falls dolefully. I turn the corner onto West Heron Street and see Mac's at the other end of the block. Outside, a shadowy figure stands smoking in the shadow of the bar's neon. There is a rush of noise, alcohol-soaked voices and a sudden glare of light as the door swings open. A one-legged man on crutches lurches out the door, teeters and falls flat on his face. The smoker stands there, looks at him and takes another drag on his cigarette. The one-legged drinker struggles to his foot and I turn and flee back round the corner.

The only other place I find open is Aberdeen's Popcorn Café. According to a *Vanity Fair* photo team I recently worked with on a story, flavoured popcorn is a very chic eat. Who would have thought that Aberdeen would offer such cutting edge cuisine? Neither member of the counter crew understands my accent. They ask where I'm from, but have no reaction whatsoever to my declaration that I'm Scottish. I am disappointed. I try to provoke them with spurious questions about popcorn varieties, but, no, they simply do not care.

True enough, I have to admit, I don't really care how any of the places I have lived got their names. Glasgow means 'dear green place,' although 'murky grey place' often seemed more appropriate for my hometown. Now, though, Glasgow does seem a rather dear, green place. Distance has driven that home. I think fondly about the fact that the city has the most parks per square mile of any city in Europe. It also, I firmly believe, has the most character per square mile. It's boisterous, it's brash and it's the only place where subway trains were designed with the assumption that no passenger would ever be taller than an adolescent hobbit.

Sitting with a coffee, way over here on the edge of the Pacific, I miss Glasgow. It's strange to think that these days I spend far more time in cities from Seattle to Montreal to Dallas than I do in my beloved hometown. The rain falling outside reminds me of home. I watch the reflections of the traffic lights ripple in the pools that have gathered on the sidewalk outside.

As I sit in a brightly lit corner of the bustling popcorn store, various staff members bring me popcorn samples, gently jolting me back to the present. I happily munch gooey toffee, chocolatey Hershey's Kiss and spicy jalopeño-flavoured kernels. Who cares what the town's named after? This popcorn is good.

I happily delve through stories in the local *Daily World* newspaper. Its pages tell of the drama of small town life. A high school football player has signed a letter of intent to play for a university in the next state. A police deputy's patrol car has been rear-ended. A Grays Harbor Undersheriff confirms that an intoxicated fisherman took five Taser gun shocks and three blasts of pepper-spray before officers were able to arrest him. It's definitely a town that refuses to go quietly.

Scottish connections are sadly lacking, so I retreat to Los Arcos Family Restaurant, a Mexican place on the highway. I order their blackberry margarita special. They bring me an entire pint of the concoction. I am impressed and much cheered. To my left, a bored wee girl slumps a table away from her parents and their jovially loud friends. Pints of margarita are likely to make folks jovial. She looks at them with embarrassment. Some things are the same the world over.

After dinner, I pop into a gas station to pick up some refreshments. Stepping into the brightly lit store, a fake doorbell chime announces my entry.

An unhurried voice comes from the back, 'Be out in a minute.'

'No hurry,' I say, scanning for the drinks fridge.

There is a crash and a series of metallic clunks. A scrawny white woman with not so recently dyed blonde hair scraped back off her face, appears out of a storeroom, pails and boxes in tow. She stops for a moment to consider me. Blue and black tattoos cover both her arms, disappearing into a tent of a pristine white polo shirt, and peeking out again above the collar.

'Be a minute,' she says.

'No hurry,' I repeat in as bright and helpful manner as I can muster.

With what seems a major effort she bundles the boxes and pails into another storeroom and plods towards me. She looks at me with fuzzy eyes as she makes her way around to behind the counter. She appears to be concentrating intently on putting one foot in front of the other. She breathes heavily. I am relieved when she makes it to the till. I put my bottles of water down on the counter's Perspex-protected lottery card display.

'That all?'

'Yes, thanks. Just water,' I offer apologetically.

'Where you from?' she asks.

'Scotland,' I tell her.

She stops what she's doing and looks up at me appraisingly. 'Well, isn't that a trip?'

I'm not sure if she is referring to this encounter or to the distance she presumes I have travelled in order to reach this gas station on the Hoquiam side of Aberdeen tonight. I say nothing while I attempt to assess the situation.

'You speak really good English for someone from Scotland.'

I have no idea if she is joking. I look at her. She attempts to meet my gaze. She looks earnest and interested, but her eyes fail to focus. She hands me my change. I thank her for the water and, for the second time tonight, flee.

8. FAR OFF IN SUNLIT PLACES:
HONOLULU AND KAILUA, HAWAII

A stray cat hovers at the ramp to the parking garage, waiting for us to clear off so it can return to a tasty snack of road-kill pigeon. The parking lot is otherwise deserted. An occasional beat-up, low-rider car cruises by on South King Street, Honolulu. The cat is alert, intent on returning to its feast.

Since arriving in Honolulu a few hours ago, I have acquired a scientist friend, Dr April, and a silver dolphin-adorned paper folder with my name glitter-penned in the corner. Both have already proved useful; the dolphin folder has provided amusement and directions to this deserted parking lot; Dr A has prevented me from turning back at the Ala Wai Canal and not even getting this far at all. The folder—upon which someone has carefully positioned the dolphin leaping majestically into a metallic blue waterline—is the programme for the Hawaii Scottish Country Dance Aloha Winter Weekend. I love this folder. It makes me feel less apprehensive about the possible public humiliation ahead. Surely, people who get their grandchildren to hand draw shiny leaping dolphins will be kind to me as I attempt Scottish Country Dancing for the first time?

Right now, however, there's no sign of anyone to be kind or otherwise to me. April and I slow slightly on seeing a very obviously closed community centre in front of us. A sign beside one door reads, 'No Hula Class Today.' We consult the folder. Inside there is a series of treasure maps with 'Treasure the Dance' written on them. I notice that the scientist is studying these intently.

'What do you think we will win?' she asks.

Dr A is sure there is a prize to be found at the end of this sheaf of clip-art-enhanced leaflets if we just pay enough attention. We study them for some time and reluctantly come to the conclusion that the prize appears to be the opportunity to keep the love of Scottish dancing alive in Hawaii. We are both a little disappointed.

There's an eerie silence as we walk past the battered dumpsters, through the empty car park towards where our treasure map indicates that we might find the Mo'ili'ili Silent Dance Center. We turn the corner, see light streaming out of a quiet, small one-storey wooden shack—and then it hits us. The Silent Dance Center is suddenly far from silent. I take an involuntary step backwards. The cat bolts. April grabs me by the sleeve before I, too, make a run for it. It's the noise that I've dreaded since childhood. The wail that kept me awake night after night. The screech that filled my brothers and me with horror. It's hideous. It's terrifying. It's the sound that even after 8,000 miles and two decades still gnaws at my soul. April gently pushes me forward. I shudder, swallow and bravely trek on as the creaky-hinge bray of violins tuning up caterwauls through the Honolulu night.

Like many things, my aversion towards traditional Scottish music is my sister Orla's fault. Her membership in various tartan-hued violin ensembles led to an awful lot of violin tuning in our house when I was young and trying to do important things like sulk, fail exams and listen to Bryan Adams records. The sound still sets my teeth on edge and provokes a maelstrom of adolescent anguish.

Soon we are spotted lurking in the shrubbery by a smiling woman in a graceful, dark, ankle-length dress. We sidle over to where she stands on the veranda. Lillian Cunningham, the chairwoman of Hawaii's Royal Scottish Country Dance Society, gestures at rows of gold doubloon-shaped name badges adorned with wee plastic jewels and explains that this year's theme is 'Treasure the Dance.'

I thank her for the glittered folder and tell her, 'I loved the artwork.'

She laughs and admits, 'It took a while to do all those dolphins.'

No grandchildren appear to have been involved.

As Lillian picks out our doubloons, April turns to me and whispers at me with raised eyebrows, 'Grown-ups made these!'

I love them for this. It increases my willingness to pitch in and support keeping the love of Scottish country dancing alive round these parts. As well as the individual treasure maps for each event, there's also another rolled up map with carefully burned corners and the programme of dances for tonight. I whip off the tartan ribbon and unroll mine. Ash promptly falls all over my white slacks and leaves a trail of murky smudges all the way down to my tartan sneakers.

When I edge nervously into the dance studio, I am the only woman not wearing a skirt or kilt. Somewhere in the folder's sheaf of papers we were instructed to wear 'aloha casual' to this part of the weekend. This afternoon Dr A and I saw a sign stating that 'The Aloha Spirit Are Traits of Character That Expresses The Charm, Warmth and Sincerity of Hawaii's People.'

'How do you wear that?' I asked the scientist.

She puzzled over this and then picked out this outfit for me, deciding that these shoes were the most sincere of my footwear options.

Everyone in the room seems to know who we are, perhaps because April and I are at least thirty years younger than everyone else or perhaps because there are only about 15 people in the room and they seem to have been doing reels together since long before my wee sister first put screeching bow to discordant fiddle strings.

This Scottish-Hawaiian evening, billed as a 'casual meet and greet social' promised 'dancing, conversation and light refreshments,' as well as the opportunity to display our aloha wear. We are soon greeted by several dancers, none of whom are Hawaiian.

A couple from Brisbane who have flown over specially for this weekend tell us, 'This is our third year Scottish dancing.'

Next a smiling trio of Japanese women come up. One in a below-the-knee blue flower print dress says, 'Marchan from Tokyo,' and bows.

The next, in a long pink flower print dress, says, 'Sachiko from Yokohama,' and bows.

The last woman, resplendent in turquoise flower print, says, 'Chieko from Tokyo,' and bows.

I say, 'Aefa from Scotland' and bow awkwardly back.

'Scotland!' exclaims Chieko and beams.

I muster a surprised return 'Scotland!' and grin back.

When the dancing finally starts, the three Japanese women will remain on the dance floor, smiling with delight, for the rest of the evening.

Before the dancing gets underway, however, instructor Bruce has to introduce the band, the Humuhumunukunukuapua'a and Strathspey Society Band, named after the state's official fish. Bruce is coerced into leading us all in repeating the name of Hawaii's foolishly named state fish. Humu. Humu. Nuku. Nuku. A. Pua. Ahhhh. It's a mouthful of a name for a snouty wee fish. Despite repeating this several times, I am pretty sure I wouldn't make it through ordering a state fish and chips any time soon.

The dancing gets going. Bruce barks curt, quick-fire instructions and everyone scurries about doing his terse bidding.

'First lady, second man,' insists Bruce.

He takes Scottish country dancing very seriously and does not tolerate any shilly-shallying in the ranks.

'Passing left shoulder! No! Left shoulder!' Bruce says, 'Reels of three.' There is a lengthy pause as he looks round with a stern frown. 'Does that surprise anybody?'

Several newly arrived Hawaiians try very hard not to look surprised.

'Good,' he says, darkly. 'After the reels, dancing couple crosses by the right hand, casts to the second place and dances a half figure of eight to the twos above. They dance in, down, below the threes, cast into second place and all three couples pass by the right hand.'

A couple of newer dancers exchange looks of mild consternation. My heart begins to thump uncomfortably. My palms sweat. This is terrifying.

I have excused myself from taking to the floor tonight in order to watch and learn. I sink back against the wall, under a tinsel palm tree that droops from the ceiling, and try to pick up some tips for tomorrow's lesson. I learn that when the dancers are doing a wee hoppity skip forward and then back to where they were, they are 'advancing and retiring.' I also learn that the dancers cannot comprehend why I am not seizing every possible opportunity to demonstrate my love of Scottish country dancing by joining them on the floor. Despite my official spectator's role tonight, there are several beckons and one rather insistent arm tug. I huddle under the tinsel fronds and fend off all entreaties. After several minutes featuring far more complicated manoeuvres than advancing and retiring, I whisper to April that I'd really like to retire completely and not join any dancing this weekend at all. But April will hear none of this talk; she is here to make sure I do not succumb to stage fright, or rather Silent Dance Center-fright, and shirk my dancing duties. I wish I was someone who could throw herself unselfconsciously into such antics, but, truth be told, I am someone who would prefer to throw herself into a vat of roiling humuhumunukunukuapua'as rather than do jigs or reels in public.

One of the things I liked best about growing up in Scotland was the fact that, other than a brief six month-interlude when my mum bribed me with Jelly Babies to attend ballet lessons, nobody made me dance in public. Towering above my diminutive Glaswegian classmates, I was happy to skulk away my otherwise relatively happy school years attempting to draw as little attention as possible to myself, so it was an enormous relief to me that nobody thought of making us show our paces at any such embarrassing national arts. We didn't learn Scottish country dancing or Highland dancing, which seemed perfectly reasonable when we lived neither in the country nor in the Highlands. In fact, if you had asked me during the 20 years I spent living in Scotland, I would have been hard pressed to tell you the difference between these two types of dance, although I might have been able to muster a suggestion that the Highland version involved swords. The only dancing I was to be found attempting was a glum left foot–right foot shuffle at an occasional school disco, an ungainly stumble round the sides of Tiffany's roller disco on a Saturday afternoon and perhaps a jokey waltz to a Corries record with my dad at Christmas. Fast forward all these years and I am the only person at Hawaii's Scottish Country Dancing Weekend who can't even do a single basic Scottish country dance step.

I attempted to get a head start on my land's legworks this afternoon as I flew out of San Francisco, the Golden Gate Bridge glowing rusty Irn-Bru-orange in the February sun below me. As the stately stripe—an exact colour match for Scotland's national soft drink—dwindled into miniature against the bottle green of the Marin Headlands, I stared at tiny, faded, perplexing pages covered in neat numbers, tidy boxes, precise circles, careful arrows, tight lasso lines. I flipped slowly through, without a sliver of comprehension dawning. If I mapped out the patterns of a disoriented bee, plans for an unnecessarily complicated heist or table revisions for a large wedding at which half the family refuses to be seated facing an objectionable aunt, they wouldn't look too dissimilar. The text throughout my in-flight reading material—the revised 1950 editions of *Scottish Country Dance*—didn't help me overcome doubts about this weekend's attempts to become a better, more rounded Scot. In 'Betty's Wedding,' they instructed me, 'First couple turn right hands one-and-a-half times and cast down one place on other side. First couple dance half figure of eight round second couple. Who move up on seven-eight.' During another reel I would theoretically be supposed to be responsible for some part of, 'Grand Chain. Pass partners twice and return to places. Turn partners, right hand. All set to partners with Strathspey steps. Each three couples dance reel of three.' 'Bonnie Glenshee' didn't look any simpler. It resembled a tricky scientific formula with three densely typed pages of instructions and four entirely unrelated-looking diagrams. I scanned with dismay other examples of my homeland's fancy footwork. For bars 13 to 16 of a reel called 'The Triumph,' I read that 'All three lead up the middle in triumph.' I first scanned this bit as 'leap up the middle' and thought it sounded like a fun dance, but triumphant leading sounds far more demanding.

The captain's voice piped through the cabin, cutting through my confusion. 'This... is Captain Mike! Welcome on board this fabulous flight to Honolulu! I'm up front on this beautiful sunny day with my co-pilot Captain Wayne. Marie, Chantelle and Lisa will be taking care of you during the flight. And if there's anything we can do up here at the pointy end to make your flight more comfortable, just let us know.' The pointy end? Surely that's not the technical name for the... um, pointy end? Captain Mike seemed to be one of those 'It's easy! Look no hands!' captains. This is not the attitude I wish for in a man behind the wheel of a 767.

As I watch the Aloha Winter Weekend dancers skirl and hop their way through a reel called 'Maxwell's Rant,' I wish I knew where the pointy end was. Or that the dance instructions were as helpful and cheery as Captain Mike. How hard can this be? The Scottish-Hawaiians told me as long as I had 'a sense of rhythm,' I'd be fine.

As I sit on the side lines in the Silent Dance Centre, I tap out Morse Code distress calls with a nervous pen, a rapid staccato beat and an increasing wallow of doubt.

'It's a lady chain, then a grand chain, followed by advance and retire. Does that sound familiar to everybody?' calls Bruce.

It seems not and various dancers glance unsurely at each other. Brisbane accents hastily whisper instructions. After a particularly interminable stretch of advancing and retiring, I duck out to the balcony.

Marchan from Tokyo comes to join me and tells me, shyly, 'In Tokyo, we have three branches of Scottish country dancing. That is 1000 people in Tokyo Scottish country dancing.'

I am amazed.

She continues, 'I was a folk dancer when I was young, then I discovered Scottish music and dancing and now I've been doing only that for the last 30 years. Scottish dancing is everything.'

An animated elderly man in an unintentionally jaunty short kilt, blue shirt and dancing shoes rushes out onto the deck. His shoulders are slightly stooped, his socks pulled up to his exposed knees.

'They said one of you is from Glasgow! I'm from Glasgow!' he exclaims excitedly.

I bound over and shake hands, just as excited to meet someone from home. I tell him about my mission to become Scottish in America.

'That's just what happened to me!' he says.

My new friend Alex Pratt was born in Springburn in 1924, the seventh of eight children, and conscripted into the navy when he was 18. After training as a carpenter and joining the Merchant Marine, the now-sprightly 86-year-old worked his way across America, reaching Hawaii in the 1970s during Oahu's building boom. He never left.

'When I moved here forty years ago, I'd never seen so much tartan in my life! I'd never worn a kilt,' he says, hitching his precariously angled Stuart tartan a notch higher. 'These reels, these jigs, these Strathspeys, this country dancing? We're Glaswegians; we don't do that! I did ballroom dancing.'

Alex's accent, undimmed by four decades on this 44 by 30-mile island, is as strong as the day he left. We are both thrilled to meet someone from home all the way over here, ten time zones away.

'Do you get back much?' he asks.

'I was just home last month.'

'How was it?' Alex leans in, eager to catch anything I can tell him about our hometown.

'It was... brilliant.'

'Were you in Springburn?'

'Not this time.'

'Ach, it's a different place now, anyway. The Springburn I knew is long gone. Did you know Springburn once produced a quarter of all the trains in the world? A quarter of all the choo choos... Springburn, I remember it so well. The noise of the train yards… The sparkies, that's what we called the electric trams… The paddle boats in Springburn Park. It was a fine place to grow up. But I wouldn't know it any more.'

I nod. I only know the Springburn that was redeveloped beyond recognition in the 1960s.

'You get to the stage,' says Alex, wistfully, 'You've been away so long, you can't really go back, you have to keep going. You know? You've turned into a…' He pauses.

I nod again. 'A tourist.'

'Aye, a tourist. Ach, but Glasgow, there's nowhere like it,' he says. 'I love it here, but there's nowhere like Glasgow.'

We both smile, thinking about Glasgow, out here in the warm Hawaii night. We both love the city we left behind decades ago.

Bruce announces 'Mrs Stewart's Jig.'

Alex's eyes light up, 'I can do that one! I can do it!' and he dashes back to join the dance.

The rest of the weekend, I see the squat, stocky 1970s apartment blocks that trudge along Honolulu's hillsides and think of the happy, excited, old Glaswegian who helped build them.

From inside we hear Bruce call, 'First and seconds set! Petronella turns as seconds set. PET-ro-NEL-la turns!'

Linda from Colorado comes out for some fresh air and takes Alex's place against the railings on the terrace.

'Back in Colorado we were the first bagpipe band to have its own dancers instead of borrowing ones from the local St Andrew's Society!' she tells me.

Her delivery tells me that this is an impressive feat and I make valiant attempts to look suitably amazed.

Before setting off for Hawaii, I read that Scottish country dancing offers all manner of benefits, from building bone density and reducing cellulite to establishing new friendships. According to Linda, however, it's actually really all about the release of what she calls 'those woo hoo endorphins.' She is as enthusiastic about this as she is about bagpipe bands having their own dancers. In fact, she seems to be pleasingly enthusiastic about pretty much everything. The website I read also mentioned that Scottish country dancing is 'a structured form of dance' appealing to those of a 'scientific' persuasion rather than 'arty' types. Unfortunately, no one's going to classify me as even vaguely scientific, so I'm out of luck, although it doesn't seem like a PhD in molecular biology has equipped April with much inclination or ability to master my homeland's dance steps either.

I ask Chun from New Jersey why he took up dancing. He gives me a look of complete wonder and doesn't answer. Not aloud, anyway. His expression says everything and his look is almost pitying.

By 8 pm, things have got a bit more boisterous inside. Two polite whoops come from the dance floor as I stand and talk with Lillian out on the deck and I'm pretty sure I heard one restrained yee-haw. Lillian tells me about all the people learning Scottishness here in Hawaii. With five Scottish organisations including a dance group and a pipe band, an annual Scottish festival, a formal Burns Supper and a book project about early immigrants to Hawaii from Scotland, the Hawaiian Scots are a busy bunch.

'We have a particularly Hawaii version of "learning to be Scottish,"' she tells me. 'At the Boxing Day dance party we discovered that exactly half the attendees had grown up outside the US, and only one person grew up here in Hawaii. Two were from Scotland; many more were from Asia. One new dancer of Chinese-Taiwanese-Filipino heritage says she is celebrating more Scottish holidays than Chinese, Taiwanese and Filipino put together. We're a lively, mixed community brought together by Scottish dancing.'

We watch the dancers whirl by the open doorway and she tells me, 'Chieko plays Scottish fiddle too. She says it gives her something to live for.'

I watch the smiling Japanese woman differently after that. I comment that the hall has really filled up.

Lillian says, 'The programme said the dancing started at 7.30, so our people didn't turn up till then.'

I thought there was supposed to be a social element to this, but perhaps Linda was right and it is really just about the woo hoo endorphins.

The band lay down their instruments for a short break. A few people mill about by a table outside, but for most of the participants, it's all about the dancing. No conversation is necessary. They take a few swigs of water and are back in their positions on the floor ready to wheel and whirl about the room for a jig called 'Machine Without Horses.'

I don't learn much during the evening—other than that a lot of Scottish dancing moves appears to be convoluted, possibly drunken, descendants of skipping. Perhaps of more immediate use is that I learn that the bulbous white squishy things that I loaded with some trepidation onto a paper plate are lychees stuffed with walnuts and cream cheese, and that they're really good.

Despite my not being entirely convinced that a morning of Scottish country dancing is a suitably enticing reason to slouch out of bed on a Saturday morning in Honolulu, I get the details of tomorrow's intensive class at the golf club and tell my new friends that I'll see them at 9 am. They all seem terribly pleased. I am pleased that they are so pleased and try a few cautious advances and a wee slip step as April and I retire from the car park.

The next morning, we drive up Campbell Avenue. It's 8.45 am and the day is already heating up. A guy in board shorts cycles along beside us, surfboard tucked casually under his arm. A Roberts Hawaii bus cruises by, adorned with a galloping yellow rabbit wearing a lei. On the back of the bus the same attitude-y bunny gives a cheeky peace sign. April and I circle round the car park of the Ala Wai Golf Course clubhouse. Parking spaces are thin on the ground.

'Come on, you scunners! We need to dance!' says April, exasperated.

By the time we find a space in the far end of the car park, this whole escapade seems less amusing. After all, I'm in Hawaii, I could be on the beach, tucking into a freshly picked pineapple for breakfast or scouring the stores for aloha wear—rather than skipping about a golf club to traditional fiddle music. April, however, is very enthusiastic. She is not about to miss out on an opportunity to witness me making a total haggis of myself. I suspect this is a large part of the reason she accompanied me to Hawaii in the first place.

A pre-dancing breakfast is underway when we eventually clamber up to the Eugene and Harriet Ichinose Dance Palladium. I'm not sure whether aloha wear was encouraged this morning, but since the weekend has a treasure theme and we spotted two skulls among the floral arrangements on the snack table last night, April has assured me that wearing a pink t-shirt decorated with silver guitars and skulls would be entirely appropriate. From the looks from the assembled breakfast eaters, the Honolulu branch of the Royal Scottish Country Dance Society does not agree. Even my tartan Converse footwear don't seem to be much of a concession in the eyes of my morning's dance partners. I'm the only one in sight not wearing a voluminous skirt of some sort, including the men.

I chat to this morning's Bruce, the name seemingly compulsory for Scottish country dance instructors on the island of Oahu. This one is a musician from the Unpronounceable Fish and Strathspey Society Band. He seems to like my t-shirt slightly better than the other dancers. I look around, but Alex has obviously taken the morning off the dance floor after last night's exertions, and is nowhere to be seen. Word has spread and about half of the 30 or so people seem to know that the only one with a Scottish accent in the dance pavilion this morning has never done a step of Scottish dancing.

Soon we're inside and straight into strenuous exercises and practice dance steps, stretching upwards, leaning forwards, lurching one way, galloping the other.

Hawaii's state tartan was recognized in 2008 and I spy it on a sprightly woman who turns out to be Mrs Herring, mother of Douglas Herring, the Hawaiian tartan designer. The designer's dad is also here. I manage to step on both their toes during the opening bars of the first dance of the morning. I'm hurtled from one dancer to another. It's like being a colt, paraded around the ring one way, then another. Soon the wonderfully kind and patient Lillian comes to be my partner, saving other people's toes from being trodden on by my inappropriate footwear.

'Try to dance on your toes. See, I'm already giving you refinements,' says Lillian encouragingly.

There's some skipping in pairs in a wide circle, then some skipping back and forth opposite a variety of people, several wee curtsey-skips and a significant amount of sideways skipping. Then it gets compli-cated. I find myself dashing round the third man diagonally opposite, pelting off in the other direction and attempting not to crash into fellow dancers. Mostly I just flail about and skip in circles around anyone foolish enough to pause even momentarily opposite me. If you sketched out the dance steps and directions of this bit of the day's first taught dance, 'Jenny's Gentle Jig, ' it would look something like a nice floral pattern with neat pearl stitches. My version looks like a five-year-old's first mangled scarf for their granny. I am just as proud. When I stagger through the first chunk of my first jig, I am exultant—I know where the pointy end is! I do an exuberant bow for the sake of April's video camera.

But as soon as I've memorized one set of moves, fish-band-Bruce adds another. Then another. And just when I think I've got the hang of all jig-manoeuvres and where I'm supposed to advance, retire, cast, gallop in a panic struck manner round the second gentleman-substi-tute, do a reel of threes with the first and the third woman, two more people join the group and I'm lost. My version of 'Jenny's Gentle Jig' ranks somewhere between a bewildered three-legged race and how I might look had I stumbled barefoot onto a patch of particularly prickly pineapples. But after a few more friendly shoves, points and yet more galloping and uneven lurching around people, I realise that I have actually done my first Scottish country dance. Suddenly, there is a huddle of people congratulating me. A couple of others sidle over to see what the fuss is about and seem genuinely surprised on hearing that that was my first-ever attempt. I take this as the finest praise possible.

After three more hours of intensive dancing, the fiddles start tuning up again. I look at April and back at the dancers assembling for another half day of dancing, we say our goodbyes and make off into the scorching hot Honolulu day.

'My sister and I always debrief after traumatic experiences,' April tells me.

We drive back towards Waikiki and I debrief, lightheaded with glee and several heavy-footed jigs' worth of woo hoo endorphins.

Some buildings opt for fierce stone beasties such as lions or dogs to guard their entrances. When we leave Honolulu's marine-themed Wyland Hotel we walk past a pair of playful-looking cement dolphins. Other than nose-butting a beach ball at intruders, I'm not sure how effective they would be on hypothetical security detail.

Dr A and I walk through downtown Honolulu where there are leis on everything from the wee figures on restroom doors to unim-pressed-looking terriers waiting outside shops. Car bumper stickers entreat us to 'Keep the Country Country' and to buy Viper Surfing Fins. Another is insistent that we 'Bring Back Assassination.' Just so we will be ready when such executions swing back into favour, a heavily made up, modelesque woman in her early 20s, sweating in the afternoon sun, invites me to 'shoot real guns at Hawaii's safest indoor range.' This is vetoed by my more sensible companion, despite the specials on offer on the all-Japanese leaflet the model gives us. Convenience stores broadcast specials on taro chips, myriad pine-apple-based edibles and Spam sushi, seemingly a major delicacy in Hawaii. Sushi, for the Vancouverite April, is the taste of home, but Spam sushi doesn't seem to be the maki she's missing. The Scottish flavours I miss most are pakora and pretty much everything on the menu at Glasgow's Wee Curry Shop. Americans are often astounded to hear that most Scots eat pakora far more frequently than haggis.

Coming from the current Curry Capital of Britain, I am curious to see the local take on Indian food. I keep my eyes open, but am quietly relieved that nowhere in Honolulu has Spam masala or Spam pakora on the menu.

We stop to watch shoals of learner-surfers paddle out into Waikiki Bay. Once the home of Hawaiian royalty, Honolulu is now a city teeming with malls, hotels and firing ranges. But it's not all Spam specialities and gun-toting tourists, the city is also home to the only royal palace in the US, King David Kalakaua and Queen Kapi'olani's 'Iolani Palace, built in 1880.

Super-social Kalakaua—or the Merrie Monarch, as he was known— was Hawaii's second last royal ruler and it's a member of his family that April and I are now trying to track down. We are on our way to pay respects to Hawaii's most loved Scot, Princess Victoria Ka'iulani Kalaninuiahilapalapa Kaw'kiu i Lunalilo Cleghorn. We know the trail is heating up when we find ourselves on Ka'iulani Avenue and pass the Sheraton that bears her name.

We find the princess in a small park on the busy corner of Kanekapolei and Kuhio Avenues, gleaming bronze and tucked behind foliage. The statue has a stately poise. Despite the ceaseless traffic, somehow this tiny glade feels strangely still compared to its surroundings. It was here in what is now the tourist tramping grounds of Waikiki that Princess Ka'iulani, Hawaii's beloved last Crown Princess, was born in 1875. The only child of King Kalakaua's sister Miriam Likelike and Archibald Cleghorn from Edinburgh, the Scottish-Hawaiian Ka'iulani was called 'the island rose' by Robert Louis Stevenson and 'the hope of Hawaii' by her people.

If you count the half-Scottish Captain Cook, Scots first reached Hawaii in 1778, although the majority arrived between 1880 and 1930, many coming out to manage or work on the sugar plantations of what became known as the Scotch Coast on the east coast of Hawaii's Big Island. Archie Cleghorn got to Hawaii early, arriving in the islands in 1851 and building a successful empire of dry goods stores. He married

Princess Miriam Likelike and created a lush tropical estate for his wife and daughter with mango, teak, cinnamon, palms, hibiscus, a banyan tree and lily ponds.

The incongruous traffic island that April and I are now standing on would have been the centre of that 10-acre Ainahau estate, a gift to Ka'iulani from her godmother Princess Ruth Keelikolani. Wild Chinese Jasmine grew all through the gardens and Ka'iulani's pet peacocks roamed all over the grounds. A fictionalised version of the princess's diary by Ellen Emerson White describes Ainahau as having 'peacock-studded shadows.' The shadows here these days are more tourist-studded and occasionally pineapple-studded. Sometimes even tourist-with-pineapple-studded, but the peafowl that once strutted about this corner of Honolulu are nowhere to be seen or heard.

Robert Louis Stevenson and his family arrived in Hawaii in 1889 and the writer soon befriended his countryman Cleghorn and his daughter. He entertained the princess with Scottish tales and legends and she became very fond of him. When the 13-year-old princess was sent to be educated in Britain, Robert Louis Stevenson wrote this poem in her signature book,

'Forth from her land to mine she goes,
The Island maid, the Island rose;
Light of heart and bright of face:
The daughter of a double race.
Her islands here, in Southern sun,
Shall mourn their Kaiulani gone,
And I, in her dear banyan shade,
Look vainly for my little maid.
But our Scots islands far away
Shall glitter with unwonted day,
And cast for once their tempests by
To smile in Kaiulani's eye.'

They never met again. Stevenson died long before his young friend came home.

Despite thinking she would only be away for a year, Ka'iulani would not return to Hawaii for eight years. She was educated in England, but visited Scotland with her father, learned about her Scottish roots and studied Scottish Gaelic. One of her oil paintings of Scotland is on show alongside her surfboard at Honolulu's Bishop Museum.

Meanwhile, Hawaii was changing. King Kalakaua had died, and his successor, Ka'iulani's aunt, Lili'iuokalani, was forced to abdicate in 1893. Ka'iulani's next major voyage was to the United States to ask the American people not to annex her kingdom. The young princess went to New York in February 1893 to plead her nation's case. Overcoming extreme shyness to speak, her poise and beauty won the hearts of America. One of her most famous quotes was, 'Today, I, a poor weak girl with not one of my people with me and all these "Hawaiian" statesmen against me, have strength to stand up for my people. Even now I can hear their wail in my heart and it gives me strength and courage and I am strong—strong in the faith of God, strong in the knowledge that I am right, strong in the strength of seventy million people who in this free land will hear my cry and will refuse to let their flag cover dishonor to mine.'

The 18-year-old's attempts were successful, Honolulu rejoiced, but celebrations didn't last long. When she finally set foot on Hawaiian soil again, four years later, the kingdom had been annexed by the US and was on the verge of being declared a republic by President McKinley. Just before leaving England for the last time, Ka'iulani said, 'I must have been born under an unlucky star, as I seem to have my life planned for me in such a way that I cannot alter it.'

Ka'iulani continued fighting for the return of the throne, but was plagued by ill health. She became ill after getting caught in a rainstorm while riding her horse and never recovered. She died on March 6, 1899, aged just 23. Legend has it that at 2 am on the night she died, Ka'iulani's pet peacocks began to scream, telling her people that their brave half-Scottish princess's fight was over.

Sitting in this overlooked spot, I think about the short, full life of this Scottish-Hawaiian heroine. A plaque beneath the figure tells her story and says she was 'Lovingly referred to as Princess of the Peacocks by her people.' I think of another quote from Ka'iulani, 'It has been a strange life, really, and a very romantic one.' While she is remembered and loved by the Hawaiians, there's little mention of her in Scotland. I reach into my bag and pull out the ribbon that held closed last night's treasure map. Amidst all the bustle of downtown Waikiki, the rainbow buses, the tourists sipping Mai Tais on the patio of hotels, I tie the tartan ribbon to one of the princess's bronze fingers, dance a few self-conscious steps of this morning's jig for the Scottish-Hawaiian princess and promise her that I'll go back and tell her other people about her.

It's hot and still as we drive out of town, along Kuhio Avenue, up to the now familiar palm-lined Ala Wai Canal. Spiny mountains rise behind the city, lush with a few puffy clouds dotted decoratively on top. We follow a green and yellow Honolulu Disposal Services truck with a rainbow Aloha State license plate. Driving out of Honolulu, motel-like apartment buildings cling to the slopes and we wonder which ones Alex built. We pass Oahu Country Club as we drive along the impossibly green Pali Highway. Vines trail down from abundantly leafy trees between jagged peaks of stegosaurus-spiked mountains.

This morning I got an e-mail. The subject of the e-mail was simply 'VISIT ME!' and the message, a phone number. At Pali Lookout I call it.

'Hello,' says a suspicious voice.

'Good morning,' I say brightly. 'How are you?'

'Well, I'm still alive.'

I tell April about my correspondent's stereotypically gloom-laden Scottish demeanour. 'He sounded a bit dour.'

'Let's go cheer him up,' she says, and we jump back into the red rental Pontiac, driving past bushes laden with pink and purple flowers to Oahu's windward side.

Pick-up trucks cruise by, blond surfer boys sprawled in the back. This part of Hawaii lives up to its clichés.

We pass Kawainui Marsh and continue on into Kailua. A dozen red and yellow outrigger canoes sit beside the murky canal. I squint in the heat at my hastily jotted directions. We turn onto Kainalu Drive and pass Kuupua, Kuuhoa, Kuuhale and Kuumele, and turn down Kuukama. We cruise down a neatly manicured street of bungalows, two-car carports, a precise line of mailboxes and perfectly hemmed lawns. A light breeze ruffles the US flags that hang from the eaves. I spy a champagne-coloured Cadillac Deville liberally decorated with statements of American pride and a hula girl sticker. The license plate simply declares, 'HULA.'

'This is it!' I say. 'We've found him!'

A trim woman in her 70s, wearing a cheerful Hawaiian shirt and a bright bandana, opens the door and tells us we can leave our slippers on the mat.

'Dad's expecting you,' she says.

We kick off flip flops and walk obediently in the direction she's gestured, through a room crammed with souvenirs, sepia prints of Hawaii's royal family and an out-of-season Christmas tree, and there we are, face to face with the reason we've come west today, Donald P McDiarmid Jr, Hawaii's freshly elected Scot of the Year.

Hawaii, as far as I know, is the only US state that elects a Scot of the Year, although both Canada and its most Scottish province, Nova Scotia, elect annual top Scots, and there are Scotsmen and Scotswomen of the Year in Scotland.

Dressed in a long-sleeved white Haipu'u Yacht Club t-shirt that states 'No Dues Bring Booze' and white shorts, Don Jr is nowhere near as dour as his phone manner suggested, invalidating our theory that it was his perfecting of this classic Scottish attitude that won him the title. He has strategically propped a printout of an article about his win from *The Honolulu Star-Advertiser*, his name badge from this year's Burns Supper and the Scot of the Year plaque itself in front of where we are expected to sit. God Bless America coasters are scattered across the coffee table beside a couple of Proud to Be an American bookmarks. The room is full of Hokus, the Hawaiian music Grammies. The word means 'star' and Don is very definitely a star in the Hawaiian music world. Not only is he the Scot of this Year, he is president emeritus of Hula Records. Trophies are scattered all round the room.

'I have no idea how many I've won,' he says as a constellation of Hokus twinkle in the mid-afternoon sun.

A champion of the classic Hawaiian hapa haole and slack-key guitar styles, Don Jr's recordings were responsible for launching the careers of scores of Hawaiian artists, including Don Ho, Gabby Pahinui and the Kahauanu Lake Trio. Although he's far too modest to say so, his work was hugely influential in the renaissance of hula and Hawaiian culture.

'Have you ever mixed Scottish and Hawaiian music?' I ask.

Don Jr laughs. 'No.'

'You don't think bagpipes would work nicely with hula songs?'

He laughs again. 'No.' He considers it for a moment. 'The chanter might work better, though.'

I put my camera down on a *Five Ukulele Songs* DVD and a Hawaiian dictionary while I pick up the Scot of the Year plaque. April and I exchange disappointed glances. We'd been hoping for a golden haggis, a silver Nessie, a tartan surfboard or a lion rampant wearing a grass skirt. This is none of those, just a perfectly decent wooden plaque with a gold bit with Don Jr's name and the outline of a piper.

'Was there a tartan carpet at the big event?' I ask hopefully.

Don Jr crushes ideas of such foolishness straight away. 'They gave me it at the annual Bobbie Burns Supper. There were about 380 people there. We don't usually go—we're not joiners, we're supporters.' He continues, 'They usually announce the winner at the awards, but one of my kids called ahead and said I had a heart problem, so they told me in advance. It surprised the hell out of me when I got the letter from the Caledonian Society.'

'How do they choose who to award the honour to?' I ask the smiling old Scottish-Hawaiian.

'They find someone who's done something for the community, preferably one with a Scottish name.'

Don plays it down. He's modest, but it is obvious that he is hugely moved by having won. In fact, he told Lillian Cunningham that it's the thing he's been the most proud of in his life—and this is a man with a lot to be proud of. Don Jr regales us with tales as birds sing in the huge ferns outside and I lean back on a cushion that reads 'If I'd known grandchildren were so much fun, I'd have had them first'.

Don Jr was born in California in 1921, but his family came west in stages over the preceding century.

'My people first went to Framboise, Cape Breton, Nova Scotia.' He pauses, 'They worked like beavers. My father was a bandleader in California. He played on 1927's *The Jazz Singer*. It was the first "talkie",' he says with pride.

Joining the dots between California and the windward side of Oahu, Don Jr tells us that his father was playing in an orchestra on a steamship that sailed between California and Hawaii in 1934 and accepted a position with the Royal Hawaiian Orchestra while on board. He stayed in Hawaii and sent tickets back to his family in California to come out and join him.

'My mother went down to the dock to meet my father off the boat and was told by a mischievous former fellow passenger that my father had got off the boat at Hawaii with a hula hula girl. That was not a good week, but the next week the tickets arrived by Western Union.'

Other than a stint in Kansas as a commissioned officer during World War II, Don Jr has lived in Hawaii ever since.

'Does Scotland feel like home?' I ask.

'Oh, yes! We've been to Scotland half a dozen times.'

There's still a tiny touch of Atlantic Canada in his accent at times. And, although Scotland seems like the opposite of the life he's built here, I can imagine him there. He's searched obscure corners of the

Highlands for traces of where his people came from, exploring single track roads near Ben Nevis for forgotten McDiarmid graves. But there's more to his love of Scotland than just his ancestry.

'I love golf. Mom loves caddying. I love driving. She loves riding. So our Scottish road trips work perfectly. The last one was really good fun. We drove from Aberdeen to Ullapool and over to the islands. All the way from Stornoway down to North Uist, all the way south. I wanted to try everything, Cullen Skink, black pudding, all those whiskies...'

Don Jr is good at being Scottish. Really, I should be pretty good at being Scottish, too, after all my mum was voted Scotswoman of the Year in 1979 and you'd think the competition for top Scotswoman would be pretty fierce in Scotland. But my mum never taught me the basics of Scottish dancing, how to rustle up a succulent haggis or a nice creamy bowl of Cullen Skink, or which tartan best matched my eyes. She never set my siblings and me straight on any of those things, not because she is unpatriotic or because she is unconcerned about our nationalistic development, but for the simple reason that she didn't know how. My Scotswoman of the Year mother—and almost every single ancestor right back as far as can be traced on that side—is Irish. Born and bred in a small town near the Silvermines Mountains and still blessed with a delightful Tipperary accent even after 40 years in Glasgow, my mum made patient attempts to teach me wee snippets of Gaelic, but it was Irish Gaelic, the language she did much of her schooling through, not the distinctly different dialect spoken on the other side of the Irish Sea. The dance steps she laughingly demonstrated beside the fire were waltzes and foxtrots she'd learned in Dublin. The recipes she shared were for Irish soda bread, not stovies or cranachan. So my mum snatching the silver rose bowl of Scottish womanhood for her charity work really was quite a coup. Just think how good she is at being Irish if she was able to master Scottishness to such a winning level during her first 14 years in Glasgow.

Don Jr leads us back through to the main room past the Christmas tree that he and 'Mom' leave up year-round and decorate for each holiday, pointing out a photo of Jacob Kaio, the only Native Hawaiian bagpiper on the islands, doing a surprise performance at the Scot of the Year's 80th birthday celebrations. At a photo of himself in uniform, he tell us of the night in December 1941 when Pearl Harbor was attacked. As an Air Force officer he had to drive the precarious, unpaved, cliff top Pali Highway by night with medical supplies.

'The only way I could see was to drive with the door open and watch the white lines. It took a while,' he says with characteristic understatement.

'Give my regards to your Scot of the Year mom,' Don Jr calls as we trundle off, clutching copies of *Don P McDiarmid Presents* and a couple of volumes of his *Hawaii Calls* radio show on CD.

We drive back past a Jurassic Park-like landscape of three-storey-high ferns. Frondy trees that I guess might be banyans shade the road. Rickety shrimp shacks lean over a dusty yard where cats and chickens scrabble and the words 'Live shrimp for sale cooked' are fading from the surfboard on which they're painted. We stop and eat volcano shrimp under a sign saying 'Do Not Touch The Turtles' alongside a wooden pineapple wearing a bra and headband. Another nearby pineapple sports shorts and boots. A tired, grubby lawn chair sits tied to the bus stop. At the next stop, there's a row of them lined up expectantly. Continuing around the coast, we round corners and see broad expanses of sand or tiny crescents of white craggy shorelines. At some, teenage boys survey the waves. At others, notices warn of treacherous undertows. There are signs for fresh pineapple everywhere and road signs for Honolulu and Pearl Harbor. Back in the city, a lemon wedge of a moon appears between palm fronds above Waikiki Beach and crabs start to pop up through the sand.

In the McDiarmids' kitchen earlier I saw a collection of car bumper stickers plastered to the tiles. My eyes caught one that proclaimed that conservative radio talk show host 'Rush Limbaugh is right.' Another queried 'Are We Having Fun Yet?' Don Jr is. He seems to have had a lifetime of it. It's quite a lesson—and one that will stick with me long after I've forgotten the finer points of 'Jenny's Gentle Jig.'

9. TILTED KILTS:
APACHE JUNCTION AND TEMPE, ARIZONA

Over 200 carefully tended golf courses dab jolts of lurid green about the sandy hems and rusty red buttes of Greater Phoenix. But the Copper State course where I want to take my first swing at Scotland's most famous game isn't one you'll find written up in guides or tourist brochures. There is no talk of these fairways around the pools of the Valley of the Sun's legendarily luxurious five-star resorts. In fact, most Phoenicians have never even heard of it. The joy of playing this covert course is something reserved for an elite few members and no one gets to play there without an invitation.

I've been fishing for leads and angling for an invite for years. Finally, it's come! I went crab fishing once, when I was 8, off the old stone pier in Ardnamurchan. Landing an invite is almost as exciting as that sole fishing experience. But this time, unlike my crab-catching debut, my jubilation has not been swiftly followed by an enthusiasm-dampening tumble into a sea full of stinging jellyfish. This is definitely progress. On that crumbling West Highland harbour wall, I celebrated success too early and was forced to retreat when my crowning crustacean achievement began to advance along the pier towards me. Decades later, as I look at my mail, I know the stings could very well still come, but I'm not going to worry about that yet.

I read the cause for today's excitement again.

'We would love to have you join us for a round of golf when you are in our area. I will mail this and wait for your reply,' says the note.

It's long, long awaited, it's postmarked 'Apache Junction, Arizona' and it's an invite to the Snakehole Golf and Country Club.

I'm not actually in the area at all—I'm in Toronto—but after all these years, I'm not going to let a minor thing like 2,237 miles come between me and my golf debut.

I've never been on a proper golf course, but I've always been partial to what North Americans call mini-golf and Scots refer to as crazy golf. Although the Snakehole is a full-size nine-hole course, it's about as crazy as golf gets. Over the years, my favourite crazy golf courses have featured a shoal of squinty-eyed sea monsters, an unconvincing invasion of UFOs and a Last Supper's worth of chipped religious figurines presiding over its holes. The Snakehole doesn't go for such gimmicks. It doesn't need to. The Snakehole has natural craziness coming out of its cavities. Literally. From a golfer's perspective, there are nine holes. From a house-hunting serpent's view, there are hundreds. Alongside these reptile roosts are the desert addresses of thousands of scorpions, tarantulas and other such venomous creepy crawlies. And in the midst of all this worrisome wildlife live the inhabitants of the Countryside Travel Trailer Resort. These resort residents make up the entire membership of the Snakehole.

Situated in Apache Junction, a wrong-side-of-the-tracks neighbourhood on the fringe of Phoenix, the Snakehole is a desert or cowboy course, where, instead of perfectly coiffed grass, lush fairways and delicately crafted bunkers, there's, well, just sand. And to prevent it from blowing and filling all useful nooks, the sand round the holes is hardened with leftover grease from local diners. This is a practical and budget-minded solution to the shifting sands problem, but it surely stirs up issues for golfers with even a semi-functioning sense of smell.

As the day draws nearer, people suggest that perhaps I should have chosen any number of amazing Arizona courses, such as the Scottish-style links at Scottsdale's Westin Kierland, where a piper closes play with a sunset set each day. Or the incredible scenery of the course under the dramatic hump of Camelback Mountain. Or either of the two challenging courses at Troon North. But I am resolute. When I play golf for the first time, I want it to be memorable and a course seething with snakes and scorpions sounds like it fits the bill.

I throw open the shutter doors of my room at Tempe, Arizona's Buttes Resort and revel in the view of the sandy slope covered in cactus and mesquite trees. A warm breeze blows down the incline and into the room, sweet with the fragrance of desert sage and acacia.

In the hotel store, less than an hour later, I survey the stock of locally made glass paperweights with real scorpions encased inside, scorpion sucker lollipops and baskets of plush toy rattlesnakes and sidewinders. Perhaps leaving my room doors open was not such a good idea.

The sales assistant sees my consternation and tells me, 'Their reputation is worse than reality. The rare few who get bitten by vipers tend to be men. Drunk guys who goad them after watching too many episodes of *Crocodile Hunter*. And only something like one in 50 scorpions actually sting.'

With these potential handicaps to play against, I'm relieved that I won't have to go it alone on the Snakehole. I'll be accompanied by Charlie, the president of this exclusive Golf and Country Club, and by my brother Mark, who, like me, has never set foot on an official golf course, unless the golf course happened to be an inconvenient hurdle between him and a nearby pub. Mark's band is touring the US and he has a couple of days off between shows in LA and Flagstaff. Somehow I have persuaded him that he should fill these precious days off by detouring via Apache Junction.

As Mark's imminent arrival proves, I have a talent for persuasion. My older brother has a talent for playing guitar. Among his many other standout talents, I particularly highly rate his ability to remember exactly how many milks and sugars someone takes in their tea no matter how many years have passed since he was last in proximity to them and a kettle. Perhaps more impressive, however, is his talent for managing to sound delighted to hear from whoever it is when he answers the phone. As someone who finds phone calls almost as appealing as extensive dental surgery, this astounds me. This and accurate tea-delivery are things I'd encourage Mark to place high on the skills section of any future job application. A man who can sound thrilled when a dental surgeon phones—and then, several years later, remember exactly how such a person takes his tea, is surely a man to be reckoned with. I feel I have chosen my golfing companion well.

Scotland is pretty short on venomous beasties. Other than Hebridean jellyfish, we have deadly adders—our sole poisonous reptile. As a kid I was more scared of a really cross woman who lived in a top floor flat in Glasgow's Marchmont Terrace and inventively cursed children playing below. Adders are not common, with only ten reported deaths in the last 100 years. The Marchmont Viper is responsible for a far greater number of vicious attacks.

When we were kids, despite the fact that we were more likely to have an encounter with a Gaelic-speaking salmon than an adder, our mum would never let us walk through the heather unless we were wearing welly boots. 'Adders hate welly boots,' our mum informed us. We had had no idea that the snakes of Scotland were so fashion-conscious. Mark and I speculated as to whether they preferred sandshoes or a nice pair of loafers. But rather than risk falling on the wrong side of such a sartorially astute serpent, on the rare occasions that we cut across the heather without wellies, Mark and I flew, as fast as our wee legs could carry us, through scratchy heather, jaggy thistles and mounds of sheep excrement, to get back to the safety of the track. Of course, this was the exact behaviour that would have any self-respecting adder startled and on the defensive, given no chance to slither out of the way of short, flailing legs. Luckily, we never met one.

The night before our golfing debut, Mark and I are in downtown Tempe, one of 22 cities that add up to Greater Phoenix and a bustling college town that seems to be populated entirely by obscenely healthy Michiganders. Neither Mark nor I have remembered to pack wellies.

I shield my eyes as the sun beats down on our terrace table as Mark and I have dinner with Toni, Amy and Nancy, three friends of mine from Tempe Tourism. I am hoping to persuade one or more of my Tempe friends to join us for the golfing excursion, although I know it's going to be quite a struggle. After all, tourism reps are usually encouraged to direct journalists to scenic or prestigious local attractions. The Snakehole has never made it onto any Tempe Tourism press tours. In fact, on more than one of my previous visits, Toni has flatly refused to stop when driving me past it.

Amy is the first to crumble, 'Shoot, sure, I'll play golf tomorrow... if I can get the morning off.'

She looks at her boss, who just happens to be sitting on her left.

Toni raises an eyebrow at Amy, 'Okay, fine, you go, but I have to work. I have to promote parts of Arizona that don't come with a 90 per cent chance of sun stroke and snake bites.'

'A flimsy excuse!' I protest.

'No way in hell you'll persuade me to join you, but I brought you a little something so you'll fit in on the course,' announces Nancy.

She drags a tartan hat out of her bag and thumps it down on the table.

Everyone looks at the hat. 'Made in Scotland' declares its tag.

'It's wool,' Toni points out, reading the heavy wool bonnet's label while fanning herself with a drinks menu. 'That might be a little warm for round here.'

'Nonsense, it's perfect desert wear,' says Nancy, brushing all argument aside, cramming the bonnet on my head and shading her eyes from the sweltering sun as she admires her handiwork.

'It's perfect,' I say, bravely. 'Just what I needed.'

Sweat begins to trickle down my neck.

'You'll need more than that to tackle that course,' guffaws Nancy. Amy begins to look concerned.

'I looked at the satellite map for the Snakehole and it just looked like dirt!' Amy laughs and waits for me to contradict this.

'Yes,' I crow gleefully, 'Dirt! Sand, scrub and dirt!'

'But, there'll be beverage carts...' Amy trails off as I shake my head. 'I don't think so.'

'You'll probably just have to cut the top off a barrel cactus and drink from that,' says Nancy.

Amy looks from Nancy to me with disbelief.

'But all golf courses have beverage carts!' she protests.

'Not this one,' cackles Nancy, taking a swig from her glass. 'This one's got scrub and scorpions instead. Enjoy that morning off.'

'Does sand not clog up the holes?' asks Mark.

I fill everyone in on the Snakehole's sand-securing strategy.

Toni makes a face.

'That's not gonna smell good,' states Nancy.

Amy is speechless.

Mark soon forgets the Snakehole's stinking sands. 'What if there's a scorpion in the hole?' he asks.

I hadn't thought of this.

'Probably will be,' beams Nancy.

I say, 'Insurance!' in a brighter tone than I actually feel. 'Anyway, this morning I was told that only one in 50 scorpions bite.'

Mark seems only partially reassured by this statistic. 'Do you not think the odds might go up substantially if a scorpion has just been woken up from a nap by being smacked on the head by a golf ball?'

'If you hit it hard enough to knock it out, the odds probably go down,' Toni suggests.

Mark looks unconvinced.

After dinner, I call Charlie.

'You're from Scotland, but you've never played golf?' he says, sounding perplexed.

I admit that that is the case.

'Alright, I'll show you some things,' he concedes.

'What should we wear?' I ask. 'Slacks? Pleated shorts? Golf visors? We want to be sure we're wearing the right things.'

'Lady, there ain't no dress code in the desert,' comes the gruff reply.

The next day, which, as luck would have it, is Friday the 13th, Mark, Amy and I are on the Superstition Freeway, heading towards Apache Junction. Directions loom for Los Angeles and the Grand Canyon. The jagged Superstition Mountains spike up to 5,024 feet alongside, stretching off into the hazy west.

It's convenient to have a local tourism professional in the car and Mark and I learn a lot about Arizona during the 30-minute drive. The Superstitions are home to quite a cast of creatures, we're told. In addition to deadly snakes and poisonous insects, local wildlife includes javelina pigs, jackrabbits, cottontails, bighorn sheep, mule deer, coyote, foxes, roadrunners, desert quail, desert wrens, black bears and gila monsters. It's a surprise to discover that, as a result of all its reservoirs, the state of Arizona actually has more shoreline than California.

'People don't think of the desert as green. It is. It's just a subtle kind of green,' says Amy.

We pass towering saguaro and chola cactus and a sign for Deadman Wash. Turkey vultures track us from the gnarled charcoal branches of mesquite trees. We make a brief detour to the old Apacheland Ghost Town and movie ranch, walking into the museum just as a recorded voice declares, 'That pig slit that damn dog's throat, using them tusks just like a razor.'

Mark and I look at each other with some concern.

'Will we meet any javelina pigs today?' I ask Amy.

'Yeah, a herd of them, chasing a beverage cart,' she snorts.

The set for Westerns, including Elvis Presley's *Charro*, the Ronald Reagan-narrated *Death Valley Days* and other classics such as *Have*

Gun Will Travel, there's nothing much left of Apacheland now, but Mark and I love the hokey ghost town, with its false fronts and saloon girl re-enactors just that little bit more because it reminds us of watching Westerns with our dad when we were kids.

As we get closer to our morning's destination, Mark and I try to think of sports that we played together in Scotland. We've got as far as an occasional afternoon's Frisbee-chucking and regular rounds of persecuting our sister Orla when we see the sign for Tomahawk Road and Goldfield Road and turn off.

The Countryside Travel Trailer Resort sits wedged between two spurs of highway, beyond the last outskirt of Apache Junction—560 trailer sites, punctuated by palm trees and scored by orderly streets. Three vast, lumbering homes on wheels trundle out as we drive in. Two ancient golf bags perch expectantly on the kerb.

Minutes later, Charlie, President of the Snakehole Golf and Country Club, arrives sporting a precise moustache, a white polo shirt, khaki shorts and a Professional Golf Association cap. Amy and I are in jeans and t-shirts, taking turns with Nancy's hat. Mark has chosen the less traditional desert colour scheme of pipe-thin black jeans, a long-sleeved black shirt and a straw cowboy hat that I suspect he acquired at a truck stop, in a card game or from an unwatched display at Apacheland.

'So you're the Scottish folks,' says Charlie with a measured gaze.

He is staring at us for so long that I say, 'Are we what you expected?'

'I don't rightly know what a Scottish person should look like,' says Charlie, inscrutably.

He continues sizing us up. Under pressure, Amy breaks ranks and admits that she is not Scottish.

Charlie looks at her intently, then shrugs.

'Right, let's get this started before the day heats up anymore,' he says and stalks off towards the highway.

We scuttle after him as he strides coolly across five busy lanes of traffic.

'This is the dangerous part of it,' Charlie adds with a hint of a smile.

A painted sign with a rattlesnake wrapped round a number 13 flag announces that we're now on Snakehole Golf and Country Club grounds. We stop and look around. It is impossible to tell where the desert stops and the golf course begins. A golf cart appears over a bit of particularly rough terrain to the south. Amy perks up. It passes and the two golfers inside wave and continue on.

'Not a beverage cart,' Amy says sadly.

Although there are assertions that the Chinese or the Dutch were the first to attack a ball with a golf-like intent, Scotland's claims to the game leave these contenders in the crabgrass. Originally called 'gowf,' golf's roots can be traced back to the east coast of Scotland in 1497. Mary Queen of Scots is said to have paused for a putt less than a century later. Legend has it that the game got its start when a few bored shepherds started punting stones into rabbit holes with adjacent sticks. Play was first recorded at Musselburgh Links in 1672. Now Scotland has more than 500 courses. Lest you think the rabbits took their ancestors' home invasions lying down, they didn't. When I worked at course-side banquets at the Gleneagles links during university days, the bunnies got their own back, burrowing in determined lines under marquee floors and dashing in the way of hors d'oeuvres delivery and tee-time. Those misty green grounds feel like another world compared to Apache Junction's oil-saturated greasescape.

The scorching morning sun bakes the desert and hot gasps of wind stir up the sand—or, at least, the stretches of sand that aren't entirely coated in vegetable oil. Ominous holes blot the sand round the straggle of scrubby creosote and bedraggled bushes that wilt round the edge of the course. Anthills erupt through the few patches of relatively even sand. While Scotland's courses are famed for their greens, the only green to be seen here are the glittering shards of beer bottles, shattered like mosaic underfoot.

'Is this the subtle green you were talking about,' Mark asks Amy. 'Heineken Green?'

Charlie says, 'We've had this golf course since 1990, all 40 acres of it. We keep thinking the State will come and take this land for houses, but we're still here.'

He gestures expansively at the sand, the scrub and the bushes, proudly. The mountains blur in the heat haze. Traffic drones along the highway. Glass shards gleam.

'Who plays this course?' I ask.

'Jim says to Bob, you should play golf. Bob maybe has one club. Jim maybe has three. Nobody's got a full set. You go to a flea market or a swap meet and you get a club. Or maybe two clubs.'

A golf cart goes by, the two people wave and their wee dogs poke their heads up from behind the seats to stare at us.

'What kinds of creatures do you get out here?' I ask Charlie.

'Roadrunners, coyotes, snakes...'

'What do you do when you see a snake?'

Charlie looks at me, puzzled. 'Well, you walk round the snake.'

'And keep playing?'

'And keep playing. Last one I saw was a sidewinder up at Hole 5. Before that, I tripped over a rattlesnake at Hole 7.'

Last night Toni told us that she'd heard the Snakehole had a 'rattlesnake rule'—that rule being that if you encounter a rattlesnake, it's perfectly okay to pick up your ball and carry it for however many steps it takes for your heart rate to get back to normal. I ask Charlie if we're playing rattlesnake rules this morning.

He just snorts.

'Rattlesnake rules? We'd get no play at all that way. See that?' he points at a swirling pattern in the sand.

'You just missed one. He heard you coming,' he says with a grin.

Mark, Amy and I look at the place where a rattlesnake was curled up in the sun until mere moments ago.

'That over there,' he gestures nonchalantly at slight ripples in the sand to our right.

'Sidewinder went that way.'

'I think that's a no,' Mark murmurs to me.

'We should be wearing welly boots, shouldn't we?' I whisper back.

The Sonoran Desert—one of the four major deserts in North America—spreads over 100,000 square miles of Arizona, California and northern Mexico. It's more than three times bigger than Scotland and is pretty much my homeland's exact opposite. By definition, a desert has less than 10 inches of rain a year. Parts of Scotland have had that amount of rain in a day.

The April sun scorches the sand beneath our feet.

'You play at 6 am and maybe get nine holes before it gets too hot. From May to October, it's pretty much always too hot,' says our golf coach as we amble to the first hole.

Mark, Amy and I peer out at the expanse of scrub. There's a ragged flag waving between two monumental anthills. Charlie makes us practise our swing with golf-ball sized rocks.

'This one's gonna be good,' Charlie says to the others as I take aim.

Charlie is mistaken. I line up my first shot with a luminous pink golf ball called a Pink Lady, whack enthusiastically and miss completely. A clump of guillotined weeds flies 20 feet.

'You should use a 7-iron,' instructs Charlie.

'I was thinking that,' I lie. I have no idea what a 7-iron is. Charlie pulls a club out and hands it to me.

'This is a 7-iron.'

My second attempt goes into a bush about two feet away. My third results in a cloud of dust. When the dust settles, the ball is gone! I am elated at having hit my first shot.

'Right, quit messing about and put it in the cup,' says Charlie.

I oblige, eventually, taking around 27 putts to get the Pink Lady in the first hole. Amy and Mark take turns, displaying similar lack of skill. Charlie takes his shot and we all gather round. There is a reverential silence as we watch his ball drive powerfully ahead into the distance between the anthills. He is a master of his course.

After a dozen clumsy putts, I get my next ball to within a couple of inches of a hole.

'It's a gimme,' says Charlie.

'A gimme?' I ask.

'It's a special desert technique. It's illegal in professional golf,' he admits gruffly. 'We just assume you'd have knocked it in with one more go.' He considers. 'Though that's probably generous.'

We all manage generous gimmes and head towards the next hole. We've only gone a few steps when the smell hits. We knew it was coming, but none of us expected it would be so... oily. I have worked in two fish and chip shops and I know this smell. It's the smell of a hundred long-battered, long-devoured fish. It's the smell of a million oil-coated calories. It's the smell of end-of-day, bottom-of-the-fryer grease.

Charlie ignores our aghast expressions. 'They put vegetable oil on it. Oil from the Moose or the Elks or the Legion. They stir in sand and oil so the rain doesn't wash it away. They add oil every other week.'

'I think out-of-date catfish was on the menu last week,' I whisper to Amy.

She sniffs the air. 'Are you sure it wasn't fricasseed squirrel?'

'I'll always associate the smell of fried squirrel with this time we've spent together,' I tell her.

At the next hole we meet an implement made of a scrap of ancient carpet stapled to a broken brush handle. After we've all botched our shots, Charlie picks up the carpet, drags it behind him round the hole and carefully smoothes all traces of our footsteps from the oil-sodden sand. After an hour on the course with us, Charlie is beginning to look like he wishes there was a similar implement for his mind.

As Mark practises his swing with a pile of pebbles, Charlie tells Amy and me about Snakehole tournaments.

'To play competitions round here, you play with your wife if she plays. If she don't, you go get somebody else's wife.' Charlie pauses. 'Or a widow lady. Then you get cake and coffee.'

'I like cake,' says Amy.

Charlie raises one eyebrow at her. Amy looks down and smoothes and resmoothes an already flat bit of sand with one nervous foot.

'See that desk over there?' Charlie asks.

Charlie shrugs one shoulder back towards the highway. There's a weather-beaten picnic table beside the wooden sign with the club's name on it.

'That's the office. That's where you sign up to join and for competitions. It costs $20 a year to be a member and you have to be a park resident. Each year we have tournaments between Canadians and Americans. But we couldn't find enough Canadians this year. And American folks had other things to do. Like playing shuffleboard. So there was no tournament. There should have been a tournament. There's always been a tournament,' Charlie studies the ground. 'None of the Americans would be Canadians. For that one day a year, they could be Canadian, couldn't they?'

We all agree. Charlie is visibly disappointed at his parkmates' refusal to better cross-border relations.

He casts a calculating eye over the terrain ahead and says to Amy, 'Hit it with a 9 and see her fly right over them bushes.'

Amy dutifully picks up the 9-iron and gives the ball an enthusiastic whack. A cloud of dust rises in the distance.

'Good work,' says Charlie.

She exclaims, 'How far was that? How FAR was that?' She is exultant. 'How many yards?'

I scan the ground with a critical eye and decide, '119 yards.'

Amy is delighted with herself.

'119 yards, yeah! That was thrilling! Finally I see how people could get so into this game,' she crows.

'Aren't you married to a golf professional?' I ask.

'Um, yeah...' she admits.

As we walk towards Hole 7, I look out over the desert, at trucks lumbering along past blue highway signs. Worrying holes speckle the ground round all nearby bushes.

I stand on a sewer lid and watch my ball bounce and ricochet off rocks 100 yards away.

'Oops, lost another one.'

Charlie tells us, 'I hit some on 5 and 7 that no one ever found. Probably a rattlesnake got it.'

'Don't go too close to those there holes,' he warns Mark who is going after a long ball. 'Just let her go.'

Mark slows.

'It makes a snake mad to be woken up,' drawls Charlie. 'And we've had the ambulance in the park once already this morning.'

Mark stops completely.

Our golf coach grins.

Charlie knows golf and he knows that we are messers. He suggests we finish early. It is getting hot and it seems wise to call it a day before we meet any of the Country Club's less welcoming inhabitants.

Huge buses with cars towed behind crawl out of the trailer park across the road. Charlie sees me watching them.

'A lot of folks pulling this week,' he explains, 'Renters go at beginning or end of month. Permanent go mid-month.'

Soon Charlie, too, will steer his winter home out onto the highway, and set a course for Idaho. Within a month or so, the snakes and scorpions will have this scrappy corner of the desert back to themselves again.

I ask Mark, 'How was your first day of golf?'

'Good. It was actually kind of fun.'

'I guess that's why people play it,' I say.

We look at each other. The thought really hadn't really occurred to us before.

After leaving Amy at the office and Mark back at the airport, I feel it's time to make up for the lack of snacks and beverages at the Snakehole, so I taxi to the Phoenician. The vast hotel sits on 250 acres and has 647 rooms, three snake-less golf courses and guests who look like they are nipped, tucked, lifted and Liposucked on a daily basis. It also has an IT butler, the perplexing offer of 'therapeutic in-room turndown service' and a legendary dessert buffet with more roomfuls of ornate confections, masterpieces of chocolate art and lavish sugary creations than even a regiment of tooth fairies on overtime could clean up after. Outside, each blade of grass stands to attention in precise regiments on either side of the path. Impeccable blond staff members in golf shorts and visors drive at regulation speed along manicured walkways. Another marches purposefully, followed by a file of neat small boys clutching tennis racquets. I walk past a freshly carved, six-foot-tall ice marlin, glistening in the heat, and watch as a chiselled blond boy catches one lone drip of water threatening to fall from the marlin's pointy snout. Attractively hued birds flutter about carefully coiffed trees. Guests lounge by waterfalls and in luxuriantly draped cabanas made of cloth so soft it looks like it was woven from the breath of baby clouds. Occasionally these pampered specimens prowl round the marlin in search of fresh canapés and champagne. It is like visiting a zoo of rich white people and seeing them displayed in their natural habitat.

Once my Grand Aunt Derry, long a patron of such establishments, insisted that the entire family went on holiday to an equivalent of this place. I turned six that week and it was the first time I had ever stayed at a hotel. Hotels were—and still are, even several decades later—a source of delight to me. Ice machines! Individual wee pots of jam with every breakfast! Numbers you can dial to make people bring pizzas and chocolate to the room the minute all responsible adults go out! My siblings and I were in awe of the extravagance of this heretofore-unknown world. Every other year family holidays were split between my parents' homelands. While Irish holidays were spent at my mum's childhood home in Tipperary, our Scottish escapades were less predictable. While most of such vacations were spent in our rusting caravan north of Crianlarich, there were also weeks at a creaky, haunted inn in Anstruther, opportunities to explore the crab fishing possibilities of Ardnamurchan, and an incredible summer on the tiny isle of Eriskay back when the only access was by prawn trawler. My family holidays didn't involve supervised sports, attentive minions or carefully controlled landscaping. No, the holidays my family went on seemed almost chosen to ensure I would tumble into a bog, be traumatised by a wild pony or lurch backwards into a shoal of jellyfish. These far-from-five-star accommodations might not have improved our tennis technique or knowledge of patisserie genres, but they provided memories that beat such things hands down. If we'd merely gone to some decadent resort year after year, we would never have stumbled on the ruins of a forgotten village, abandoned during the Highland clearances. We'd never have seen Aunt Honor tumble headfirst into the River Cononish—something that I remember in fine and hilarious detail and something that Aunt H insists happened long before I was born. We would never have witnessed our always impeccably dressed and dignified granny's expression as a succession of burly Hebridean fisherman hoisted her like a pudding and bundled her from one fishing boat to the next to the next to the craft that was going to take us all to Eriskay. We would never have heard her spluttering with indignation as she was plunked down on the final deck, her fur-fringed Sunday hat still perched jauntily on her head. All the ice marlins in the world can never trump memories like that.

To my delight, I'm in time for the dessert buffet and quickly set to it. Three chocolate-spattered minutes later, having consumed more than a herd of famished javelinas, I still feel it's necessary to save a couple more choice offerings for a wee afternoon snack. This, I realise, five minutes later, as I mop melted chocolate off all my belongings, is not a clever thing to do in a desert.

Back in Tempe, three-storey bars with iron railings tower on either side of Mill Avenue. 'Go Devils!' encourages a sign above an ice cream place. 'I Love Hoebags,' says one of a 20-something panhandler's hand-written signs underneath. His other declares, 'Yeah, I'm a Retard.' On the other side of the street and at the other end of the intellectual begging spectrum, another sidewalk solicitor is reading

Nietzsche. Stars and stripes hang from lampposts and Arizona State University Sun Devils merchandise is on display in every third window.

I've always been rather jealous of people who moved away to college towns. Mark went the 45 miles to Edinburgh. Most of my American friends packed up and went off to school. When I went to university, I moved two doors away. I lived in a basement apartment with my school friend Caroline and Bob, a paranoid parrot she acquired when she went to a pet store, stoned, in search of a chipmunk. We whiled the days away becoming experts on daytime soaps and seeing who could outspin the other in swivel chair endurance tests. Reared on tales of my parents' social whirl and away-from-home university romance, my allegedly academic years rather paled in comparison, although the pride Caroline and I felt at having taught a green-cheeked conure to squawk the theme tune to *Home and Away* is something that neither of us will ever forget.

'Where are we off to?' asks Therese the cab driver.

I tell her that I'm off to investigate rumours of a Scottish pub out on the southern fringes of the city.

Therese had no idea there was any such thing round here. 'Next time I'm asked to recommend a Scottish pub, I'll know where to send them.'

'Are you asked often?' I ask hopefully.

Therese considers. 'Well, no, nobody has ever asked that before.'

She tells me that Tempe is the smallest place she's ever lived. We drive 20 miles and cover slightly less than one inch of my map of Greater Phoenix. In the same time, we could have gone halfway across Scotland's central belt. Before the Second World War, Phoenix was a sleepy Southwestern town surrounded by fields of cotton, lemons and oranges. Now it sprawls across 400 square miles.

Finally we reach the Tilted Kilt, which seems like a tartan oasis among ubiquitous identikit strip malls and bungalows. I take a deep breath of desert air and walk in. I'm expecting to feel homesick, but merely feel very tall as I'm greeted by a tiny waif of a server wearing a low-slung mini-kilt and matching tartan bra. Her co-workers all sport the same attire. They look as though they pilfered outfits from fetish store mannequins or Japanese hipsters. I felt underdressed when at the Phoenician. However, in the Kilt, my tank top alone would provide enough material for seven complete staff uniforms. Before I can consider ordering a pint of locally brewed Kiltlifter Ale, I'm ID'd by another miniscule server.

I ask her a few questions about the menu and the bar, but she just answers each one with a laugh and an 'Oh, I dunno.'

To my relief, people capable of having a conversation arrive. Toni has brought her husband Jeff and her workmate Tony along to meet me for dinner. As they join me, the server returns and spills most of my drink on the table.

The Glaswegian word 'glaikit' comes to mind as I look at the menu. It's adorned with a glassy-eyed, red haired woman in the Kilt uniform. She's carrying a tray, off which a pint of beer is tumbling. The lack of basic waitressing ability here certainly seems accurate. They've also managed to capture a complete lack of any discernible intelligence. So far, so authentic. It's a tough decision between Fat Bastard's Meat Loaf, Danny Boy's Shepherd's Pie, the 'Classic Caesar made the same way our clan did in Tijuana,' a Braveheart Burger and Braveheart's Chopped Salad.

Typo-strewn limericks, of the kind that intellectually stunted 13-year-old boys might scrawl on school desks before passing out after a couple of pilfered shandies, are painted in a pseudo-Celtic font on the wall. I'm tempted to move straight back to Glasgow and open a trashy Arizona-themed bar with scanty snakeskin uniforms and a menu crammed with cringe-inducing supposedly desert dishes as cultural revenge. But, although I might bluster and complain to Toni, Jeff and Tony about this one-dimensional stereotyping, I get it. When I was a kid, we very occasionally went to Glasgow's then lone American restaurant, the Back Alley. It was where I first got a taste for the US. The Back Alley fed me my first clichéd views of America and I devoured them—every obvious yellow cab, skyscraper and NYPD cop car they could plaster across my sightlines. I thought it was brilliant. Then again, I was nine. The Tilted Kilt won't give any starry-eyed nine-year-olds their first taste of another culture, but possibly impressionable under-10s aren't this chain's intended clientele.

At the till in the Tilted Kilt, the pint-sized server is struggling with the challenge of ringing up two drinks and a salad. She has got all four bills completely wrong. None of us has a bill for anything we were actually served. She keeps smiling and waits for us to accept our seemingly inescapable financial fate and hand over some token cash.

'Where are you from?' she asks as she waits for me to pay for three portions of unconsumed Guinness Beer Sauce Nachos.

'I'm Scottish.'

'Scottish, British, American, whatever,' she smiles brightly, if I can use a word such as 'brightly' to describe someone who would be outshone in an intelligence test if pitted against a carrot.

As my cab glides along Red Mountain Freeway towards the airport, the desert sunset has turned the sky into a blur of wild reds, intense purples and inky blues. I think about having finally crossed golf off my Scottish to do list. I think about returning to Arizona to play a course with less grease and more beverage carts. I think about having escaped both the Snakehole and the Tilted Kilt without injury, despite forgetting my welly boots. I turn a souvenir scorpion paperweight from the hotel store over in my hands. It's surprisingly heavy. I'm not a fan of insects, especially ones with anatomy specifically designed to inflict pain, but, feeling brave after all my Arizona escapades, I hold the paperweight up for a closer look.

'Ha, you didn't get me!' I crow silently at the encased scorpion.

Then, somehow, I don't know how it happens, I lose my grip and the paperweight falls weightily, painfully, on my foot.

10. GAELIC WITHOUT GROANS:
FORT WORTH, TEXAS

Since setting off on this journey to Scottishness, I have done many things I had not previously imagined attempting. I've Scottish Country Danced in Hawaii, breakfasted on Scotch in a Memphis churchyard and sunk a hole in one beside scorpions and sidewinders in Arizona (with the help of a few gimmes.) I've come up close to a tossed caber in Northern Oregon, been shown the Scottish Way in Illinois and encountered an array of colourful Scottish-American charac-ters including state-sanctioned Scots, Scottie dog devotees and sporran specialists. I've donned a feather bonnet, a terrier ensemble and various lengths of tartan attire. But there are still a couple of crucial components of Scottishness for me to explore on this side of the Atlantic. When I open my e-mail, I find that I'm on my way to crossing off one more.

'Let me tell you all the things that might put you off first,' says the message. 'Texas heat is not for the faint-hearted. Or for the easily burned. It is mostly triple digit temperatures and usually no rain to break the heat. This year is an inferno and we are having a drought.'

I scan further down the page and realise that this next step in learning how to be Scottish might not be as easy an escapade as I had hoped; inhospitably toasty temperatures are just the tip of the rapidly melting iceberg on this e-mail's inventory of impediments.

'If you are thinking of a vacation and seeing other parts of the state, be aware that Texas is very large and it can take a day or more to drive from one part to another. I teach to give myself the discipline to learn. I am not fluent. I am a learner-teacher.

There are many, more fluent learner-teachers in Toronto, Ohio, Washington, DC, Seattle, North Carolina, not to mention Cape Breton. This is the back of beyond for learners.'

And there's more. 'Most baby beginners are glassy-eyed after three hours. Even experienced learners are wiped out after an immersion weekend.'

My correspondent finishes her barrage of assumed learning deterrents with, 'I have four cats.'

I already feel slightly glassy-eyed. Even though I tend to tuck cats into plus columns, it's not quite the upbeat, persuasive course information I was looking for in my search for a beginner's Scottish Gaelic class.

The note then offers a distinctly slimmer set of reasons why I might want to head to north Texas. 'Now here's the flip side, so that you can make an informed choice: I have a pool, I am a good teacher and I live on an acre southwest of Fort Worth. There are lots of stars and it is normally quiet and peaceful.' It's signed, 'Tioraidh an dràsda, Jonquele.'

I have no idea what 'Tioraidh an dràsda' means and a Texan cat ranch during a heatwave seems like a challenging place to further my Scottish education, but it should certainly be a memorable lesson. I write back and book a place on a Gaelic immersion weekend. Stars, cats and a swimming pool versus an exhausting, sprawling inferno? Sign me up.

When my sister Orla learned Gaelic as an extracurricular subject as a teenager, she traipsed about various picturesque parts of the Inner and Outer Hebrides—and some slightly less picturesque parts of Glasgow. I will be learning in what is now described as an 'exurban area' but once was ranchland, and before that, buffalo hunting grounds for the Wichita, Caddo, Comanche and Lipan Apache tribes. When Orla learned Gaelic, she wrote an impassioned article in *The*

Glasgow Herald about the decline of Gaelic. My literary take on this trip to Texas may not end up extending too much further than a few postcards proclaiming, 'Cats! Big hair! Hot!'

Scots poet Hugh MacDiarmid was a leader of a linguistic renaissance in the 1920s, arguing that the country needed its language back in order to move forward. But the poet wasn't fighting for Scottish Gaelic. Our national poet, Robert Burns, didn't write in Gaelic. Dialogue in Sir Walter Scott's bestselling Victorian romance novels wasn't in Gaelic. Because Gaelic isn't the only ancient Scottish language struggling to be heard. Burns, Scott and MacDiarmid were champions of the language that the majority of Scots have spoken since the 11th century. They were champions of the Scots language.

Linguistically, Scottish Gaelic perches prominently on the Celtic language family tree alongside Irish Gaelic and Manx. On that tree, Breton, Welsh, Cornish and the now extinct Cumbric qualify as first cousins. But the Scots language can be found in a different part of the linguistic forest entirely, dangling from the outer branches of West Germanic, a descendent of that tongue's great-grandchild, Frisian, and a sibling of English. Scots is a language full of splendid words such as breenge ('a forceful, but clumsy rush,' according to my Scots dictionary), shoogle ('a shake, push or nudge') and scunner ('an irritation or disgust or an object or situation that provokes such a sensation').

Of course, many of our Scottish forebears did indeed speak Gaelic, but the majority of the ancestors of most Scots and Scottish-Americans last had a chat in Gaelic around one millennium ago. But if we're going back that far, we might as well delve a little deeper and rifle through the bookshelves of history for a few other Scottish phrasebooks while we're at it. If we want to learn the languages of our ancestors, we've got an intimidating choice. As well as Gaelic, we could pick Pictish, the language of the Picts, the people who lived north of the River Forth and were Scotland's first recorded chatterboxes back around the first century AD; Cumbric, the language of the Britons of Strathclyde in southwestern Scotland; perhaps a few Norse phrases to represent the Vikings who pillaged their way into the Scottish gene pool between the years 794 and 1266, settling in the Orkneys, Shetlands and Northern Isles; and the stocky Old English of the Northumbrian kingdom of Lothian in southeastern Scotland.

The Gaelic-speaking Scots tribe arrived on the scene from what is now Ireland around the year 500 and settled in coastal Argyll, calling it Dalriada. Five hundred years later, Pictish and Cumbric had been drowned out by their vociferous new neighbours, and the breezy, well-watered kingdoms of the Scots, Picts, Britons and Northumbrians had merged to form Alba—pretty much Scotland's precise cartographical predecessor.

As part of the deal to annex the northern reaches of Northumbria to Alba, the Northumbrians were permitted to keep and use their language. And this was a language with legs. Sturdy legs that outran consonant-crammed Gaelic. Soon power followed, slipping from the Highlands down to Central Scotland, via Scone, Dunfermline and Stirling and reaching Edinburgh in 1437. As far back as the 1100s, Old English had become the language you'd hear bandied about by King David I (1124-1153), his children King Malcolm IV (1153-1165), Prince Henry, Princess Claricia and Princess Hodierna, and other surprisingly named members of Scotland's royal family. An influx of Norman noblemen in the 12th century brought with them minions who spoke a similar Anglo-Scandinavian-influenced dialect known as Inglis, tipping the balance further in favour of English. Before the 13th century had come to a close, Gaelic was on the wane—the Highlands, South Ayrshire and Galloway its last outposts.

In the subsequent centuries, Inglis developed differently north of the border with England, influenced by trade with the Netherlands, by the political 'Auld Alliance' with France, by Latin terms used in literature and law, and by the slew of words, such as brogue (from bròg, the Gaelic for 'shoe') and slogan (from sluagh-ghairm, the

Gaelic for 'army cry'), that percolated into common parlance from Gaelic. By the end of the 15th century, this offshoot of Old English, now called Scottis or Modern Scots, was the language of the country's literature and education and it seemed there was no stopping this mutated marvel.

But the lack of a Scots translation of the Bible and the move of the Scottish court to London in 1603 took the wind out of Scots' loquacious sails. The parliamentary Treaty of Union in 1707 deflated things almost entirely as the aristocracy and middle classes strove to speak the language of the suddenly more socially acceptable south. However, Gaelic continued to be the language of the Highlands and Islands and Scots remained the language of the Lowlands—and the spoken language of the majority of Scots. And that's pretty much where it stands today.

Growing up in the Lowlands, it simply never occurred to me to learn Gaelic. Learning how to cling desperately to the walls of Finnieston Rink in a grim approximation of ice skating and studying the fashion statements of Scottish bands such as Goodbye Mr Mackenzie and Altered Images provided far more conversational and social possibilities for me as a teenager. In the Glasgow of the 1980s, you didn't hear anyone speaking Gaelic—other than a scatter of people, including my wee sister and Ishabel, her Hebridean teacher. Gaelic's less than prominent place in our daily lives did not deter my determined younger sister, who has subsequently worked her way to fluency in a handful of other dead, dozing or otherwise limited languages.

But despite the more recent reach of Scots, it's my Gaelic-speaking ability that, outside Scotland, I am asked about. The dearth of even a basic Gaelic sentence in my vocabulary often takes people aback in the US. It's frequently assumed that Scottish Gaelic punches the same weight as Irish Gaelic in terms of reach, relevance and recent usage. While I can usually distract people from the topic by uttering a sentence featuring some obscure Scots words and a quick succession of enthusiastically rolled Rs, it seems that, for Scottish-America, an arsenal of Scots expressions and an accent is not enough, so it is Gaelic that I must add in order to become a Scottish-America certified, 100% Scot.

Two months later I've packed my finest heat wave outfits and a textbook called *Gaelic Without Groans* pilfered from Orla's childhood bedroom on my last trip home. It is unclear whether the typical Gaelic tome or the language itself usually comes with complimentary groans, but I am happy to avoid such annoyances either way.

'An accent can really open up the world to a person,' drawls Webb, a South Carolina horse breaker I meet at the departure gate.

He and I have really hit it off, bonding over a delight with each other's accent.

'With certain accents,' declares Webb, 'People like you. People trust you. With accents like ours, life is easier. Life is sweeter,' says Webb.

When Webb says this, it sounds more like 'Lah-eff is sweeedah.' It certainly is when Webb says pretty much anything.

'They say my family came to the Carolinas from Scotland sometime in the 1700s,' he says. 'I always heard my family was descended from a Mary Queen of Scots. Have you heard of her?' Webb enquires.

I admit that I have indeed heard of Scotland's most famous monarch, the impetuous Mary Stuart, who ruled from 1542 till 1567. I mention that Mary was executed by her cousin Queen Elizabeth I of England. Webb looks shocked.

'Well, her being family, that wasn't very nice,' he says.

Decapitating your cousin would apparently be a dreadful breach of etiquette in South Carolina.

Webb tells me about horse training and Roscoe, his favourite mule, and I am captivated. Webb's drawl is delicious. I could drink it. It sounds like horses are fond of his accent, too. Webb modestly admits that he's done 'jus' fine' in the horse breaking business. With much prodding, I discover that he's done significantly better than 'jus' fine' and horses he's trained have won pretty much every type of event at which you might hope for a horse to hurry, including the Kentucky Derby and the Belmont Stakes. I wonder how equines feel about Scottish accents. I haven't attempted a conversation with one since my unfortunate introduction to the critters on that Hebridean bog 30-odd years ago.

'Oh, they'd like it fine,' reckons Webb. 'Like I do.'

A thought suddenly occurs to him. 'You know, when you're in Texas, you might get your Gaelic with a Texas twang.'

'Do you think the horses would prefer that?'

Webb grins. 'Maybe, but I think they'd like a South Carolina twang jus' that li'l bit better.'

Just before we board, I read a message that has just landed in my inbox and realise with some horror that there will now be a Gaelic song component to the weekend. Jonquele has signed off on this e-mail 'Le gach deagh dhùrachd,' which could mean anything from 'You are going to be really awesome at Gaelic airs' to 'You will soon burn to a crisp under merciless Texan skies,'

As we prepare to take off, the captain warns us to expect 'isolated weather cells and a few pockets of nasty bumps.' I am much more concerned about having to sing Gaelic airs in public. Singing in public is one of my least favourite activities, along with listening to Americans shout 'Freedom' when they realise that I am Scottish and being gnawed on by diminutive horses.

To distract myself from such concerns, I examine *Gaelic Without Groans*. The cover boasts an ecstatic pink Highland cow perched in a rowing boat. The cow appears quite at home in such a craft. It looks as if it has spent its life roaming heather-tangled hillsides, dreaming of the day when it will have a seagoing vessel of its own. The cow bobs on a teal-coloured wave, face angled expectantly forwards. I open the book somewhere above East Pennsylvania just as the seatbelt signs come on and we encounter a succession of those nasty bumps and a couple of significant shoogles. The book states earnestly that it has tried to offer its lessons in as 'palatable' a form as possible 'in the belief that in the presentation of Gaelic in a popular and attractive form lies the best hope for the continuance of the language.' Presumably the euphoric bovine is another such tool in Gaelic's survival-strategy arsenal.

By the time we reach northeast Texan airspace, I have learned Gaelic proverbs that the book's introduction assured me will help me understand 'the Gaelic speaker's mind set.' I'm unsure what 'A big head on a wise man, a hen's head on a fool' or 'She is neither tiny and pretty nor big and ugly' tells me about the Gaelic psyche. The book advises, 'Wise words are usually hard to grasp, but show something of the Gaelic speaker's outlook on things. In time the reader will, we hope, be quoting them with gusto.' As we encounter a few more weather cells, I contemplate learning the Gaelic for 'Were today yesterday,' 'I am no scholar and I don't want to be—as the fox said to the wolf' and 'It is a pity for the one who goes to the shore when the very birds are deserting it.' I don't know when exactly I will quote them or the Gaelic tongue twister that translates as 'There has never been a broad grey fat ram' with or without gusto.

Growing up, one of the only sayings I heard regularly was a catch-phrase used almost daily by my Scottish granny. At just four foot ten, my Lanarkshire grandmother was known as 'Little Granny,' sized up in comparison with our loftier, five foot eight Irish 'Big Granny.' The titles caused both sizes of grandmother immeasurable displeasure.

Little Granny justified every loss, failure and disappointment in our lives with the consolation that 'What's fir ye'll no go by ye.' Knowing that whatever was destined for us would not pass us by soothed away all sorts of worries at having been snubbed for some opportunity or other, and was used to justify many shocking instances of lethargy on my part. The adoption of this lazy laissez faire phrase as an unofficial family motto says a considerable amount about the mind set of the Mulholland clan.

Reading through the vocabulary section, I realise that when pilfering a book from my sister, I should have checked when it was published. It turns out that *Gaelic Without Groans* first tried to make the language palatable in 1934. I'm delighted to learn the Gaelic for 'tip top' and 'rascal,' but suspect I will have less use for 'prohibitionist' and 'fruit sandwiches.' There is no vocabulary for any other kind of sandwiches. What sort of mind set explains a culture with only fruit sandwiches? As I find words for 'hair restorer,' 'means test' and 'home-spun cloth' but no further sandwich terminology, I am thankful that my homeland has devoted the decades since publication of this book to expanding its sandwich selection. Without Coronation Chicken sandwiches, my life would have been a far less flavoursome thing.

Another section of the book offers a few colourful curses, including 'Marbhphaisg ort!,' which translates literally and cold-bloodedly as 'May a shroud be upon you!' A few pages on, the book refers to the Outer Minch, which sounds like a far more obscene thing to have said in your presence, but is actually just the name of the body of water that separates the islands, where the bulk of the shroud-threateners live, from the parts of Scotland where we prefer insults such as 'nippy sweetie' (a cross woman), 'teuchter' (a Highlander) and 'tumshie' (a turnip). The book also offers the word for 'wireless,' which seems impressively up-to-date, but the fact that this entry is immediately followed by 'wireless set' reveals that the word has merely come full circle and back into usage. A fruit sandwich renaissance is probably just round the corner.

At 7 pm, Dallas Fort Worth airport is a seething mass of people darting off to their gates, but outside on the blank cement walkways it is deserted. And hot. Startlingly, almost incomprehensibly hot. It is so hot that within twenty feet of leaving the terminal building, it feels like my hair is sweating. This, it appears, is what a Texan heat-wave feels like. It is a pity for the one who goes to the shore when the very birds are deserting it, I think to myself, as I breenge, beet red and sweating, towards a lone downtown shuttle idling a hot hundred feet away.

A big, orange sun bleeds into a crimson horizon. Starlings surge overhead in a joyous swirl as the van rattles in the direction of George W Bush Turnpike.

Our driver lurches into an unexpected five-lane lane-change. The two other passengers and I cling grimly to the seats in front of us as he guns towards Dallas whistling an off-key version of 'All Shook Up.' 'Injured in a wreck?' enquires a billboard we hurtle past.

Downtown Dallas is as far as I'm going tonight; I head into exurbia tomorrow.

At the hotel, Deshawna checks me in and says, 'Well, that's another hot day in Dallas done and dusted. So many scorchers in a row. I'm cooked.' She asks, 'How 'bout Scotland? Is it very hot?'

I laugh. 'No. It rains a lot.'

Deshawna breathes in audibly. 'Oh, my. Rain. Wow. You have rain? Rain...' She trails off, imagining this. 'I'd love to live somewhere with rain.'

I've never thought about rain from a Texan perspective before. Anyone who grew up in Scotland simply made sure that 90% of their garments had hoods on them and took umbrellas whenever daring to don the other 10%. I never thought we were particularly lucky to get drenched on a near daily basis. But on my way here this evening, I saw the earth crumbled to dust in flower beds, seared trees withering on the sidewalks, a spectrum of faded browns and greys, not a lick of green in sight. Once again, the US makes me think differently about home.

'How about if you got rain five days a week?' I ask.

'Really, it rains that much in Scotland? I think I'd take that Scottish rain. I'd take buckets of it.'

At a mere 42 storeys—30 storeys shorter than the nearby Bank of America Plaza—the hotel is still pretty lofty. If suddenly and inexplicably deposited in Glasgow's East End, this hotel would tower almost 300 feet above Scotland's tallest occupied buildings, the 267-feet-high, identically grim 'Gallowgate Twins.' I've always been awed by the soaring skyscapes of North America. While my American and Canadian friends barely blink at a Van der Rohe, a Van Alen or a Gilbert, I gaze in amazement at these incredible vertical creations and romanticise skyscrapers in the same way that North Americans romanticise the castles, keeps and medieval constructions of Europe. The grass is always greener. Although obviously not in Texas during a heatwave.

From my 42nd floor room, I see the city glow and sprawl, and finally fade into the darkness of the surrounding black-land prairies. Once I tire of marvelling at the near endless lights, the mind-boggling dimensions of this city, I compose an e-mail to Orla stitched together from Gaelic Without Groans.

'Orla Og, Tha Texas anabarrach! Agus mòr. An seo, tha dith-dhealg, ach cha robh reithe leathann liath riamh reamhar.'

'Young Orla, Texas is tip top! And big. Here, there is wireless, but there has never been a broad grey fat ram.'

After a morning marvelling at downtown Dallas's high rises, I trek through the sweltering heat to Union Station, scurrying to shade whenever I have to wait for traffic. Even 30 seconds standing under those merciless Texan skies and I begin to feel like I've been poached. I scorch my hand pushing the brass push-plate of the stiff oak door into the train station. I was not designed for this climate. I leave Dallas on a blissfully air-conditioned train and head west to Fort Worth, a city that promises it's 'Where the West Begins.'

Despite more than a decade of travel writing, my knowledge of Texas is not from tourist boards. It's not from the barrage of press releases that thunk into my inbox each morning. It's not from lovingly compiled country music press trip playlists. It's from growing up in Scotland, watching Westerns at home in Glasgow with my dad. Texas might be as staunchly All-American as it gets, but it makes me homesick and makes me wish my dad was here. And that he had brought along a suitcase full of wearable air-conditioning.

Fort Worth, the 18th largest city in the US and officially the fastest growing city in the land (when considered independently of its brash conjoined city twin, Dallas) started life in 1849 as a military fort on what was then the frontier. Although the fort was vacated in 1853, the town had been established and soon won the right to be the county seat—allegedly by stealing whisky from the competition and then bribing voters with these ill-gotten gains. Perhaps Glasgow should try that with Edinburgh if ever a vote for the capital comes up.

Once the half-Scottish, half-Cherokee trader Jesse Chisholm had blazed the eponymous Chisholm Trail south from Wichita, vast herds of Texas longhorn cattle made for the city and pistol-toting cow-boys caroused in Hell's Half Acre, this cowtown's infamous red light district. Businesses moved in to meet the drovers' needs and Fort Worth became the trading hub for the entire northwest of the state. The railroad reached Fort Worth in 1876, promoting the city from just another stop on the trail to the final destination for cattle drives.

Fort Worth went from strength to strength. The city next struck it lucky in 1917 when an oil 'gusher' was sprung on a farm 90 miles west. Soon there were hundreds of wells in the vicinity. Operators, promoters, speculators and refineries followed. Today, Fort Worth has a population of 700,000, the last remaining cattle stockyards in the US and a lot of cool-sounding museums that I am far too hot to consider visiting. Anyway, I have been warned by my soon-to-be host and Gaelic teacher, not to expect too much as Fort Worth 'is still a far cry from European cities,' which is precisely what I have always loved about the cities of the US. The grass is always greener. Even in Texas during a heatwave.

Once off the train and on the streets of Fort Worth, the heat is huge and heavy. When the wind blows it's like being chased by a furious oven. I fear that one or more of my limbs may melt. I have cut my sightseeing schedule down from an extensive city walking tour to one vital stop, but by the time I reach the National Cowgirl Museum and Hall of Fame, my interest in the history of the American cowgirl is outpaced by my keen new interest in air-conditioning.

'What are you even doing out today?' says Margaret the matronly museum concierge, shaking her head. 'Girl, it's too hot to do anything other than sit smack in front of the air-con.'

I do a swift tour of cowgirl costumes, bits of rodeo and movie tack and associated troughs of fillies on film memorabilia, giving a wide berth to the interactive Bucking Bronco attraction. I sidle towards the exit, thinking that I'll leave encounters with cantankerous colts to Webb. Margaret, however, has other ideas.

Ninety seconds later, I clamber nervously onto the back of my first ever such mechanical monster and brace myself. Margaret flips the switch and nothing happens. That's when I realise with a mixture of relief and disappointment that the bronco does not actually buck. In fact, it only reaches a turgid lurching pitch if I shoogle back and forwards frantically to budge the great lumbering beast along its obstinate mechanical haunches. As the camera rolls and I make a self-conscious fool of myself, Margaret calls helpful instructions such as 'Ride 'em, girl!,' 'Holler!' and 'Whoop!' I do as I'm told, awkwardly whirling a pretend lariat above my head and ricocheting from side to side, a pained grin stamped on my face.

'Who...' Lurch. 'Sees these...' Judder. Creak. 'Videos?' I pant.

'Just the Internet,' Margaret reassures me.

After I stumble off my imaginary steed, I watch the video. Myself and my unwieldy ride have been superimposed onto an ancient black and white reel of a bucking bronco kicking its heels around a rodeo ground. Plinky piano saloon music plays as I humiliate myself on screen. It makes painful viewing, and not solely because I threw my back out while obeying Margaret's demands to 'Giddyup' like I meant it. Only in the footage of my panic-struck stagger through my first attempt at Scottish country dancing in Honolulu have I before managed to look quite so foolish on film, but I'm sure my dad will be proud of my first roping scene.

Leaving Fort Worth as the light starts to fade, Adam the Moroccan taxi driver tells me he likes it here because the heat is so 'homely,' an affection surely only felt by those brought up on the hem of the Sahara.

'What are the things about Scotland?' he asks, looking at me in his mirror. Before I have a chance to answer, he bursts out, 'Whisky! And drinking!'

Adam is pleased with himself.

I smile and nod, happy not to have to hear about *Braveheart* or freedom for a change.

'What are the things about Morocco?' I ask before *Braveheart* has time to rear its ugly blue face in the conversation.

Adam says, 'You don't know any?'

'Camels? And, um, couscous?' I offer.

Although he keeps his sights locked on a Ford Mustang unpredictably weaving ahead, I can see Adam is surprised by my extensive knowledge of his land.

'You know these things? Excellence! And Scotland also has...' Adam pauses. 'The monster! This sizeable monster!'

'Yes! We do have a sizeable monster!' I say with pride.

'More Morocco, please.'

'Morocco has, um, fez hats!'

'Yes! Hats!' Adam beams. 'And you have the meal of the stomach of the sheep!' He frowns slightly. 'This is a strange thing to do to a sheep.'

I cannot argue with this.

'We have Merguez sausage. Sausaging, this is a better thing to do to a sheep.'

We drive out into the dusty, flat ranchlands west of the city. Engrossed in our competition, it takes three cruises along the same stretch of highway before we finally find the turn off.

Adam and I survey Jonquele's wide brick ranch house with its sun-scorched lawn and forbidding gates.

'What do you know about this lady?' demands Adam. 'You know as much about this lady as you know about Morocco?'

I tell him about her love of Scottish Gaelic and her four cats.

Adam weighs this up. 'Okay. I also like cats.' He says, 'I drive off when you wave you're okay. You look. You decide she is an okay lady and then you wave. Okay?'

Three plaintive hemp kittens woven into the doormat look up at me. A Texas spiny lizard scuttles up the mosquito screen as the door opens. I squint in the relentless sunlight as the door opens.

Before my eyes have adjusted to the dark inside, a loud voice booms, 'Fàilte! Welcome to Texas!'

Based on the hemp kitten committee and the welcome, I decide she is an okay lady and step in. I look back at Adam and wave. I'm sorry to see him go.

As I lope through the main house behind Jonquele, I glimpse shelves crowded with dolls, sofas draped in colourful quilts and heaped with fat cushions, corners silted up with dolls' houses. Bookcases are laden with books and games. It's a house where you could mislay an entire language and never find it again. A Manx cat called Shelby darts onto a table, threatening to topple its teetering tower of books and papers. Another beastie slinks by, haunches low to the ground, as we pass.

Across the courtyard, Jonquele's 'playroom' boasts banks of sewing benches where an army of quilters can stitch away, or, on weekends such as this one, a platoon of Gaelic students can study the language's most palatable proverbs, plus, of course, make feeble attempts to sing Scottish-Texan airs during a heatwave. It feels very strange finally to be here, this unlikely outpost of Scottishness in exurbia. Not as strange as, say, debating better sheep usage with a Moroccan taxi driver, but strange all the same.

Jonquele has shoulder-length, recently greyed hair, cheerful blue-framed glasses and a big, generous laugh. She describes her ancestry as 'West European,' a mix of Irish, English, Welsh, French, German and Scottish. When opting to adopt an ancestral language, she could have chosen High German, Welsh or Latin and would probably have had more people to chat with in the neighbourhood. And yet she picked Scottish Gaelic. I have to ask why.

'Music. That's how it started. I heard a song by the Irish group Clannad. And I just thought, 'What in the cat's hair language are they all speaking?''

That cat's hairy language turned out to be Irish Gaelic.

'Then it got me thinking,' says Jonquele. 'What do they speak in Ireland? Irish. What do they speak in France? French. What do they speak in England? English. What do they speak in Scotland? English.' She pauses for effect. 'And I thought, English? Well, that's not right! It was a Eureka moment.'

Realising that something was linguistically awry, Jonquele hunted down Scottish Gaelic and took to it with gusto.

'I loved the sound of the language,' she lights up. 'The way it flowed.'

I feel pleased to have picked such a passionate teacher. Jonquele obviously feels she's doing good by spreading Gaelic and she's doing it for love, not money, which is probably just as well considering the surely shallow pool of possible Gaelic students in northeast Texas.

Jonquele shows me to my quarters, a room set up for her 'quilting girlfriends' when they come to stay. I've never had any quilting girlfriends, which, looking at the lovingly stitched creations draped over a row of four single beds, I now realise was a foolish mistake.

Nestled on pillows jubilantly embroidered with the words 'Quilt Party!,' under a prim, decorative wooden cat that holds a sign in its mouth that warns, 'Vigilance,' I look out at the hot, muggy darkness. Flotillas of knobbly wee lizards dart up the screen. Gargantuan bugs hurl themselves again and again at the cobweb-shrouded outdoor light. The pool practically steams in the heat. I wonder what Orla's view was like when she learned Gaelic on the island of South Uist. I suspect there was less of an emphasis on quilting, a lower lizard count and a slightly chillier average water temperature. I wonder about the two days of Gaelic classes ahead of me. Surely, having spent the first half of my life in Scotland, I will have some sort of bonus native advantage over my fellow students? I wonder whether those bugs can get in. I scan the screen nervously, checking for any holes. 'Vigilance,' the wooden cat reminds me.

It's 7 am and I'm standing beside a plucky Prickly Pear cactus, the only living thing in this scorched Texan landscape. The grass around me is patchy and yellow. The muffled gurgle-squeak whistle of an Eastern Bluebird percolates through the singed air. The temperature vaults upwards in aggressive jolts. I duck indoors. A brilliant emerald hummingbird whirs frantically round each tiny trough of an empty bird feeder just outside. Beyond, the pool blurs in the intense heat.

Lisa, my sole fellow student, arrives, dashing into the air-conditioned room, and I offer the paltry dribble of Gaelic that I learned in Memphis, 'Madainn mhath, y'all!'

Lisa looks surprised and says, 'But I thought Jonquele said you were gonna be a baby beginner! It don't sound like this is your first lesson!'

I reassure her that 'Good Morning, y'all' is the extent of my Gaelic and she looks at me with confusion. Then it clicks.

'That accent... You're not from Texas! You're Scottish!' She says accusingly. 'But... if you're Scottish, why don't you already speak Gaelic?' Lisa is perplexed.

I hesitate. Should I break the news that just over 1% of us speak Gaelic? That 99% of us couldn't tell our 'achs' from our 'anabarrachs'? I don't want to dampen her enthusiasm for learning the language.

'Somehow I missed out, but I'm sure I'll catch up in no time.'

Lisa's eyes narrow. 'You reckon? I already got seven Sundays of Gaelic classes on you, missy,' she says.

Across the sewing bench, Lisa and I size each other up.

On the dot of nine, Jonquele bustles into the room with several unruly stacks of paper in her arms. She has paired bright pink and custard striped tracksuit pants with a daffodil yellow tank top. Her glasses perch quizzically on the brim of her nose as she surveys her two pupils. She closes the door with a decisive shove that indicates that my first ever Scottish Gaelic class is now in session.

'Okay. If y'all are ready, let's start. We're gonna need our Gaelic names,' she says.

On her first lesson, Lisa became 'Ealasaid,' which is pronounced something like 'Elisudge' and is the Gaelic for Elizabeth. I'm already graced with a Gaelic-ish name, so am permitted to stay 'Aefa.'

Jonquele, however, does not stay 'Jonquele.' This, she points out quite reasonably, is because in Gaelic the golden jonquil flower is referred to as 'the plant that vomits.' I didn't realise that the daffodil so often felt so poorly. Rather than being known as the Puking Plant, Jonquele became 'Uiseag,' which sounds like 'Ooshak' and which has no correlation whatsoever to the nauseous narcissus; Jonquele's Gaelic name means 'Skylark.'

Damn, I wouldn't have stuck with 'Aefa' if I'd known I could so easily have metamorphosed into Tufted Puffin or Shorty or Tip Top for the weekend.

'Okay, here's how you pronounce this here language. Ls are kinda tongue flips,' Skylark says. 'It's not how you speak in Texas. When I say 'em, I have to put my Gaelic brain on. This is a language in which you actively use your nose. Ns are nasalised. Dh is like gargling. Gh is like deeper gargling. Ch is an angry cat noise.'

As Skylark wades through the gargles, catfights and nasal acrobatics required for Gaelic, I am aghast. That pink cow on the boat lied; this is not a palatable language! Lisa has had seven weeks to digest this obstreperous collection of consonants. I'm really not sure that I can develop a taste for such a hard-to-swallow language in just one weekend.

'If you speak German, you got some of these sounds hiding around in there,' Skylark continues. 'Fh is silent. Rs are to be enthusiastically rolled.'

Ahah! I can name a few random woodland creatures in German and, unlike these Texan Scots, I can roll my Rs with gusto. And, when

I think about it, not only am I a talented gargler, but I regularly torment our cat Beastie, making her twirl her wee whiskers and hiss. Texans are not known for such tongue trilling or gargling and Lisa doesn't look like a cat person.

'Do you have cats?' I ask, innocently.

Lisa looks puzzled. Before she can answer, Skylark has swept on with the lesson.

'H makes the word look big and long and hairy but it's just a flag,' she says. 'Ignore them Hs. And vowels, well, I tell you, the Gaels didn't go though the Great Vowel Shift of the 17th century,' says Skylark with a laugh.

Lisa, who has obviously used her seven weeks of Gaelic well, understands this joke and adds, 'That's cause we're stubborn and we don't like change.'

During the morning, I attempt to learn the verb to be, tongue tripping over the unfamiliar sounds.

'Sibh is y'all,' says Skylark, 'That's the polite form for elders or strangers.'

Pronounced 'shiv,' I struggle to store this in my brain, alongside the silent Fhs, gargled Dhs and hairy Hs. Lisa chirps through the declension, racing ahead of me. Soon it's time for me to construct my first Gaelic sentence.

'Just use whatever part of the Gaelic you got,' encourages Skylark. 'It don't matter if the sentence goes all cattywampas.'

My first sentence is short and accurate. 'Tha mi caillte,' I say. 'I am lost.'

I am unclear as to whether this is cattywampas or not, but Skylark and Lisa applaud. I am as pleased as a cow in a rowing boat.

With a sheet of cartoons, Lisa and I play verb charades, taking turns to asking 'Dè tha mi a dèanamh?' 'What am I doing?.' It feels an apt question. We vie for obscure activities with which to stump each other. I run. Lisa skips. I get her with jumping. But she gets me with fighting, climbing and winning. I briefly think I am finding my way, but then we start on participles and I lose all Gaelic direction once again. By lunchtime, I have learned that Lisa is far better at Gaelic than me and that I have a decidedly hazy grasp of participles in any language.

Skylark knows her languages and she is, indeed, a good teacher. So far, all she warned me of has come true, from the multitude of cats and the toastiness of Texas to the fact that immersion learning is exhausting.

We lunch out by the pool. It is 105 Fahrenheit in the shade, or 40 Celsius, which counts as rather toasty however you measure it.

Skylark looks round, 'The heat's burned the peaches and the grapes. There's nothing in the well. The pool's down inches every day. The animals all come by. They're all drinking from it. In the last week, I've seen a hawk and a coyote drinking there.' She adds, 'The one day it rained during this drought, I had some of my quilting girlfriends over. We all ran outside, arms outstretched. It was almost biblical.'

I'm fascinated by this unfamiliar heat, the parched opposite of Scottish weather.

Talk turns to the Old Country. Lisa and Skylark both talk wistfully about the Highlands, although neither Skylark nor Lisa knows where in Scotland their ancestors came from or whether they were High-landers or Lowlanders.

'My people, the Stuarts,' says Lisa. 'They got halfway to Mississippi and they couldn't shed the Old Country fast enough.'

Her ancestors might have been eager to leave all traces of their homeland behind, but their Fort Worth descendent feels very differ-ently. Now Lisa organises Clan Stewart Society of America booths at Scottish festivals and games, learns Gaelic and dreams of the day she can join Ed Miller's annual 'Folksong Tour of Scotland.' The Edinburgh-born Miller hosts radio shows on Austin's Radio KUT-FM and his Scotland is a significant link to the country for Lisa. She talks of him with some reverence. I am delighted to discover that Ed insists his tours are 'not a search for the Scotland of *Brigadoon*, *Braveheart* and the Loch Ness Monster.' Instead, he offers his take on Scotland's 'music, people, history and landscape.' The tours even spend time in the Lowlands, which is startlingly unusual in the misty Highlands-centric land usually fêted by Scottish-America.

'Ed organised a house concert with a Scottish folk singer,' says Lisa, 'And I was so excited to meet someone over from Scotland. I even got up enough courage to speak a few words of greeting to him in Gaelic. He thought I was a loon! Then he realised that I was speaking Gaelic and said something about it not being spoken anymore.' Lisa looks downcast at the memory. 'I was sure disappointed, but that just can't be right. Some folks must speak it, so I'm still studying away.'

Skylark has been to Scotland once. She was well prepared for the trip, both linguistically and sartorially, travelling with a wardrobe that included a tartan Tam O' Shanter hat and an Aran fisherman's sweater. Lisa's wardrobe also boasts such items. I am amazed at these two Texans with their Scots Gaelic and their Scots garb. Other than during my recent trip to Oregon, it has never occurred to me to model such an ethnic ensemble.

After studying the language for all those years, Skylark was hugely disappointed that people in the Outer Isles weren't speaking Gaelic when she got there.

'I'm pretty sure they start speaking Gaelic as soon as the tourists are not around,' she says.

She may be right, although maybe she was just looking in the wrong place. It's ironic that Glasgow rarely features on the itineraries of Scottish-Americans when it's one place outside the islands where you might actually fall into a conversation in Gaelic. I tell Skylark and Lisa about Glasgow's Gaelic school, its Gaelic centre, its Gaelic choirs, its Gaelic bookshop. I can see them watching intently. There's a look of relief on both their faces. Their dreams of talking Gaelic flicker back into life.

But, for Skylark, there was obviously a lot lost on that trip to the Isles. It was not the homecoming this Texan Scot had dreamed of. With some Spanish ancestry, Skylark then thought of retiring to Spain but the romance was destroyed there, too.

'I got mugged in Barcelona. It made me think. I came home. I drove the back roads. I thought again. And I saw the beauty and the romance right here.'

The three of us sip our iced tea contemplatively.

'Well,' says Skylark, 'That was before we started having wars with people who fly planes into buildings.'

The rest of the day is devoted to Gaelic song, which means that Skylark sings like her namesake and Lisa and I coo along like apologetic pigeons. Skylark is a founding member of the a capella ensemble Cór Gaeilge Texais and is particularly proud that this Texan Gaelic ensemble appeared at something that sounds like 'the Feeble Fobble' in Belfast. Skylark looks as pleased as a Texan in a brand new Tam O' Shanter as she tells us about this glorious accomplishment. She chooses a sheet of lyrics from the worryingly large selection with which she has equipped us.

'This one is a puirt-à-beul, a jig for the mouth,' she says.

A jig for the mouth! What a delightful description! I find this a splendid concept and at that moment a genuine love for Gaelic begins to take hold. A language with descriptions such as this must never die!

Skylark sings us the mouth jig, followed by a tongue-twister called 'Tha Mulad' and a beautifully forlorn number called 'Buain na Rainich,' which is about a fairy's ill-fated love for a human girl and which translates roughly to,

'It is a pity that I am not with you again

We would be tuneful

I would go with you to the ends of the earth

Sailing on the crest of the waves.'

Skylark sings and I immediately feel mournful. My modern Scottish cynicism is no match for the power of a Gaelic lament. I start pining for things I've left behind: my long-suffering partner, my cat, my mum.

As introduction to a traditional 'waulking' song, Skylark reminisces about 'the croft lifestyle,' and explains how in Scotland neighbours gather to work the new wool by 'waulking,' a process of kneading by hand to shrink and thicken. Waulking has one interesting industrial setting ingredient—urine.

When shearing's done in Scotland, Skylark tells us, you call your neighbours and they all come around with steaming buckets of pee in which to dunk the wool. She makes it sound like we all still slop the contents of our bladders over to our neighbours on a regular basis. I am lost for words. In any language. I think about how my mum would feel if she knew this was how our lives were being portrayed over here in Texas. She would struggle to maintain her legendary levels of hospitality if Joan from round the corner carted a pot o' pee with her when she came for dinner or if Frankie from next door sloshed up the steps with a flagon of fresh pee as a friendship gesture. While I have to assume that hygiene, sense and my people's olfactory delicacy have all called a halt to neighbourly pee-provision, it seems that in the past many of them really were generous pee-gifters. What in the cat's hair was going on with that?

I was not the only Scot unaware of both our peeing prowess and the fact that up till recently Scots were dutifully still peeing their parts in Hebridean communities. In the book, *Life of Pee, The Story of How Urine Got Everywhere* by Sally Magnuson, the Scottish author reports with astonishment that urine is behind the distinctive 'designer smell' of Harris Tweed. Like Ms Magnuson, I had no idea. It took a Texan to tell me.

Skylark is now talking about an Arizona-based Gaelic teacher originally from the Isle of Skye. She says, confrontationally, that when this Islander reached Glasgow she was 'pretty much brutalised for speaking Gaelic.' She glares at me. This is quite obviously entirely my fault. I have exposed myself as a representative of modern Scotland, the evil land that brutalises Gaelic speakers and refuses to pee in buckets.

While this exploration of Scottish-America has turned me into something of a champion of the Lowlands, it doesn't mean that I don't love the Highlands. The Highlands start just 20 miles away from the creaky old house in the west end of Glasgow that I grew up in, but 20 miles really is quite far in a country that's only 37 miles wide at one point. Despite its impressively determined midge population, the area has always had an irresistible allure. But, actually, for me, for a substantial part of my childhood, I didn't even know the area to the north of my hometown was called 'the Highlands.' We didn't go to the Highlands for weekends, we went to 'the Caravan'—an approximately two-square-mile area north of Crianlarich and just short of Tyndrum, around the fern-filled clearing where our decrepit 13-foot-long Sprite caravan sat rusting into the mountainside. The ferns acted as helpful camouflage against Forestry Department sightings of our illegally parked accommodation, as helpful insulation against the weather and as consummate breeding grounds for a particularly voracious subspecies of Highland biting midge. At the Caravan, we would while away the occasional sunny spells with our own Highland games—complicated battles based on skilfully knocking empty Tennent's Special beer cans off rocks on the banks of the River Cononish. My mum would amaze us all by skimming stones right across the river, often to the alarm of a sheep innocently grazing on the resilient heather on the other side. At night, we would perform great feats of strength by attempting to topple my brother Mark out of his bunk whenever he had just nodded off. It was like tossing a snoring caber, but far more dangerous and infinitely more amusing.

My dad was in charge of cooking on our expeditions north. Never one to give up too soon, traditional Highland food consisted of extremely burnt potatoes and determinedly charred sausages, cooked on an open fire on the riverbank when it was dry, and hacked-open cans of Spam and crumbled McVities Digestive Biscuits when it rained. We could not have dreamed up food more delicious or exotic. Traditional music up there, far from plug sockets and the torment of Orla's fiddle orchestra albums, was my mum singing 'My Lagan Love,' my dad singing 'The Loch Tay Boat Song,' or Brian, the youngest, breaking into peals of his sudden and delighted laugh, while the rain battered the roof of the aged fibreglass trailer and the midges multiplied endlessly outside.

The Caravan and its environs were a magical place where, if we lay still long enough, we would see deer loping down to the river for a drink, where we could scamper along hoof-trodden sheep trails through the heather to explore the ruins of an 18th century village, abandoned during the Highland clearances, and where we could plant a rowan sprig one season and by the next, the relentless rain would have propelled it to truly majestic heights. Today, a tree planted by my sister Ciara towers 60 feet above a bristling profusion of lush green ferns, a few ancient moss-claimed tyres and the rusted base frame skeleton of what once was a much loved 1970 Sprite caravan.

Night has settled like a sauna over North Texas. I perch on the bed under the gaze of the vigilant cat and pick up Bill Bryson's book *Mother Tongue*. In the first chapter, Bryson joyfully reports the Scottish Gaelic word 'sgrìob,' the word for the 'itchiness that overcomes the upper lip' just before the drinker takes his first sip of whisky. It's a delightful concept. I can feel myself falling for this language with its anticipatory whisky itches and mouth jigs.

It's late afternoon on Sunday and I have learned that there are almost as many prepositional pronouns as there are Gaelic speakers. By the time we reach the 132nd pronoun, it's my brain rather than my upper lip that has succumbed to an itch. Before I can take full account of this litany of language—and the fact that, in Gaelic, all numbers ending in one or two count as singular—Skylark picks up a dictionary, the snappily named *Dwelly's Faclair Gàidhlig gu Beurla le Dealbhan*, first published in 1901.

'With this 'un, you can have a lot of fun just looking up words for 'sheep',' she says.

Much like throwing pee parties, this does not seem like the most fun activity. Then I try it. Skylark is right! There are pages and pages of words for sheep. This is fun! There are words for a small or inferior lamb, draft gimmer or crooked hogg. For a short-tailed ram, pet ewe-hogg or three-winter ewe. You can even narrow your conversational sheep requirements down to 'a female after weaning but before her first shearing,' 'a yearling of a wether after its first Halloween' or 'a barren twinter if not put to ram.' And then you can do the same for cows! And, presumably, pigs! The precision you can achieve in Gaelic really is most impressive. According to Skylark, who has counted, Dwelly's lists '87 different types of cow,' offering clarification as to whether they're on their third calf or just had one or whether they're a sturk, which, it turns out, is an adolescent heifer. Words for old women are just as extensive, she tells me. What a splendid language! I remember Olive, a friend in Glasgow, saying that she'd heard there were dozens of words for 'love' in Gaelic; from a word for the love of a friend to one for the love of a wife. Or, my dad suggested, for the love of a friend's wife. I'm quite sure *Dwelly's* has a word for that, too. With its exhaustive ovine, bovine and amorous vocabulary, Gaelic puts Glaswegian to shame, although proportionally we have more insults to other parts of a sentence, which seems a more useful thing for any language spoken in my hometown.

I leave Jonquele's playroom thoughtful, glassy-eyed and newly expert in ovine terminology. A sign in the Trinity Railroad Express depot warns passengers to 'be aware of people who appear lost, loiter, stare or watch others, pace or appear nervous or jumpy.' After a weekend of Gaelic immersion, this describes me to a silent over-heated T.

I take a seat in Riscky's Barbecue in Fort Worth Stockyards, famous for 'calf fries' and 'steak on the hoof.' 'Forget those French things!' proclaims the menu. 'Our original Texas Fries pardner up with sweet onions and spicy jalapeños.' A few minutes later, approximately half a heifer and three barbecued sturks are delivered to my table in a Texas-shaped straw basket. Should I consume this portion in its entirety I, too, will be Texas-shaped.

Polish immigrant Joe Riscky opened his first restaurant in 1927, selling homemade barbecue lunches. I wonder do later generations of Risckys pine for whatever Old Joe left behind before he hit the Mississippi? I wonder how many generations need to go by for 'old countries' to be shrouded in selective, soft-focus mists of time? I wonder how much of home I have airbrushed over the years? I wonder could they have crammed any more calf fries in this enormous crater of a carb container?

The heat continues to scorch down. A dusty herd of longhorns ambles along the street outside. A country song called 'Where I Come From' plays on the radio. The band sings about various things they miss and are proud of back home, including car park brawls, a lack of access to education, and moonlight, the latter something the song-writers clearly feel is strictly limited to skies over the southern US.

I think back to Skylark taking another look at home, the rethink she had to do, post-mugging and post-Highlands disappointment. I think I'm ready to rediscover my own backroads. The moonlight and opportunities for car park punch-ups there really are tip-top.

11. BLOODY BRIGADOON:
NEW YORK CITY

Because it seemed as though my journey to Scottishness should experience one of the most visible and, to many Scots still in Scotland, risible, elements of Scottish-America, I am in New York for Tartan Day.

Tartan Day? 'What is Tartan Day?' you might quite reasonably ask. And plenty of people have asked—including the girthy Ohioan who overflowed my armrest on my flight here this morning. My feeble attempts to explain what T-Day is all about fail to clear up confusion, even when I resort to 'Divide St Patrick's Day by 1000 and turn up the bagpipes.'

The truth is, I don't really know what to expect. I know that Tartan Day is a big deal in Scottish-America, with such days featured on calendars from coast to coast. And I know that New York's celebration offers the highest bagpipe and Scottie dog count. And I know that I'm really looking forward to standing on Avenue of the Americas, dwarfed by skyscrapers, feeling proud of my homeland.

Wading through a sea of kilt-clad pipers and tartan-bedecked Scottie and Westie dogs on 45th Street, I overhear a woman with a Glaswegian accent say, 'This isn't Scotland, this is bloody *Brigadoon*! It certainly isn't the Scotland I come from.'

'Och, it is! It's just like Glasgow,' says another cheerfully, 'It's shambolic.'

'Aye, that's true.'

The two women grin and then raise appreciative eyebrows at the sight of dapper Scots actor Alan Cumming, grand marshal of this year's parade. Alan stands with a jovial, kilted, silver-haired man who I suddenly realise is Bob Winter, Glasgow's Lord Provost and my parents' neighbour.

'Just join the march,' suggests Bob the Provost after we have swapped news of various family members.

An officious woman with a clipboard, whose task seems to be to prevent precisely such shocking departures from official Tartan Day etiquette, frowns and shakes her head at this. I've only seen it once, but I'm pretty sure Brigadoon had fewer clipboards.

A stern pipe major on the corner barks at his troop of bagpipers, 'Attention! Don't look at the photographers! Don't stop for the photographers! Don't stop for anyone! If anyone gets in your way, run them over!'

Pipers immediately begin to jostle and fall into ranks all around me. I am in imminent danger of being squished underfoot. I duck as a burly piper beside me adjusts his substantial paunch and then looks stoutly forward. I dart out of the way of his gargantuan gut and to the corner where Little Brazil Street meets Avenue of the Americas. While I await this mighty display of Scottishness, I admire the scatter of flags and Scottish saltire hats that pepper the parade route.

Beside me, an out-of-breath woman, obviously in a rush and desperate to cross the street, asks a traffic cop, 'Is this the demonstration?'

'No, ma'am, it's a Scottish parade.'

She stops panting for a moment. 'It's a what?'

'A Scottish parade.'

'Why do the Scottish need a parade?'

The policeman shrugs, 'I don't know, lady. I really don't know.'

Why do we need a parade? Officially it's to celebrate Scottish history and culture. Unofficially, I suspect it's just because the Irish have one. Other than to bolster Guinness sales and increase pick-up rates among inebriated 20-something US college students, Irish-America doesn't really 'need' a parade either. But the 150,000-participant, 2-million-spectator Saint Patrick's Day Parade leaves Tartan Day limping in its shamrock-strewn wake, by around 1.99 million spectators and by alcohol sales figures larger than the GDPs of several small-to-medium-sized countries. There are some obvious reasons for Saint Patrick's Day's dominance of New York's spring Celtic celebration calendar. Clearly, a 261-year head start gives something of an advantage when it comes to drumming up spectators but, more importantly, it's far, far harder to turn a dram of Scotch whisky tartan-coloured than it is to add a few wee drops of lime food colouring to a Guinness. When it comes to novelty-coloured beverages, Scottish-America definitely drew the short straw.

Held on the Saturday closest to April 6th, Tartan Day's current date commemorates the 1320 Declaration of Arbroath, Scotland's equivalent to—and alleged inspiration for—the US's Declaration of Independence. Scotland's 14th-century Declaration stated, 'For as long as but a hundred of us remain alive, never will we on any conditions be brought under English rule. It is not for glory, nor riches, nor honours that we are fighting, but for freedom—for that alone, which no honest man gives up but with life itself.' Sentiments worth celebrating, except that, since Scotland lost its independence in 1707, all these years of Tartan Day parades seem a bit like celebrating a hard-won divorce while still married to the same domineering spouse. The Declaration was pretty awesome as constitutions go, especially Middle Aged ones, and had some radical wee touches such as believing in equality for everyone, whether they were Scottish, Greek, Jewish or even, incredibly generously, English.

Like Saint Patrick's Day parades, Tartan Day parades began in the US. The first Saint Patrick's Day parade was in 1737 in Boston. The first Tartan Day was held as a one-off, parade-less celebration in New York on July 1st 1982, marking the 200th anniversary of the repeal of 1747's Act of Proscription, the law that forbade Scots from wearing tartan. In 1998, the parade had just two pipe bands, while today Tartan Day is marked with parades, pipers, paunches and shoals of excitable Scotties from Brisbane to Buenos Aires to Albuquerque.

However, unlike Paddy's Day, the spectacle hasn't caught on to the same extent back home and you won't find troops of plaid-clad Texan cheerleaders shivering along Edinburgh's Princes Street, traumatised by the temperatures. Organised tartan-themed activities in Scotland are rather meagre, with the main Scottish news item on Tartan Day usually featuring an amused but perplexed report on the New York event and perhaps a segment on the determined efforts by the people at East Links Family Park to dye their flock of sheep tartan, a feat only slightly simpler than attempting to make a malt match clan colours.

From the corner of Little Brazil Street, I hear the wail of massed bagpipes waft into earshot. It's a powerful sound, building and echoing through the skyscraper canyons of Manhattan as it nears. I find a slightly muddy Scottish flag discarded on the street corner and wave it enthusiastically, craning to catch a first glimpse of this platoon of pipes.

As the bagpipes draw nearer, a trio of inebriated, 30-something New Yorkers pushes past me, partially obscuring my view.

'Bagpipes!' howls the woman, batting a belligerent strand of chestnut hair out of her eyes as she jams on a pair of sunglasses decorated with a Scottish flag.

'Charles! Fiona! We should take bagpipe classes,' exclaims the sliver-thin guy on her right.

'Ohmygod, Cordey, so much yes!' says Fiona.

'Beats pottery class,' drawls Charles.

'We should march with them!' says Fiona.

'But that would interfere with our drinking time,' Charles points out.

'Nix all marching,' says Fiona.

A kilted Alan Cumming steps nimbly into view, a representative of a far edgier, more modern Scotland than that which usually takes pride of place in Scottish-America. Bob the Provost grins and waves amiably alongside, his ceremonial gold chain gleaming in the afternoon sun. There is a polite cheer from the crowd.

'Alan! Alan, we love you! Guy beside Alan, we love you too!' scream the three in front of me.

'Kiss me!' shrieks Fiona, jabbing at her 'Kiss Me, I'm Scottish' badge.

'Alan, I want your babies!' shouts Cordey, waving frantically.

A straggle of older men in Revolutionary War outfits and exceedingly disreputable kilts teeter into sight. One sports a mini kilt worn at least six inches too short, much like the abbreviated garments worn by the waifs at the Tilted Kilt, except it's on a 70-something year old man with terrifying knees. Another wears his in what I assume to be an unintentionally revealing low-at-the-back, high-at-the-front-style.

A delegation from the Scottish Parliament walks past. The crowd applauds politely.

'Yes! YESSSS!' screams Fiona. 'I vote for Scottish equality! I demand equal menu billing for haggis!'

'Scotland!' shouts Charles.

'Freedom!' bellows Cordey.

I am enjoying their Scotch-sodden commentary on the spectacle so much that, for the first time on this Scottish-American odyssey, I only frown slightly at this Braveheart reference.

Countless clan organisations and nearly 30 pipe bands march past—from the Breezy Point Catholic Club Pipes and Drums to the NYC Correction Department Pipe Band, plus dozens of individual pipers, including one lone representative of the secretive-sounding FBI Pipe Band. The majority of pipers are American, but there are three from Pakistan's Jaffray Pipers, 45 Scottish kids from Scotland's St Columba's School Pipe Band and a posse from the Hong Kong St John Ambulance Brigade. As the noise of the pipes fades up towards West 50th Street, shrill yaps approach. A mixed pack of around 60 Scotties and Westies amble up the avenue, followed by a dozen hefty men from the Tartan Army—fans of the Scottish football team—staggering along with a 600-pound, 24-foot-long caber, the world's largest such stick.

'Toss the caber! Toss the caber!' Fiona, Charles and Cordey chant.

'What is this?' an elderly Jamaican passer-by asks me, with tones of amazement.

'It's a Scottish parade,' I tell her, my answer nearly drowned out by irate drivers backed up along Little Brazil Street.

'Why do the Scottish need a parade?' she asks me.

'Er, it's our only chance to convert people to the bagpipes.'

She thinks about this.

'Scotland!' screams Cordey.

Fiona says, 'We are so taking bagpipe classes.'

The old lady nods, 'Seems like it's working.'

'Bar first, bagpipe lessons later,' says Charles firmly.

'Scotland!' screams Cordey again.

The Jamaican lady looks at them with wonder, 'This is a weird amount of enthusiasm for a bunch of white people.'

'Ooh, Charles, there's a hot pipe major coming up,' murmurs Cordey to his friend. 'I really like aesthetic of the bagpipes,' he adds. 'The sound is ghastly, but the look is good.'

'You'll get a skean dhu knife in the chest,' says Fiona.

'I think I'm getting tartan tinnitus,' says Charles.

The parade stops momentarily and four teenage girls do a Highland dancing display. Cordey and Fiona attempt their own version and then collapse into giggles.

'What is *that*?' blurts Fiona, peering at the avenue.

Holding up the rear of the parade, Tartan Day's supposedly glorious finale rumples into sight. It looks like the combination of an unmade bed and the ghost of a baguette. It looks like a last minute Halloween costume thrown together by a depressed entomologist. It looks truly awful. It's three people draped in white sheets with cartoon features scrawled in marker and it's meant to be the Loch Ness Monster. There is a silence while the crowd takes this in. A Scottie dog with a

Nessie hat would have been more impressive than this bedraggled bedspread. I am astounded. Even Fiona, Charles and Cordey appear to be speechless—although I suspect they may just have finally become too intoxicated to see through their Scotland sunglasses.

This nyaff of a Nessie is a shocking missed opportunity. We could have so easily have won some points over the Saint Patrick's Day parade here, because in the Rock, Paper, Scissors contest of mythical creatures, Nessie should be able to beat a pack of leprechauns with her eyes closed. Or with one plesiosauric tail flick. Or with one rhomboid fin behind her back. Instead, Tartan Day finishes with a whimper and three people shimmying northwards under a badly painted sheet. I watch as one third of Nessie ducks out and nips into a store. Two of Nessie's remaining four legs start doing a wee dance. I cower with shame under the awning of an adjacent Irish bar. As the Scottish Ambassador, I'm going to have to put mightier monster parade representation at the top of the ambassadorial To Do List before anyone Irish witnesses this sorry sight.

But there was one thing that was truly mighty today, that tugged at my cynical heartstrings, that moved me and occasionally even silenced Fiona, Charles and Cordey. It was the sound of the massed pipes, filling the canyons of Manhattan.

I walk away from the crowds and the terriers, tartan and discarded saltire flags, and I realise there are still a couple of things I have to do to become a 100% Scot. I have to encounter a Highland cow up close and, even though it may well interfere with my drinking time, I need to learn to play the bagpipes.

There are far more piping teachers in the US than you might think. It's a surprisingly popular profession, with people offering their piping services in every corner of the land. Since I'm in New York, I first try a New Jersey fire fighter and bagpipe teacher who piped in the movie *Dead Poets Society*. In the two weeks it takes him not to return my messages, I work diligently on designs for mighty Nessie costumes and on perfecting a tartan liquor with which to win over the Americas. Next I approach a Salt Lake City pipe major and tutor who writes romantic, historical bagpipe fiction—a substantially larger literary genre than you might think—and lists her favourite books as *Harry Potter* and *The Book of Mormon*. She also thinks the better of ever getting back to me.

Finally, just when I am despairing of ever playing pipes, I send a plea to a kindly sounding Louisianan who believes that 'anyone desiring Pipe Music should be able to have it.' Within half an hour, there's a student piper syllabus and the offer of a $60 practice pipe in my inbox. Within another half hour, I have a ticket and I'm off to New Orleans.

12. KILLING THE CHANTER:
NEW ORLEANS AND GRETNA, LOUISIANA

When people hear that I'm a travel writer, they are often envious. Admittedly, travel writing has more glamorous moments than many of my previous jobs, such as my brief career as a haggis chef, the two days I lasted as a glowstick seller at kiddie pop concerts and the summer I spent dressed as a storybook lion at a book fair. There, my daily storyline appeared to revolve around busloads of tough urchins from some of Glasgow's harder corners wrestling me to the floor in order to yank off my tail. Travel writing definitely outglams those occupations, but people rarely realise just how much of a travel writer's life is spent delayed at gates, overnighting in shuttered airports and skulking in dingy underpasses, willing the arrival of elusive downtown airport shuttles.

I'm in Louis Armstrong International Airport in New Orleans, the day before my first bagpipe lesson. My friend Maggie has flown in to join me for 48 hours. We spend the first two of those hours in a grim underground parking lot waiting for our ride downtown but, with no children from Possilpark in the vicinity and neither our tails nor whiskers in danger of removal, I can't complain.

When we eventually reach downtown New Orleans, we stroll to Canal Street, the eastern hem of the French Quarter. The street is grand, wide and punctuated by scatters of palm trees, white table-clothed sidewalk cafés and the occasional neon alligator. Aged maroon streetcars roll by, rumbling through the humid evening, windows open to breathe in the promise of imminent rain.

By the time we cross Canal, we realise that this is a city seriously committed to intoxication. What an impressive number of very drunk people there are on the streets on a Monday evening! In Scotland, we reserve such advanced levels of drunkenness for royal weddings, cooking sherry promotions and the appearance of any rare glimmers of sunlight. New Orleans obviously rolls out this degree of mayhem on an average Monday. We watch as one would-be smoker makes seven fumbling attempts to light his cigarette, burning his nose and staring at the match with surprise after each failed attempt.

We consult our crumpled map. Earlier, when we asked Candace, our hotel concierge, for directions to the French Quarter, she appeared to think we had, in fact, asked about the success of her recent nude calendar shoot. An easy mistake to make. She anchored the hotel's stack of maps with her ample bosom as she talked us through her portfolio

'I only do tasteful nudey work,' the 50-something calendar girl informed us, flicking from August to September, a month that revealed her every asset in stark detail.

'See, tasteful,' beamed Candace.

'Such an interesting, ehm, arrangement,' I said, acknowledging the tangle of limbs.

'Wonderful lighting,' said Maggie, grabbing a map while Candace rearranged her cleavage.

Our liberated map leads us along Royal to Bienville to the famed Bourbon Street, which displays levels of inebriation higher than any I have seen since the terrifying night I coincided with Irish high school exam results night in the west of Ireland. The things I saw would put you off education entirely.

Blues, Cajun and Zydeco blare out of bars and into a melee of sound mid-street. A group of bleary-eyed teens stagger along the street, stopping occasionally to vomit into green neon-lit doorways.

In the binge-drinking Olympics, Ireland and Scotland might take the gold and silver, but New Orleans gets the bilious green.

Red neon blazes 'Oysters' and 'Hand Grenades,' yellow proclaims 'Hurricanes' and 'Zydeco' and blue announces 'Daiquiris' and 'Gumbo Ya Ya.' It's a brilliant shock of colour, noise and character. We admire a red neon sign that states, 'Big Daddy's World Famous Love Acts.'

'Wonderful lighting,' says Maggie.

Leaving Bourbon Street behind, we pass a dreadheaded woman rocking out on reggae flute, a straggly duo concentrating intently on heartfelt folky guitar and a sliver of a man interpreting country classics on the xylophone.

Night has fallen on the Crescent City with a delicious sense of possibility. There is a mischief and an irrepressible energy on these streets and I love it. We stroll the streets until we're sure that Candace has finished her shift.

Back at the hotel, we slink past the lobby, the wilted plants and the thankfully bare concierge desk and slope upstairs, cursing the overbooking that decanted us here instead of at our chosen residence around the corner. Along a sepia-hued corridor we reach our room and Maggie turns on the dim lights and a large, grubby bug scuttles along the peeling wallpaper.

Maggie, a former stunt girl, occasional member of a Toronto kazoo quartet and composer of electronic music, is one of my closest friends. We've been through a lot together. In addition to helping each other weather breakups, work hiccups and some ill-advised haircuts, we once survived a week together on a cruise ship that ploughed its way through both a Category 2 hurricane and a nasty outbreak of gastroenteritis. You really get the measure of a person when you see how they deal with being surrounded by waves of storm swell and of projectile vomit. I know her well enough to know that cohabiting with cockroaches is a definite deal breaker.

'Was that a...' says Maggie.

'No, no, no, that was just a, ehm, a Louisiana Beetle,' I assure her, watching the gargantuan roach flail defiant limbs at us from behind the sagging luggage rack.

To distract from the number of such six-legged guests that may be sharing the room with us, Maggie and I scour the Internet to learn about bagpipes.

We discover that the bagpipe originated in Scythia, played the Romans into battle and wailed its way across Europe during the 12th and 13th centuries, becoming an integral part of Scottish life by the 1400s. Across Europe, the pipes' distinctive screech and volume made them a natural choice when wanting to intimidate the pants off anyone you wanted to battle, beat or otherwise subjugate. It certainly worked on me and my wee brother Brian when we were kids being wrestled into front row seats for our sister Orla's appearances at traditional Scottish music concerts.

An article on the bagpipes in the Portland, Oregon Highland Games programme called 'What's That Beautiful Sound?' says, 'It's even been said that with the right weather conditions, and played loud enough, the Highland Bagpipe can be heard from 10 miles away.' They say this as if it is a good thing. People of Oregon, you worry me.

Until my recent emotional encounter with the pipes when watching *The Queen*, I would have been quick to side with Alfred Hitchcock who said, 'I understand the inventor of the bagpipes was inspired when he saw a man carrying an indignant, asthmatic pig under his arm. Unfortunately, the man-made object never equalled the purity of sound achieved by the pig.' But, for me, something has clearly changed. Irish poet WB Yeats said, 'I firmly believe that distance adds enchantment to the bagpipes.' And he is right, although not in the way he originally intended. The distance of decades, many thousands of miles and a whopping great ocean has made me change my tune. It's as if somebody rustled Hitchcock's poorly pig into the nearest doctor's office and got the wheezy wee beastie an inhaler.

Catching a fragment of a piped lament or slow air is such a rare occurrence over here that now I begin to understand why the call of the pipes is just that—a call—which is amplified to weeping-on-strangers'-shoulders level when a Scottish or Scottish-ish audience has consumed several drams of whisky. And it's a plaintive call because it's one that can't easily be answered when you're dashing down Broadway, moseying up Main or stomping along East 4th. I'm not going to admit it to anyone back home but, after all these years away, to hear the pipes' mournful skirl in the depths of the canyons of Manhattan, on an achingly blue morning in Memphis or from the tattered back row of a grimy Oregonian cinema does something I could never have foreseen. It gnaws the strings of my cold, cynical, starred, striped and maple-leafed heart—and knits them into a snug wee tartan bonnet. The U.S. has made me love the pipes.

But it's actually surprising that the pipes ever came to be seen as a symbol of Scotland at all. Rewind a handful of centuries and you'd find bagpipes equally popular across the bulk of European soirées and skirmishes. When they arrived in Scotland, the pipes had one lone determined drone—that constant underlying hum that underlies all pipe tunes, but the Scots so loved the pipes that they added two more drones, the medieval equivalent of turning it up to 11, and the Great Highland Bagpipe had arrived. As civilisations progressed, the bellicose blare of the bagpipe fell out of favour across Europe, replaced by quieter, subtler pipes—ones you could play and not bother hung-over people in every village within a two-mile radius, but the Scots stubbornly kept going full blast. And so the bagpipes headed towards extinction in musical repertoires across much of the rest of the continent, but lumbered on like belligerent diplodocuses across the Scottish musical landscape.

But those on adjacent floors of this fine hotel don't need to stock-pile extreme decibel earplugs just yet; beginner pipers don't actually start on a Great Highland Bagpipe. Beginners start on a practice chanter. Although I've arranged to buy one from Pipe Major Bob tomorrow night, I am a little hazy about what it actually is.

Online, Maggie and I find intimidating images, instructions and even a sonnet inspired by the chanter. We see that it looks like a squeaky miniature CN Tower. Or a piece of drainpipe that collided with a reed. Or a bike pump rammed viciously into a pogo stick. The Internet implies that once I have a chanter, I jab both it and a 'blow pipe' into the bag part of the bagpipes. This inflatable bag part is called a 'goose.'

Maggie, scarred by my recent admission of how haggis is cooked, says, 'We can guess how that got its name.'

None of these items sounds as though they will be found perched at the top of Approved Cabin Baggage lists. I suspect I'll have to allow a bit more time for security if I decide to travel any type of musical poultry.

'You better allow a lot more time,' says Maggie, 'It says here that the bagpipes are still listed as a weapon of war.'

The next morning I'm on the St Charles streetcar as it creaks through the city from the French Quarter towards Carrollton. Inexplicably, Maggie has opted to explore some drone-free side of the city, so I head west solo. The aged tram chunters along the avenue like a cartoon train, juddering past grand antebellum houses with pillars, plantation shutters and verandas. The houses of this neighbourhood have picked from an appetising paint palette of white, cream, taupe and various degrees of poached salmon. They look like they should be served on platters with lace doilies. Wooden porch swings sway in the lazy breeze. Ornate railings edge the lush lawns of stately double-galleried 19th century homes. Live Oaks, maples and streetcar wires glitter, still laden with beads: the metallic blue, red, green, silver and black remainders of February's Mardi Gras parade. Tartan Day could take some lessons in celebration from that obviously exuberant spectacle.

I look at Pipe Major Bob's piping syllabus for the first time. There are gracenotes, taorluaths and tachums. There are pages and pages of music with scales, dots, cuts, strikes, throws and doublings. There are grips, leumluaths, triplets and birls. The Gaelic phrase, 'Dè tha mi a dèanamh?'—'What am I doing?' and the only one I currently remember from my weekend in Texas—runs through my mind. Once again I am about to wade out of my depth and into Scottish-America. Who knows what cross-cultural revelations lie ahead? I am excited to learn. I vow to listen and keep my mouth shut, well, as shut as is possible when taking up a wind instrument.

Across the aisle, two middle-aged convention wives in floral capri pants start a loud conversation and distract me from my looming lesson.

'Did you do the alligator tour?' brays the blonde.

'Oh, my, yes,' says the other from behind her bob. 'We did the half-day tour. Saw a big ol' gator out there in the mud! How people can live out there, I don't know!'

'Our tour,' says the first with a tiny tinkle of a laugh and a blonde flick, 'Took all day. We saw so many of those brutes I lost count.'

Her companion smiles tightly. 'Did you do the plantation tour? Such a window onto the Old South.'

'No, I did the Hurricane Katrina tour instead. Forget windows. The Katrina tour, I feel like I actually lived it.'

All around, locals sit silently, as the two women attempt to outdo each other.

I explore Carrollton and discover that the low-lying riverbend neighbourhood was once part of New Orleans founder Jean-Baptiste Le Moyne de Bienville's lands, but became something of a pleasure resort for New Orleanians when the streetcars linked it to the city in 1836.

I amble northeast alongside those streetcar tracks, away from the protective grassy shoulders of the levée, inhaling the warm, earthy air of South Carrollton Avenue. Turning onto Oak Street, I pass the charmingly faded Mr Louis' barber shop, venerable Mr Buddy's Hair and the now-shuttered Austin's Dresses For Special Occasions. Outside the Maple Leaf Bar, 20-somethings in short-sleeved shirts, tattoos showing on impressively muscled arms, model serious expressions and equally grave facial hair statements.

Over a coffee at Z'Otz Café, I see that *The Gambit* newspaper has ads for chocolate voodoo dolls, making New Orleans the ultimate destination for those who want to simultaneously do damage to someone and to their teeth. Revenge really can be sweet.

'Good morning, my sister,' says a flamboyant man with an approximately 11-inch waist and one permanently raised eyebrow, as he slinks along the sidewalk and by my table.

'You jus' keep right on doin' what you're doin',' he smiles, tracing a blessing with one nonchalant finger.

Unsure of the appropriate response to this, I stutter, 'Amen,' and smile back.

People in New Orleans smile a lot. They also, it seems, treat road perimeters as more of a suggestion than any legal absolute. I watch as the third driver in an hour rolls onto the kerb outside the coffeehouse, slightly denting the newspaper box. He then slouches inside the coffee shop, unperturbed.

The latest kerb encounterer has a dazed expression and a thatch of sandy hair sticking out from under a thick knitted hat. When he comes back out, he walks by me three times, looking like he's trying hard to remember either which item of street furniture he rammed his truck into this morning or how to put one foot in front of another. On his third and final considered perambulation, he finds his vehicle and rummages around the seat. He ambles back and hands me a painted postcard.

'It's Free Art... What day is it?' he asks as he hands me the card.

'Tuesday.'

'It's Free Art Tuesday!' he says, jubilantly.

'I love Free Art Tuesday,' I say.

'Awesome!' he beams. 'If you hold it up to the light, you'll get the message.'

Obediently, I hold the stiff card up to the light, looking at its turquoise and yellow watercolour blobs. Letters scrawled backwards
on the back show through in the sunlight, informing me, 'TREES
BREATHE. PLANT MORE TREES.'

'I'm trying to bring tree people together,' says my tree friend earnestly. 'I wanna save the trees. The sky's getting hotter.' He points
at the cloudless sky. 'The trees are dyin', man. It's like tradition. We
need tradition and we need trees.'

'I like trees,' I offer.

'Right on, man!' He breaks into a huge, craggy smile. 'I knew it! I
knew you'd like trees when I saw you!' He is delighted. 'Maybe I'll see
you at a show somewhere down the road. Maybe a tree show. Yeah,
a tree show, man,' he says as he walks back to his truck.

'I hope so,' I grin and wave. He waves back at me until the truck
weaves out of sight, narrowly missing several other seemingly surprisingly situated kerbs and a couple of pedestrians.

In Blue Cypress Books, I browse through titles such as *Anti-Italian
Sentiment and Violence in Louisiana 1855-1924*, *The Lost German Slave
Girl* and *Literary Levées*. There's absolutely nothing Scottish on the
shelves, although there is a cat that looks just like Muffin, the grumpy
Glaswegian tabby of my youth, snoozing on the Alternative Religions
section. Dipping into books on city history, I read that, historically,
New Orleans has had significant Native American, Caribbean, African,
Spanish, French, Irish, German, Italian, Greek, Croatian, Filipino and
Acadian populations. There's no mention of the Scots. Unlike in so
many US cities, the Scots must either have played a very minor role
in New Orleans' development or swiftly woven themselves into the
fabric of New Orleans society.

I mooch along to Carrollton Cemetery where German, French and
Irish names decorate the rows of brick barrel-vaulted tombs, sar-
cophagi and white marble slabs. There are Zieglers, Ruhlmans and
Gebharts; Trosclairs, Duplaisirs and Comeauxs; Murphys, O'Dwyers

and Doodys. But there are no obvious Scots here in this city where I feel so at home.

A few blocks south, I meet a local writer called Lovell, which is pronounced, in true New Orleans-style, 'Lo-vehhhhl.' It appears that the further south you go in the US, the longer it takes to pronounce names. Over an iced coffee at an outdoor café on Maple Street, we talk about the alligator cheesecake Lovell is planning for dinner, the Crescent City's dearth of Scots and how chatty New Orleanians are.

'People here are so friendly,' I say.

He corrects me. 'We're not so much friendly as we're nosy. In N'awlins, we are just dyin' of curiosity. Now, tell me, what does your partner do?'

This is my fourth visit to New Orleans and once again I'm won over by its warmth, its characters, its deliciously treacle-slow pace. It's a city that seems to have time for people, one that doesn't seem to let minor obstacles or the clock get in the way of coffee, curiosity or gossip.

I'm sorry not to join Lovell for alligator cheesecake and some more insights into the New Orleans psyche, but there's just an hour to go until I become a piper and I need to prepare myself. I sit down at what was the Marine Bank and Trust until the Stock Market crash of 1929, but is now a café, stocked with a wealth of pastries, a treasury of ripped flyers and an abundance of slouchy writer types.

My plans this evening are not what most visitors have on their Tuesday night schedule on a visit to New Orleans. It is definitely a strange choice when there are Hand Grenades to consume, Cajun and Zydeco to appreciate and live love acts on show, but for me, tonight's expedition is the only option. Picking up the pipes is almost the final piece in the Scottish-American puzzle I set myself all that time ago in Oregon: the plaintive call that made me realise that I'd lost something more of myself than simply some corners of my accent, easy access to haggis and an acceptance of average summer high temperatures in the low teens. I've made it all this way—across states from New York to Hawaii and from Washington to Georgia. After this, my next stop is Gatlinburg's Scottish Parade. I imagine it as a kind of graduation, but one where bluegrass battles it out with bagpipes as I march down Main Street.

The catch is that I have only just begun to like the bagpipes. I worry that being surrounded by a dozen of them in someone's living room might make that fuzzy new pro-bagpipe feeling recede. A semi-detached house on a residential street seems a strange pick for massed pipe playing. Do the people at numbers 8129 and 8133 not mind? Do their pets?

When we were kids, my parents bravely insisted that we all learn a musical instrument. Orla swiftly mastered the violin. Mark took to the trumpet like a New Orleanian to a kerb. Brian tackled the cornet with as much gusto as he did everything, from talking to general mischief to inventive methods of waking up his older siblings. The cornet definitely added extra effectiveness to his early morning arsenal. I'm surprised, though, that he didn't pick the bagpipes. The prospect of that volume would definitely have appealed to him.

I managed to set a somewhat ignominious record by failing Grade 1 piano five times, much to the fury of the tiny but ferocious, ruler-wielding Sister Catherine-Louise. After failure five, I was in the market for a new instrument, ideally one that was less cumbersome than the ones my siblings had to lug with them each day and one that was relatively unobtrusive in a school orchestra setting and so could safely mask my lack of musical coordination. More importantly, I wanted one that would keep my knuckles beyond the reach of diminutive Glaswegian nuns. Bagpipes were obviously too unwieldy, too audibly obvious and all but guaranteed to enrage members of religious orders into attacking me with classroom stationery, so I picked the flute. I hope that somehow those five reluctant years of woodwind will stand me in good stead tonight.

The sky starts to cloud ominously as I walk up South Carrollton Avenue. I pass a house with a veranda strung with hammocks and am startled by a sudden screech, 'Ayee-Ayee-I'm gonna getcha!' I am only slightly reassured when I realise the threat was issued by an enormous emerald green parrot, bobbing on a post like a caffeinated Cossack. Dozens of stray cats roam the streets as I approach Pipe Major Bob's house. 'Save yourselves, cats, while there is still time,' I want to tell them, but they are probably too busy assessing whether the parrot is bluffing or not. Number 8131 is suspiciously quiet, but a metal bagpiper doorknocker tells me that I've found the right place.

A figure in a blue polo shirt leans out of an upper window. It's Pipe Major Bob, or perhaps, this being New Orleans, that should be Mr Bob. He sees me. The cats and I have missed our chance to bolt.

Bob, a soft-spoken, unflappable engineer, ushers me to a seat at the dining table. As Bob bustles about, I admire the mantelpiece's family photos, flutter of wee US flags and collection of mauve knitted thistles. As someone who has often ended up on the jagged end of a thistle, I approve of this Louisiana knitted variety. A stern selection of Scottish songbooks including *The Methodist Hymnal, Hymns of Praise* and *The Balmoral Reel Book* perch on the piano.

Bob tells me he took up the bagpipes in the 70s. When I ask him if he's Scottish, he gives a genial grin, shakes his head and admits that his ancestry is Welsh and Irish, but his wife is 'more recent.' Her family arrived in Louisiana from Hawick in the Scottish Borders in the 1930s.

He shrugs, 'Me? I just like the pipes. It's the same with most of the band. We're just folks who love the sound of the bagpipes. There's not much Scottishness here in New Orleans, although there's an Urquhart Street in the Ninth Ward. It's about the only Scottish name for a street I can think of in New Orleans.'

The band consists of 'five or so,' plus students, so it's not a huge operation.

'We play at a few events, but we mostly play here,' says Bob.

'Do the neighbours not complain?'

'Well, nobody's shot at me yet,' grins Bob, handing me my new chanter.

I now own a bit of a bagpipe! A wee piece of a weapon of war! As I look in a pleased and slightly perplexed manner at my new instrument, more band members arrive.

'I'm not the new guy anymore,' crows Scott when he sees me staring with confusion at my new pipe.

'How is it going?' I ask.

'I've learned two lines in two weeks,' he says, proudly.

It seems progress is not likely to be swift.

'When might I get promoted to the pipes?' Scott asks.

Bob does a sum, 'If you learn a line every week, in ten months you'll get some bagpipes.'

I clutch my chanter. Grimly. I revise my ambitions for today's one-hour lesson.

A slight woman in her 50s with cropped peroxide hair, an easy smile and a white t-shirt featuring a dancing Kokopelli stick figure, has been playing the chanter for three years. She has still not ascended to the glorious heights of a full set of pipes. I ask her why she started playing.

'I heard 'The High Road to Gairloch' at the Kilts of Many Colors Cancer Walk. For two weeks, it was going round my head and then I thought, "Wouldn't it be cool to be able to play that?" I said it to a friend and she dared me to join a band. And here I am.'

She smiles with the satisfaction of a dream acted upon.

'Is Luke coming?' She asks Bob.

'He'll be here in an hour.'

'I'll probably be gone by then,' says Scott with something that seems like it could be relief. I wonder whether I'm imagining it.

The others disappear off next door, leaving me to start learning how to play the pipes.

Following Bob's example, I stuff the chanter in the corner of my mouth and clunk the end on the table. Bob nods encouragingly. I take a deep breath and blow. I make a truly hideous noise. Bob recoils slightly. I try again. My efforts still sound like retching seagulls. It must be broken, I think. There's no way anything could possibly sound so ghastly. Bob thinks so, too, and wonders if he put the reed in wrong. He takes my chanter, changes the reed and gives a wee puff. He plays beautifully. I try again and emit reedy shrieks like a parrot suffering some terrible indignity, possibly at the paws of a posse of street cats who had finally had enough of empty threats. From the next room, I hear Duchess and Scott belt out a perfectly acceptable version of something stirring and martial. Pitying all wildlife in the area, I check to make sure the windows are closed.

Eventually I screech to the end of an approximation of the chanter's nine-note octave. It sounds at least eight notes too long. I gasp for breath, fingers clenched over the sound holes until it feels like their pattern will be forever cut into my fingerpads, thumbs clinging desperately onto the back.

'You're killing the chanter,' says Bob, frowning at my death grip.

We try again and Bob flinches.

'I'm going to have to unleash Luke on you,' he threatens.

Based on Scott's look of relief and the threatening shape of Bob's eyebrows just there, I imagine Luke to be a dark, brooding hulk, basically Brando with bagpipes. However, 20 minutes later, a slight, lithe 30-year-old with tousled brown hair and a raspberry pink shirt that states 'Desire' bounces into the room. A ball of compressed energy, Luke tumbles into tales about the months he spent learning at the Piping Centre in Glasgow, about playing 'Minstrel Boy' and other assorted Irish airs on the bagpipes for Grand Order of Hibernians events, about the two years he spent with the circus. I relax and wonder what Scott worried about. This sunny peripatetic charmer is sure to be an excellent chanter tutor. And then, suddenly, everything changes. A grave look clouds Luke's brow, the small talk is over and the serious business of chanter playing starts. Within a minute I realise I should have left with Scott.

Luke harangues me through botched octave after botched octave after botched octave. Without allowing a second to gulp breaths between ghastly screeching blurts, Luke makes me stagger through the scale, over and over, barking out instructions; 'No crossing noise! Clean it up! Elbows out! Again!' Each time I think I can't manage one more puff, Luke has me climbing all nine excruciating notes of the octave again. And again. And again. This is bagpipe boot camp. This is torture. This makes Sister Catherine-Louise seem like a merciful deity. But, by the 123rd or 124th octave, my squawks begin to sound like something almost musical.

'What's a birl?' I ask in a desperate attempt to distract Luke.

'Two strikes on a low G,' he says, demonstrating. His fingers pirouette and dance on the keys. A wonderful whir comes from his chanter, like a blackbird chirping its delight at having just snacked on a really awesome worm. It is sweet, melodic and soothing to the ear. I rest my chin in my throbbing hand and soak up the sounds.

Luke's voice grates through my reverie, 'Another octave.'

Eventually, after three hours of relentless octaving, I plead to be allowed to give up. My thumbs, wrists, ears, lips, jaws, teeth and brain hurt. Luke grudgingly relents and I slink back through to the living room, massaging my left thumb. Luke joins Bob and the others around the table. Their expressions are solemn, their hands and fingers are poised. At a nod from Luke, they all place the ends of their pipes on the table, Luke's chanter points straight ahead, Bob's points Popeye-like out of the side of his mouth. They launch into a spirited version of 'The Bridge of Scotland.'

They break off after a couple of lines and Luke instructs, 'Let's exaggerate that out and hold just a little more... Three... Four...'

And they're off again.

I attempt to pick up my glass of water, but my fingers don't work. It will be a while before I join in or manage to drink anything without the aid of a straw.

Bob drives Luke and I east through the city. We drive through Gert Town, Tulane, Tremé-Lafitte, St Claude and reach the dark streets of the Lower Ninth Ward where half the houses remain boarded up and abandoned, post-Hurricane Katrina.

'Before the hurricane, there were 500,000 people in the city. After-wards there were just 380,000 of us,' Bob says.

Bob points out some of New Orleans' architectural styles; the free-standing, sliver-thin shotgun shacks, the side-by-side 'double shots,' the camelbacks with their smaller second-storey additions perched above their kitchens. By what I presume is a strange coincidence, Luke lives on Urquhart Street.

As Luke unloads his tiny trick bike from Bob's SUV, he says to me, 'I want you to practice in an hour and in 24 hours.'

I hear the ruler in his voice and shudder.

Back in the hotel room, Maggie attempts to be supportive as I demonstrate my new skills. I try to marshal my numb thumbs into position.

After I emit a few reedy squawks, I say, ruefully, 'So much for killing the chanter, I think it killed me.'

Maggie says, 'It doesn't sound like it was a fair fight.'

The Louisiana beetle peeks its scaly head round a wizened standing lamp. As I start to squawk through another painful octave, the beetle flees. Maggie looks like she is similarly inclined.

We wander out to find food. At the French Market on Decatur Street we see signs that entreat us to 'try a huge muffaletta,' 'grab a gator po'boy sandwich' or 'get some hot stuff.' We contemplate Rabbit in Gravy, Seafood Gumbo and Shrimp 'n' Grits, but turn our noses up at smudgy jars crammed with cherry red pickled pigs' lips and balk at the fierce flavours of the 'Walk of Flame' with its battery of searing sauces. We tuck into the N'Awlins Café and Spice Empo-rium's Creole Jambalaya, Cajun Dirty Rice and Crawfish Étouffée. We sail from one stall to the next, sampling sustenance from Pork

Boudin blood sausage to Gator Kebabs, although with my chantered hand, I can barely pick up a fork. Changing tack to try liquid Louisiana specialities, my clumsy attempt to open a can of local Big Shot Fruit Punch ends up in an archipelago of crimson punch stains over everything I'm wearing.

'That Big Shot sure had plenty of ammunition,' says Maggie helpfully.

The French Market serves up Louisiana history on a plate. In the 1700s, Native Americans came to Decatur Street to trade herbs and spices such as sassafras. The Acadians, from what is now Nova Scotia, further spiced things up in the late 18th century with their piquant gumbo, étouffée and jambalaya. New arrivals from Spain, France, Italy, Germany and the Caribbean brought their culinary contributions to the Crescent City. African-Americans brought coffee and pralines. The market is history by larder, which seems a fine way to digest information.

A regiment of pralines catches my eye—and my taste buds. I know this flavour! In Scotland, we'd call this 'tablet' and we'd find it at a church bake sale alongside a wilt of deflated scones, some half dead geraniums and a lumpy, one-eyed sock puppet made by someone's absent-minded granny. Here it's a chic sugar fix adored by tourists. Scotland really needs better bonbon ambassadors. Even the name 'praline' comes from a 17th-century diplomat, César du Plessis Praslin. Modern pralines are the delicious descendants of sugarcoated almonds that Praslin's chef created for his employer's soirées—they're ambassadorial appetisers, of sorts. Once pralines emigrated to the new French colony on the Mississippi, almonds became pecans, cream was added to sugar and butter and they became the sweet treat du jour. In pre-civil war days, free black women known as pralinières sold the confectionaries around the French Quarter. Today, there are famed local praline makers, such as Evans Creole Candy Factory, who have been baking up batches of the buttery stuff since 1900.

While this American cousin can claim aristocratic ancestry, Scotland's common confection takes its name from 'Rose Tablets,' sugar lozenges flavoured with red rose juice, which are first mentioned in

The Edinburgh Pharmacopoeia, published in 1784. This early pharmaceutical tome informed the reader, 'These preparations are chiefly valued for their agreeableness to the eye and palate. Some, likewise, esteem them, medicinally, as light restringents, and look upon them, not undeservedly, as an excellent addition to milk in phthisical and hectic cases.' Having seen the city last night, swarming with hectic cases and people obviously suffering from a variety of phthisical afflictions, praline-manufacturers are obviously onto a good thing down here.

'Fancy a light restringent?' asks Maggie, offering me another praline.

I munch pralines and mull. I understand the food here; it has striking similarities to Scottish snacks. Like my homeland, New Orleans has a sweet tooth and a fondness for the deep fat fryer.

Since Maggie has to leave in the morning, we head back to the hotel without any late night hurricanes or hand grenades, but I won't be packing up just yet. I've found a lead on something Scottish on the other side of the Mississippi.

I was not supposed to be on the number 108 bus from the Algiers ferry dock to Jefferson Parish's Wilty Terminal this morning, but when I ambled down to catch the ferry across the Mississippi to Gretna, Louisiana, it wasn't there and I had to get one to Algiers, three miles north instead. The guy sweeping the floors—and the only New Orleans Regional Transit Authority employee on the premises—told me, 'Sometimes that ferry run, sometimes she don't.'

Today she obviously don't and, as the number 108 hurtles down rundown streets and under murky underpasses, I question whether don't might have been the better option for me today, too. On top of some concerns about whether this is the right bus, the bus driver has not instilled confidence in my decision to travel via Jefferson Parish. At the ferry dock, she terrified one would-be bus passenger proffering a large note by telling him, 'If you gonna be stupid enough to walk about with that kind of cash in yo' hand, yo' gonna get shot.

You wanna get shot? Put yo' money away.' The would-have-been passenger fled back into the ferry terminal.

We've only gone a couple of blocks when the bus lurches to a halt. The driver stomps to the back to berate the only other passenger, a teenage boy wrapped in an immense sweatshirt and headphones the size of muffalettas.

'The bebop is a distraction, boy. That is for your listening pleasure. I,' she informs him with an emphatic finger, 'do not find it a pleasure.'

The young offender fumbles to turn the music off, hoisting up his sagging jeans in panic, mumbling, 'Sorry, ma'am' and cowering from her wrath.

Once we're on our way again, we pass boarded-up buildings and sunken-looking low-rent apartment blocks where hollow-eyed residents are propped on sagging stoops. We pass the WJ Fischer Charter School where a chipped sign states that they are 'soaring to excellence' and where the ten-foot-high chain-link fence topped with razor wire is approximately ten feet higher than you'd hope was necessary at an educational establishment. One would have to plan one's soaring very carefully to escape without getting snagged on a fence like that.

I'm going to Gretna, 'a small city with a big heart,' according to its official website, because I think I've finally found a Scottish link. It's tenuous but it's the only Louisiana lead I've got.

The city of Gretna government website considers it major news that 'On Wednesday afternoon, a chartered Mid-American Coach parked downtown and 47 German tourists came to Gretna!' There's not much else on the official site, but it lists the alleged ferry schedule from New Orleans to Gretna and has a link to the lunch menu at a local café, where pretty much everything, including the Seafood Stuffed Artichoke, is fried. On the basis of this admittedly rather limited research, I have imagined Gretna to be a slow-paced small town riverside delight, a combination of iced tea, shady oaks and scenic sprinklings of Spanish moss—pretty much *Steel Magnolias* on the Mississippi. I get out at a scatter of bus stop signs and a shabby portacabin under a neglected bit of expressway. On the other side of two lanes of traffic, drab brown buildings squat under a gargantuan billboard that extols the virtues of Golden Flake Louisiana Hot Sauce Fried Pork Skins. There are no shady oaks, unless the graffiti-defaced, half-burned bench is descended from one, and the beat-up vending machine is all out of iced tea. Perhaps I got the wrong bus. Perhaps I got off too early. Perhaps I should have spent the day searching for the perfect praline on the other side of the Mississippi. I am spotted skulking between bus bays by a beaming bus official. She beckons me into the heavily barred portacabin.

'How do I get to Gretna from here?' I ask

Her look is both curious and slightly pitying. 'Girl, you in Gretna now. This here is Gretna.'

'I thought Gretna was... Isn't there a...' I don't want to say 'nice bit,' so I try 'old bit' and 'historic bit.'

The beaming bus lady doesn't think so. Then she remembers there's some 'old stuff' down by the river, but she's never been. She sends me along the expressway 'a ways' to something like 'Hoopylong' with a smile and a 'Don't worry, I'm here.'

I scuttle away a tad nervously, anxious at not knowing if I'm going beyond where tourists should sensibly tread or if I'm even going in the right direction. I pass 20 minutes of bungalows with scrappy lawns and tired cars rusting in their driveways.

Just when I'm pretty sure I'm lost, I see a schoolyard crammed with small children wearing floppy, wide-brimmed hats and a sign that says 'Huey P Long Avenue.' I exhale with relief. The fact that there are children wearing ridiculous headgear surely means I have reached safety. I sidle on as houses and cars get increasingly mani-cured and garden ornaments reach new heights of twee with every half-block. Further down 'Hoopylong,' I pass the 1905 Texas Pacific Railroad Depot with its Illinois Central Railroad caboose outside, the 1923 Jefferson Memorial Arch and a three-storey brown, cream and white courthouse and square that could get extra work as the backdrop for any movies set in the 1950s. Beyond the square, the levée rises. Downtown New Orleans hunkers low, distant and blurry on the far side of the Mississippi, hazy in the midday heat.

At the German-American Cultural Center, I learn that Gretna was a major port of entry for German immigrants. So much so that this part of Louisiana was once known as 'the German Coast.' To drive this Austro-Germanic point home, the first two lines of 'Edelweiss' repeat relentlessly as I wander through the museum. Laid out by those German immigrants in 1836, the First World War forced this little German town to tamp down its German identity. When the Second World War struck, German-language newspapers were closed, Germanic street names changed nationality, German foods were re-branded as Dutch and the speaking of German was prohibited. Today Gretna's Germanity is to the fore once again, proudly celebrated by at least 47 visiting Germans. I pick up a leaflet about 'the old German town of Gretna,' which promises me 'One of the Nation's largest National Register Historic Districts' and a 'Unique Experience, Like Being in a Time Machine.' It also tells me that I will find the town 'Entertaining & Educational.' These leaflets obviously never made it as far as Wilty Bus Terminal.

'Here's another pam'plet for ya,' says a soft-footed, septuagenarian docent who has snuck up beside me. She hands me a ferry leaflet. 'Not that it's much use. That ferry don't do much runnin'. Or some days it runs one ways and don't come back. People come over here and get stuck.'

The docent seems quite pleased about this turn of events.

'Is that how you ended up here?'

She stares. 'No, ma'am. I got the bus from Indiana.'

The second line of 'Edelweiss' swells to what feels like its 700th emotional conclusion.

I ask, 'Do you have German heritage?'

The docent of the German-American Cultural Center looks genuinely puzzled. 'No, I'm Choctaw Indian. From Indiana. I got no German. No German at all. Why, you got some?'

'Nope. I'm Scottish.'

'There's not much Scottish here. It's all German, German, German. Oh, hold on... There's the blacksmith's shop! It's in the back of the Historical Society. On Valentine's Day they have a Scottish player playing the bagpipes.'

The blacksmith's shop is in fact the reason that I'm here; the sole Scottish lead I've located in this part of Louisiana. At some point—way before it became socially, linguistically and culinarily unacceptable to be German—the wee German town of Mechanicsham began calling itself Gretna after Scotland's Gretna Green. The book, *Louisiana, a Guide to the State,* compiled by writers from the Works Progress Administration Federal Writers' Project and published in 1941, says, 'Among the earlier settlers of Mechanicsham was a justice of the peace who not only issued marriage licenses and performed marriage ceremonies by day, but cheerfully accommodated elopers, largely from New Orleans, at any hour of the night. As the years passed the name of the town gave way to 'Gretna' after the famous Gretna Green, in Scotland, near the English border, for centuries a haven for run-away lovers.' The town was officially incorporated as 'Gretna' in 1913.

But, I puzzle, why would 19th century Louisianans have heard of Scotland's tiny Gretna in the first place? And did that quill-happy justice of the peace moonlight as a blacksmith? And did anyone think that the Dutch were really dastardly enough to be the ones responsible for a creation such as German Schwarzsauer goose giblet stew?

'Edelweiss' is still playing mercilessly as I walk back out to Huey P Long in search of answers. I manage to get lost in the tiny town, turning on Lavoisier instead of Lafayette. On 2nd Street, I meet Sevilla.

'You,' she informs me with an imperious eyebrow, 'Are not from here.'

And Sevilla would know such things. Her steamship captain great-great-great-grandfather 'came down here from the bowels of Kentucky in 1812' and fought in the Battle of New Orleans three years later. Sevilla and her ancestors have obviously been keeping a close eye on comings and goings ever since. Before Sevilla deigns to give me directions to the blacksmith's shop, she has found out who I am and what I'm doing in her town.

'I'd invite you in for tea, but I have to go down and see what's going on at the courthouse,' she says before striding off.

On Sevilla's instructions, I soon find the Gretna Historical Society Museum, a pleasing row of one-storey whitewashed houses and a stocky 1859 wooden firehouse. The museum is manned by 83-year-old Amery, who—at about 5 foot 1—is also quite stocky. His arms are spiderwebbed with age-blurred anchor tattoos, his neat mahogany slacks are hoisted high by a huge prize rodeo belt buckle. Born in 1918, he married his high school sweetheart in the school church when he was 20. They still live in Gretna.

'I just never thought of living anyplace else,' he says.

We start the tour where we are, at the 1845 Lily White Ruppel Creole cottage.

'This was the White House, because the Whites lived here. That was the family name, White. The White Family,' Amery informs me. 'But these ain't the old floors. Mice all came up through the mortar and ate the wood until there weren't no floors left.' Amery frowns at the floor. 'Gretna was a German town, one time. When the Germans came up the river, New Orleans was gonna charge them $5 a head to get off the boat. Here was free. So they got off here. Here, Gretna. Gretna used to be called Mechanicsham.' Amery pronounces this, 'Mech'n. Eek. Ham.'

In the Ignatius Strehle House, an 1860s Creole Cottage, the museum has a schoolroom, the sheet music for a splendid-sounding ditty called 'We Threw the Overalls in Mistress Murphy's Chowder' and a 'War Room' where artefacts include a rusting Civil War musket, found buried under the floorboards of the house. It looks worryingly like my chanter.

'It musta been buried by Ignatius Strehle. Old Ignatius musta hid it. What do you think happened to the handle?' Amery asks, through gritted teeth.

'It was the mice, wasn't it?'

'Yes,' he grimaces. 'The mice ate the handle off that musket. I hate them mice.'

'What's that?' I ask, pointing at a small speaker on a display case.

'It bleeps to keep pests away, but too quiet for folks to hear.'

'I can hear it.'

'You can hear that?' he says with a look of wonder. 'I spent 46 years pile drivin'. Now I don't hear much.'

'It sounds like a herd of chirruping wee mice.'

'Oh, I wouldn't like to hear that,' Amery's forehead creases with worry. 'I wouldn't like to hear mice.'

Our next stop is a Creole Cottage from 1840, the home of the town's first German settler, Claudius Strehle, presumably Old Ignatius' dad. Claudius' daughter Kittie taught at the school in Gretna for 57 years. The leaflet from the German-American Center backs this up and adds that Kittie the 'educatior' was 'youngest of nine and last to reside at the house.'

'All them dishes and all them things 'sposed to have come over here from Germany,' Amery tells me.

He points out his favourite things; a no-nonsense foot massager and a terrifying ear plunger. He picks up the ear plunger and makes a playful lunge at me. Amery is spry for an 83-year-old. I dodge, narrowly missing having my nose plunged. He pulls an ancient pair of Victorian ladies' laced boots out of a dresser.

'Kittie was a big woman with small feet,' he states. He gestures at a place where the leather has worn away. 'Musta been a bunion.' He frowns. 'Or a mouse.'

We walk through the narrow back door and there it is, William D White's blacksmith's shop. A red brick pathway leads to a low wooden building with an Old-West-style false front. It's maybe 25 feet long, with a corrugated metal awning across the length. Broken wagon wheels and random lethal metal implements loll against the clean wooden boards. A horseshoe hangs above the doors. Inside, a wooden sign that says 'Weddings Done Here. Guaranteed Until The Fire Is Out' rests across a mahogany rocking chair and church pew bench. More skewers of metal await inside, plus a fireplace and a cradle of various hammers and anvils.

A tattered and oft-stapled sign on the door asks, 'Why Gretna?' Before any potential brides or grooms can ask themselves the same question and head to somewhere more traditionally romantic, the sign hurries on to answer, citing the 1754 English legal change that sent under-21s north to get hitched in Scotland where nuptials could be conducted for those just 16, 'often with excited parents in hot pursuit.' The sign explains that Gretna Green was the first village after the Scottish border and 'the first building was the Ole Blacksmith Shop' where the blacksmith would swiftly marry couples. But that one-stop wedding and horseshoe shop still seems awfully far from this burg by the bayou. How did inhabitants of a tiny town on the Mississippi even hear of Scotland's barely legal bolthole?

It turns out that Mechanicsham had already gained a reputation as a place for rushed romantics when a play called *Gretna Green, or Matrimony in Scotland* appeared in the early 1800s and caught the imagination of Louisiana's theatre-going public. Soon people started calling the town Gretna and the local blacksmith saw a chance to expand the business beyond simply melding metal. The board confidently states that this wee tool-strewn shed offers the same 'romantic aura' as Scotland's Gretna, which seems reasonable if you've ever been mired in traffic on the A74 motorway at Gretna or stuck in line for sustenance at its Welcome Break service station.

'There's a weddin' anvil and a workin' anvil,' Amery tells me, struggling to lift the copper hammer that sits on top of the workin' one. 'Because here's still a working smithy.' Amery manages to hoist the foot-long tool and smacks it off the metal with a juddering clang. He lets go with some relief.

I ask if I can have a shot.

'Will you manage her?' asks Amery with some concern.

I pick up the hammer with both hands. It weighs about as much as a small dollop of goose giblet stew.

Worrying about how often Amery has to wield this obviously considerable weight, I ask, 'Do many people come to see the blacksmith's shop?'

'Before Katrina, we got a lot of folks coming from out of town, but since New Orleans don't get too much tourism now...' Amery trails off. 'She did pretty good damage, Katrina. We used to have a pecan tree there, over a hundred feet high and a hundred years old and Katrina came by and took her.' Amery looks sad. 'But last Valentine's Day, we had 21 weddings!' he says, brightening. 'We had us a lady bagpiper. The bagpiper lady was bagpiping folks to the blacksmith's shop and the Justice of the Peace was marrying them. Then the blacksmith said "Two pieces of metal melded together, two people melded together", then he hit the anvil and gave 'em their scroll and that was them. Just like you do 'em in Scotland,' Amery beams at me.

I do not tell him that in most parts of Scotland, weddings infrequently feature forges.

There is an impressive range of fried items on the menu at Common Ground, which is a neighbourhood restaurant, bar and shoeshine. After wrestling with the choice between fried mushrooms, deep fried onion rings, fried sliced potatoes, fried cheese sticks, deep fried artichokes and fried crab cakes, I tune into the conversation between two staff at the bar.

'I looked cute,' says one.

'Uh-huh.' Her co-worker is unconvinced.

'No, I was wearing jeather. That's like jeans and leather.'

'Oh my goodness, cute!'

'That's what I'm saying!'

I tuck into my fried chicken and a coffee that I'm sure would have been fried if there was any way it could possibly have been dunked in boiling oil.

There are rules in restaurants and cafés in Louisiana, I am learning. At a table nobody talks to you or interrupts your intake of fried items, but the minute you're on your feet or outside, random strangers can no longer hold their restraint-to-curiosity ratio in balance and you're fair game. Outside, the shoeshine guy is lounging at a table across from a shy 20-something with an enthusiastically tattooed neck, and a doughy white guy in his mid-30s and a collar-up polo shirt. The doughy guy gets his greetings in first.

He and his friends hear my accent and make the usual obligatory startled enquiry, 'Where you from?'

'Scotland.'

'Scotland? Awesome!' they exclaim in near unison.

'You like it here?' asks the shoeshine guy.

'I do. People are friendly and the food reminds me of home. We fry a lot of stuff, too.'

'We fry pickles,' boasts the young guy.

'And pork skins,' adds the shoeshiner.

I raise the stakes. 'We deep fry pizza.'

'No!' he says with some awe.

The trio is obviously impressed. I have scored substantial fry points for Scotland. Before we can delve any further into our common high cholesterol culture, I see a milky orange-coloured Glenn's Taxi crawl slowly up to the kerb and have to say my goodbyes.

'Where you from?' asks the driver, shrugging his entire body in time to some hard driving blues on the radio.

'Scotland.'

'Ayeeee, Scot, y'all! You...'

He trails off and leans his head out the window to shout at the US Mail lady.

'Hey, Peggy! You deliver that mail! You deeeee-liver, girl!'

'Do you know everyone around here?'

'I'm a cab driver. A cool cab driver. I know people. I know people. If I see a knucklehead, they gonna stay right here on the corner.'

'You didn't leave me on the corner.'

'You cool, you cool, you no knucklehead. You like Gretna?'

I nod enthusiastically.

'Gretna's cool... as long as you're cool. But, me, I'm not from here. I'm Mr Mississippi. I got me a place across the state line. I got me some acres with a fishing hole. No one can see me from the highway. I get me a drink. I get naked. I can be butt naked, fishin' and drinkin'. Ain't nobody can lay their eyes on me. Ayeee! Oh yeah, I'm livin'.' Mr Mississippi laughs like a motor trying to catch.

Every time I arrive back in Glasgow, I'm happily surprised by how staunchly pro-Glasgow the taxi drivers always are. I was charmed when one told me he could never live anywhere other than Glasgow because it was 'the best cheery wee city in the whole world.' Gretna's cab drivers apparently echo Glaswegian drivers' enthusiasm for their home, but raise it with tales of naked fishing exploits, although perhaps that's simply because the Scottish climate is not quite so conducive to such pursuits.

We pass back under the Ponchartrain Expressway bridge and back into Algiers. It looks very different now that I'm here with Mr Mississippi. Now the streets don't look so menacing. Corners that seemed edgy just hours ago come to life with his commentary.

'This place right here, CC's, this is where you come party. You should party here tonight!'

'I'll party on my next visit,' I promise.

'Aeeee! Yeah! You come here, you let your hair down, girl, get out there on the floor and do the bus stop with everybody else.' Mr Mississippi laughs that chug of a laugh again. 'Everybody's out dancin' the bus stop. I'm 60 years old and I'll be right out there with you. See there? That's Maria's, best seafood in the world right there. You want something good to eat? You stop right there. Some fresh fish to fry? You stop right there. You come back on down here, get you a convertible, let your hair down, and we're gonna eat fish and I'm gonna teach you how to dance.'

I could probably do with some dancing lessons to add to my repertoire alongside 'Jenny's Gentle Jig,' but they'll have to wait till next time. We pull up outside the Algiers ferry dock. My thumbs are still numb as I fumble for the fare.

'Sheeeeet, yeah, girl! Now get outta here!'

In the last few days I've already learned so much. I've learned that neon, cheesecake and kebab are all acceptable forms of alligator, that bagpipe-provoked thumb injuries are surprisingly incapacitating and that Gretna has particularly voracious mice. I've also fallen a little further for this city of irresistible character and characters. I grin all the way back across the Mississippi, as the afternoon heats up, sticky and muggy, and the spray mists my face. I feel so at ease in this southern city, the place with the least officially in common with Scotland, but the one that feels most like home.

Back on the other bank, I go into a wee corner grocery. The counter guy, a debonair character in a figure-hugging white t-shirt, maroon corduroys and matching bandana, snaps to attention when he hears me speak.

'Where you from?'

'Scotland.'

'Oh my. Oh my! Oh my!'

He pours my coffee and escorts me to a table outside.

'Okay, lady, talk to me with that Scotland Scottish accent all day. Whatcha doin' in my grocery store? You're coming back, right? You should move into the building across the street and have coffee with me here every morning. You're moving here, right?'

I sit on a sagging plastic lawn chair on St Charles, sip my coffee and think that one day I just might.

13. LAND OF MY HEART FOREVER:
GATLINBURG, TENNESSEE

At the airport in Seattle, Courtney and her daughter Caitlin are in the check-in line in front of me. I ask Courtney if she has Irish heritage and she looks confused.

'No.' She shifts the toddler to her other hip. 'Why?'

'I just thought that because of Caitlin's name.'

'Caitlin is an Irish name?'

'Yes. It's a version of Catherine in Irish.'

'I had no idea. I was going to call her Grace.' Courtney looks at me. 'What does Grace mean?'

'Um, grace?' I suggest.

Courtney thinks about it. 'Yeah, maybe.'

My name means 'radiant,' which would have given me a lot of pressure to glow during my formative years if I'd bothered to look up its meaning before last week. I'm pretty sure my mum put a decent bit of thought into such matters, even though she had quite a few of us, but I never knew I was supposed to shine at above average wattage. My siblings, Golden Princess, God of War, Noble One and Dark-Haired Beauty, were encouraged to glow just as much as I was.

My namesakes straggle back through myth and pre-history and include a legendary woman warrior, a wild princess prone to viciously battling her wee sister, a goddess who stole an alphabet of knowledge from the gods and an evil stepmother who turned her stepchildren into swans for 900 years. It's a lot to live up to. Shining might be easier.

I'm on my way to Gatlinburg, Tennessee's Scottish Festival to take my place in the Scottish parade that first sent me on this mission, way back in Oregon. It's the final symbolic step in my journey to Scottishness, which, right at this moment, as I wait for a flight to Houston and then another on to Knoxville, is making me feel unexpectedly emotional. Perhaps my quest to become 100% Scottish is not quite on a par with epic Celtic sibling rivalry, thieving goddess antics or the avian shenanigans brewed up by jealous stepmothers, but it feels hugely satisfying to have finally got to this stage of my expedition. To feel that all that bagpiping, Gaelic acquisition and whisky consumption have been leading to something. To know that all those hours on highways, on overly air-conditioned buses and crammed in middle seats have added up to something more than air miles and a lifetime's aversion to toilets that travel faster than 20 miles per hour. Now I just have to get to Gatlinburg, have a Highland cow encounter and then I'll be ready for the parade the day after tomorrow. Perhaps I will channel some of my namesakes' cunning, sleight of hand or impressively effective cursing vocabulary for this saga's final chapter. I'm sure that even a couple of vowels from an ancient alphabet of knowledge could come in handy in backwoods Tennessee.

Many hours later, I land in Detroit, which would be great if this plane hadn't been supposed to land in Texas and if there seemed any possibility that I might still be able to catch a connecting flight to Tennessee. My first visit to Michigan is not a relaxing one. The violent thunderstorms that re-routed me here have made it a long shot to get on board the sole remaining East Tennessee flight tonight unless I run, according to an earnest airline rep, 'like a angtelope.' This weather event has also filled all seats on flights that might be in any way useful tomorrow and the day after, so making like a mispronounced gazelle is my only chance.

It's late and it's been a long day but I take off at an ungainly lope, lugging an unwieldy book and laptop-filled bag and trailing a tartan hoody that is clearly intent on tripping me. My paces have more in common with a panic-struck blancmange than with anything remotely related to the speedier members of the bovid family. With six minutes till my flight closes and 'final calls' resounding through the departure areas, I bolt through the concourse, screech past a black granite water feature that spurts jets of liquid in a splutter of frantic directions and pelt past banks of jumbotron TV screens all set to identically dire weather warnings. My soles squeak on the polished marble as I take a sharp left towards Terminal C with just two minutes to go. I sprint into the connector tunnel where lights change in time to music that I can just hear over my thudding heart, from quiet turquoise to soft green to gentle violet. I pant through a pan of subtle colours as the minutes tick away. But half way through, I begin to flag. I check the time. My flight closed two minutes ago. I feel my chances of making Tennessee tonight recede, my plans for making the acquaintance of a Highland cow fade, my dreams of taking my hard won place in the Grand Scottish Parade evaporate. Angtelopes have it easy; they don't have to contend with reduced Michigan to Tennessee flight schedules and airport terminals designed by people more concerned with aquatic art than convenient gate locations. I peter along for three more minutes and finally lurch to a hunched stop, lungs heaving. I feel a huge, quiet thud of despair as my hopes of making the flight flicker out. There will be no waking up to a Tennessee morning for me tomorrow, no Scottish festival full of Highlands-loving hillbillies, no glorious marching finale to my Scottish-American quest. A particularly melancholy hue of blue undulates overhead as the music soothes to a standstill and the tunnel settles into silence. I nudge slow inches along the moving walkway, crestfallen. Is this where this adventure comes to a close? A slow-mo dead end in Detroit?

But, just at that moment, just when I'm ready to hang up my tartan and concede defeat, the lights overhead burst into a fierce display of fiery reds and invigorating oranges. A victorious and rather surprising xylophone version of 'Chariots of Fire' breaks out, swells and fills the underpass. I feel a sudden jolt of energy. Dammit, I've made it this far, I'm not giving up yet. Maybe the pilot decided to wait for me. Maybe the flight is as delayed as I am. Maybe destiny has saved me an aisle seat. I pick up my paces and my three tons of reading material and race out of the tunnel, bags whipsmacking against my legs. I gallop through the concourse. At the far end of the deserted terminal, the gate agents see me, jump to attention and spur me on.

'Run, girl, run!' shouts one, scooping the air in urgent circles to urge me on. 'We're holding this for you! We're clinging on to this plane's tail till you get on it!'

'Come on, you're so close!' calls the other, stretching her arm out for my boarding card as I approach. 'You're gonna make it! You're gonna make it!'

'Lucky you got them long legs,' says the first as I wheeze past her and onto the jetway.

'Congratulations! I sure hope Tennessee is worth it. Now, run!'

I pound along the jetway and bound onto the plane, narrowly avoiding knocking myself out on the diminutive doorway. I sink into my seat, the last passenger on board the day's final flight to the Volunteer State, exhausted, but beaming. I've made it! It's all back on; the cows, the festival, and most importantly, the Parade! Despite the stressful circumstances, I got a good feeling about Michigan, plus a fine opportunity to reassess the inspiring qualities of the xylophone, and for that this state will always hold a special place in my heart.

The plane is very small, only slightly bigger than something you might get free in a box of Cornflakes. The windows are so low that to see the runway lights of Detroit Metro Airport I have to bend over like a curious orang-utan or slide down so low in my seat it looks like I am trying to surreptitiously remove my pants. And this doesn't seem like that kind of flight.

The blue lights of DFW twinkle below me and I'm off from the Midwest to the Midsouth. Across the aisle, a fellow passenger is so engrossed in a magazine article called 'Loving your man, Losing your mind' that she doesn't notice my potential pantslessness.

So this is it, the glorious finale of this quest that started all those months ago. I've explored, endured and experienced so much in my endeavours to become fully Scottish. So what do I hope for in Tennessee? Well, I hope I'm not allergic to foolishly fringed Highland cows. I hope I'll get adopted by a clan for the parade, like I've been adopted and made feel so at home by the US. More immediately, I hope I can actually get into my motel room when I reach Gatlinburg at 1 am.

I arrive in Knoxville at midnight and walk purposefully through the near-deserted building. I'm an hour away from Gatlinburg, but I know the way. Detailed instructions were left on my phone in an accent as delicious as Tennessee barbecue sauce. 'Come out of the airport and look to the right. Do not look to the left. Just right. You got that? Right. Ah'right. Ah've got you wrote down. Ah'll be there. Ah'll see you.' After listening to these directions at least ten times, I know them off by heart and I'm excited to meet the owner of this delightful voice.

As I walk out into the silent Sevier County night, looking determinedly to the right, a white taxi van rumbles into sight. All available exteriors, including the van's tinted windows, roof and, presumably, undercarriage, are plastered with stickers. As it cruises by me, the passenger side window proclaims 'KIM' in gigantic white letters. The taxi makes a slow U-turn, revealing a gargantuan 'TIM' on the driver's side. The taxi shudders to a halt and, for a second, all is still. Then the door opens, the Dodge creaks and, with a great heft, a huge man hoists himself out and towers to his feet. This mountain holds out his hand for my bags, which instantly look tiny, light and doll-sized.

'Well, welcome to Knoxville,' beams Tim.

I manage an excited squeak of a response.

A tiny slip of a woman with tidy hair sticks her head across the seats and pipes up, 'And y'all are welcome to "Severe County"...'

'So it's not Seh-vee-ur County, then?' I ask.

Tim and Kim think this is hilarious.

'No, ma'am, it's not,' guffaws Tim as I clamber into the cab. '"Seh-vee-ur," oh my...' he repeats, shaking with laughter.

'Oh my!' titters Kim.

My mispronunciation is clearly one of the funniest things anyone has ever said in Tennessee.

Kim, Tim's wife, is from West Virginia, which she says is 'Like Tennessee, but not as pretty.' Tim was born and bred in Gatlinburg.

'It's not that big a town,' he tells me. 'Maybe eighty-five hundred people. You'll find that people are just real down to earth. If you've heard the expression, "redneck people," well, that's who we are. Yep. We got mountain heritage. It ain't changed, in some ways, since how people used to live back in 1800. Yep. We got no high society, no high falutin, just all these friendly country folks.' He pauses and adds shyly, 'It's nice.'

We drive Sevier County backroads for an hour, passing the Texas Roadhouse, Food City and the Gas'n'Go, bright blares of neon on otherwise inky midnight country roads. I stare through Smoky Mountain Taxi stickers at slivers of rural Tennessee lit up by these sporadic sudden reveals.

Signs appear for Dollywood, Dolly Parton's butterfly-adorned backwoods theme park and temple for those with strong convictions about country music, country cooking and Christianity. I've always been a huge fan of Ms Parton, on account of both her music and wise words such as 'Money can't buy you happiness but it sure can buy you something pretty to be depressed in.' But, judging by the photos on the signs, if I was to take such advice while shopping at Dollywood, I'd have a wardrobe entirely adorned with butterflies, rhinestones and religious statements, which, in my case, might actually contribute to depression.

'Dolly's done a lot for this area. Ain't she, Tim?' says Kim.

'Yep.'

'She's done a whole lot.'

'Yep.'

'She's from up by Caton's Chapel, ain't she?'

'Yep.'

'Her momma still alive?'

'Shoot, yep, her momma's still alive!' Tim grows animated and then bashful. He says to me, 'Actually, I'm third cousins with Dolly. My momma and Dolly's momma's momma were cousins. My momma was a Parton.'

Before I can squeal with glee at this revelation, I'm jolted right out of my seat with fright as the taxi fills with an ear-splitting blast of 'IT'S PEANUT BUTTER JELLY TIME, IT'S PEANUT BUTTER JELLY TIME, IT'S PEANUT BUTTER....' Tim calmly cuts this cacophony short by answering his phone. My heart continues to do terrified somersaults for several more miles of Highway 441.

I'm still wide-eyed and fearful of any more incoming calls as Tim recommends that, once in Gatlinburg, I start with Bennett's or Hogs and Honeys for barbecue.

'That's hogs, as in bikes,' adds Tim, helpfully.

'But, Tim, maybe she'd like breakfast first. Barbecue ain't breakfast. Do you like breakfast?' Kim asks me.

'I do.'

'Well,' says Kim, 'You're in pancake heaven in Gatlinburg.'

I mention that since I'm allergic to gluten this might actually be pancake hell for me. Kim frowns when I say 'hell' and says nothing else for the remainder of the journey.

We reach Pigeon Forge, the town before Gatlinburg. So many Country Revue shows! So many neon-emblazoned motels with rooms for under $20 a night including breakfast, cable TV and passes to a choice of gun ranges! Such a staggering bounty of fast food franchises from the most extreme end of the calorie scale! Pigeon Forge appears to be a fine place to shoot, sample cut-price country cabaret and court heart failure.

The outskirts of Gatlinburg are a far less fluorescent place. Tim judders the Smoky Mountain Taxi over an afterthought of a bridge at the edge of town and up a patchy driveway to what initially looks like a neglected, closed down motel, but turns out simply to be a very, very neglected motel. A couple of thin exterior lights sputter on and off above the shuttered office.

Tim and silent Kim drive off and I'm alone in the East Tennessee night. The motel is eerily still. It feels as if it was abandoned around 40 years ago and is now inhabited solely by mildew, some rare Appalachian fungi and perhaps a few malevolent bunnies that are partial to human blood. The office is completely dark but there's an envelope with a keycard taped to the door with my name and 'Room 411' scrawled on it in direct contravention of everything I learned about guest safety during my years working in hotels. By the elevator, vending machines sell obsolete disposable cameras that passed their sell-by date twenty years ago and varieties of painkiller that haven't been handed over a counter since 1974. A line of empty Coke cans and two carefully placed cigarette butts rests on top.

My room is on the dark, wooded, unlit side of the building, accessed by an exterior walkway. A densely treed hillside slopes up, feet away. The air smells of earth and rotting leaves and has a nose-assaulting mustiness very similar to the mushroom lasagna served on my first flight this morning. There's an unsettling, muffled silence, occasionally underlined by an insistent drip. I have plenty of time to consider what could be dripping in the darkness as I try repeatedly to get my room key to work. Checking the envelope again, I see a scrawl that says, 'Prblem? Margo room 202.'

I walk down two flights and knock.

Eventually, a bleary, make-up strewn face peers round the door and stares at me. I blurt out my name and rooming issues. The woman continues to gaze wordlessly at me. A man's voice rasps something indistinguishable from inside. I have a horrible feeling that I knocked on the wrong door.

Then the woman turns and yells into the darkness behind her, 'Shuddup, Billy, 's a girl, a girl for a key.' She stands clear of the door and turns her back to me with a final, 'Shudd-uuuup!'

Although I'm relieved that this has turned out to be the right room, I find a lot about the situation disconcerting. The dank darkness surrounding me. Not being able to get into my room in the middle of the night. The fact that it is now starkly obvious that Margo is naked.

Margo turns back to me and looks down, seemingly surprised to find herself nude. She hands me a new key card.

'Try this thang. It'll maybe work.'

It doesn't.

Back on the fourth floor, I groan, hugely reluctant to wake Margo again. If it wasn't for the cold, the damp, those bunnies, I'd almost consider sleeping here. Sighing, I trudge back down.

'I'll jus' get clothes or somethin',' Margo slurs.

I stand on the landing for five minutes and begin to wonder if she has passed out, but Margo eventually returns, wrapped in a duvet.

'Shuddup, Billy,' she shouts into the silent room as she steps out to join me.

I follow her along the chilly walkway in her trailing duvet. We stand in the lift as it ascends the two floors, Margo chatting away as if this is all perfectly normal. As, of course, it may well be. At room 411, Margo puts my keycard in the lock and I have that moment of dread you have when standing on a fourth floor landing beside a drunk motel manager wrapped in a duvet and you suddenly wonder if you just put the card in upside down, but the door doesn't open for her either. Margo looks at the card, the door and then the darkness in the direction of the ominous drip, concentrating fiercely.

'Well, darn, this ain't even the right room! I gave you the wrong room number! You should jus' have tried all the doors.'

Thirty seconds later, Margo and her duvet have gone back to bed and I'm in room 412. A nicotine-hued halo emanates from one battered orange standing lamp in a corner, giving the fake wood-panelled room a permanently sepia tone. Walls are unintentionally two- and sometimes three-toned, with a spectrum that ranges from viciously scuffed to tobacco spit-stained. Furniture is similarly inclined. These moteliers really have perfected derelict trailer home chic. This is the ideal address for people who like 3-watt bulbs and for their tissue dispensers to come with built-in bottle cap openers.

I wake up to the sun trickling through the windows and the sound of a cheerful selection of Tennessee birds. Motel corridors that seemed menacing last night now feel light and friendly. Even the threadbare stags' heads pegged at unpredictable intervals around the property seem to have a more hopeful countenance. After ploughing through a breakfast trough of gloopy grits and gravy, I sit out on the balcony. The weak morning sun makes valiant efforts to clear misty mountain ridges that ripple off to the southeast but it can't quite shake off the haze. The Little Pigeon River gurgles happily towards the centre of town. Even the damp air smells less compostable than last night. Thin strains of upbeat country music waft up from a parked pickup truck below. I begin to feel positive about this town where vending machines are frozen in the time before Dolly and Kenny's first duet and the dress code includes duvets. It's amazing what a bit of sleep, sunlight and the strategic use of a tissue dispenser bottle opener can do.

Down at ground level, Steve Earle's 'Hillbilly Highway' plays as a smiling man in his 30s, a trucker cap and denims unloads his truck while he asks me about who I am and why I'm in his town. Chip turns out to be the day manager.

He tells me, 'Me, I've lived all my life between these traffic lights,' he says.

He sees me look confused.

'That's how you find your way in this town. Town starts at Traffic Light 1 and goes all the way up to Traffic Light 10 before you've gone right out the other side. Coming back here, just keep countin' down the lights.'

As Chip's truck reverberates to slow guitar finger picking, I set off to explore.

Gatlinburg is pretty much as far east as you can go in Tennessee without tripping over the border into North Carolina. And there are far less clumsy ways to cross into the Carolinas. The town weaves along the banks of the Little Pigeon and Roaring Fork Creek and up the densely treed slopes of various misty South Appalachian mountains with a history of bluegrass, grist milling and moonshining. It's flanked on three sides by the Great Smoky Mountains National Park, the most visited national park in the US. Opened in 1934, the 521,000-acre park changed the fortunes of this town by bringing millions of tourists in. The creation of the park also forced the relocation of hundreds of mountain folk, marking the end of a hardscrabble way of life in places such as Cades Cove, which was settled in the early 1800s and was once home to more than 600 people. More recent history, of course, has been made by that perky and prodigious fourth of twelve children born in a rudimentary shack up on Locust Ridge, Dolly Rebecca Parton. In Parton's Deli, at Traffic Light 2, her cousin Dennis takes my order.

I begin to form the suspicion that a majority of the residents of Sevier County are related to the Big D. There certainly is a plethora of Partons about. It's one of the same few dominant family names that feature over and over on business names. Upwards of 90% of Gatlinburg appears to be run by members of the Ogle, Reagan and Parton clans.

Mr Parton 'don't do no coffee,' so I have an ancient-looking glass bottle of Orange Crush instead and watch an occasional pick-up truck slide by towards Traffic Light 1 and the edge of town.

The 1970s deli has polished pine walls and ceiling, original gleaming cranberry tile floors, pristine white Formica banquettes and jars of Pepperoncini and Dill Strip pickles standing to attention on the worn counter. Flyers for Dollywood perch alongside. It's a meticulously kept place that has clearly been scrubbed and shined fiercely every day of its three-plus decades.

Alongside an ancient photo of the Gatlinburg Police Department, a pinboard has a yellowed notice that generously offers, 'If you don't know Jesus, I'll take the time to introduce you,' for those who fancy being saved once they finish their soda. Up on the wall, there's a t-shirt for sale that commemorates Parton's 30th anniversary in 2004. I wonder why there are so many boxes of t-shirts underneath, so many years after the date, and what kind of person might buy such an item. Surely very few people are that daft?

Back out on the Parkway, I tuck my new Parton's 30th Anniversary shirt into my bag and walk north in persistent drizzle. Dilapidated businesses with questionable punctuation hope for customers under rusty signs with fonts that remind me of brands discontinued in my childhood. I pass The Manger, home of Living Faith Television, and a sign stating, 'Jesus Talk Live!' Given the town's disregard for punctuation, I wonder whether this is a description, a boast or an entreaty. Windows of the town's many dozens of t-shirt stores are crammed with the same identikit religious range, including sectarian outfit options such as, 'Deal or no deal, Jesus is the only bet,' 'Exposure to The Son May Prevent Burning' and 'COPS—Christians Obediently Preaching Salvation.' The storekeepers of the Smokies know their market and that market obviously does not allow for any freedom of religious expression or deviation from emphatically evangelical duds. Further up the Parkway, the first of a quiver of weapon shops bristles with 'Good deals on gun, knives and swords.' Across the street, Medieval Blades offers 'Knives, Air Soft Guns, Self Defence and Tobacco Accessories,' which certainly covers all my souvenir needs. There are many shoulder-length mullets, many of them modelled by people in 'Jesus Saves!' and 'What Happens at Deer Camp Stays at Deer Camp' t-shirts. There are also more mini golf courses than I can count. And, as Tim promised, there is not much in the way of high society, very little evidence of high or even medium falutin and plenty of delightful, friendly country folks. Really, small town Tennessee seems not that dissimilar to small town Scotland when measured in terms of friendly locals, confrontational-casual, faith-based clothing and quantities of rain, although Scotland has fewer officially sanctioned weaponry boutiques.

I pass the Tennessee State Bank, Smoky Mountain Nascar Racing Collectibles, a clunky animatronic Tyrannosaurus Rex, Ripley's Moving Theatre, Ripley's Believe It Or Not Museum and Ripley's Haunted Adventure where spookings come courtesy of 'real special effects with wax.' Between Traffic Lights 5 and 6, as I pass Ripley's Aquarium of the Smokies, I'm given a blotchily printed American Sign Language guide that offers the words for 'sweetheart,' 'ok,' 'drink,' 'no good,' 'God' and 'I Love America,' but has been so shoddily photocopied that it actually simply features blobs of ink and illustrations that look like people punching each other repeatedly in the face. Probably as punishment for wearing boxers without Biblical text.

'I love you,' says a drunk in a 'Pick Jesus' t-shirt outside Corky's BBQ.

As he reels closer, I put my hand up to stop his approach. I hope this is the universal sign language gesture indicating lack of interest and not 'Splendid, we will have many children together,' but just in case he's intent on hashing through reasons we're not going to work the doesn't get the message, I duck into the restaurant.

Inside, the bartender doesn't understand my accent at all. I squint at the sign language leaflet and consider trying to adapt my newly acquired vocabulary to sign, 'God, sweetheart, I love drink,' but would just look I'm trying to give myself a black eye. I point at the menu instead.

Consulting my 'Gatlinburg Trolley Routes' map, I notice that the legend includes wee symbols for parking, traffic lights, restrooms and marriage license centres. I hadn't realised this town was such a hitching post. I don't find Gatlinburg quite as romantic as many other visitors apparently do.

My lunch is delivered and I thank the server. The wizened 60-something-year-old guy at the next table stares.

'You ain't 'Merican!' he exclaims.

'No, I'm Scottish.'

'Well, I'll be...'

We chat for a while and then he interrupts, asking, 'Why don't you stay, we'll get us a cabin up in the woods, have us a shackload of kids?'

Tempting. And, unlike the candidate outside, my latest admirer actually has a few teeth! This seems like an improvement until the restaurant's revolving countertop fan changes direction and sends a blast of my lunch companion's distinctive scent my way. I guess the shack on offer may not rise to indoor plumbing. Despite having some doubts about the appeal of spending the rest of my life raising a clan of backwoods babies, I don't want to be rude, so thank him, but tell him I'm already spoken for.

'Well, when you find a woman who ain't your cousin round these parts, you want to grab them fast.'

That seems fair enough and goes some way to explain the need for the town's easily accessible marriage license centres.

'My ex-wife, she was my cousin. My high school sweetheart, too. We only found out on the night of our prom,' he says with a defeated shrug.

I feel bad for nixing his chances of finally marrying outside the family. It would certainly be an unexpected ending to this adventure, but maybe not one my other half would be terribly pleased about. My suitor belches loudly and we go back to eating our food.

Two hours later, I trek a muddy trail through the National Park. There are five of us on what the Gatlinburg Scottish Festival and Games schedule called a 'Mountains Stroll.' I'd think of a more energetic description if I could just catch my breath. So far the pace has been more martial than I had expected. I'm bringing up the rear, lagging a shack's length behind the rest of the troop, despite two of my fellow strollers walking with sticks. It really is little wonder I nearly missed my flight last night.

I'd thought East Tennessee would be hot and sunny in mid-May and so didn't bring any cold weather attire. I shiver in my thin tartan hoody and wonder idly which tartan it is and whether I can acquire a warmer one.

Trees cover all the mountain ridges. Everything is very green with the occasional splash of a scarlet tanager or the custard flash of a hooded warbler in the canopy above. Our hike leader tells us about the kinds of creatures likely to be in the vicinity: white-tailed deer, black bears, elk, wild turkey, groundhogs, copperhead and timber rattlesnakes and 30 species of salamanders. I stop on the trail to take a photo of a spindly, yellow Carolina lily with pleasing cayenne splotches on its delicate petals while the others are up ahead looking for bear tracks. Afraid of what might sneak up on me while I'm setting up the shot, I snatch a hasty picture and scuttle back to the group, but there is nothing more threatening than one dead tiger moth and an old bear paw print. I encountered more wildlife on the motel balcony earlier, where a red cardinal popped up to check on me every so often and an enormous shiny-butted bee seemed determined to befriend me. Or eat me. It was hard to tell which.

The hike is led by Dan, a former Ohio police officer, current treasurer of Clan Smith USA and a serious sword enthusiast. Dan's precise black moustache, stern eyebrows and brisk pace successfully mask a friendly disposition that only reveals itself once the hike comes to an end. His enthusiasm for his ancestry, Gatlinburg's Scottish Festival and 18th-century broadswords is strangely compelling. Well, it must be: by the time we're back in Gatlinburg, I have been persuaded not only to show up at the town's Mill Park at 7 am tomorrow, but to take sole charge of the Scottish Festival's merchandise stall once there. I had only planned to go for a couple of hours in the afternoon, to save my energy for the parade, now I'm going to spend most of my the day selling promotional items in a muddy field out by the high school.

Over lunch Dan talks about his German, Irish, Scottish and English heritage. Although he's never been to any of his ancestral homelands, his predecessors are obviously guiding forces in his life. He has two kids, one who lives in Germany, the other in London. Despite their addresses, which seem like reasonable proof of at least some passing curiosity about the lands of their forebears, Dan's disappointment in their lack of interest in their heritage is palpable.

'They don't care about where they came from,' he says sadly.

I don't argue. By now I know how vast a gulf can separate those carefully preserved, romanticised Old Countries from the living new countries they evolved into.

The server comes round to take our order. Today's special is a grilled cheese sandwich.

Dan frowns. 'I don't like hot cheese. I only like cold cheese.'

'But this one has sweet onions. And pickles. And the cheese melts real nice. You might like it.'

But, no, Dan only likes cold cheese and no developments in grilling and garnishing can change that. He orders, his cheese remains cold, his sandwich status quo remains at room temperature.

Back at the motel, I make myself a drink. This trip has been full of surprising revelations. Tonight's discovery is that iced tea goes surprisingly well with gin, but today I've also learned that a town can be contained by its traffic lights and that I'm easily swayed into festival-stand servitude by men with military moustaches. I sip my newly invented Smoky Mountain Iced Tea and weigh this up, in between practising appropriate marching steps for tomorrow evening's Grand Parade.

It's 6 am and the sun is out, creeping slowly over low ridges of the Smokies. Many raucous birds find this most pleasing and are cawing their wee heads off. The empty coke cans and cigarette ends that adorned the painkiller supplies box when I arrived the other night still stand to attention outside. Each morning Margo and Chip shuffle in and out past them and obviously see no reason to dislodge such a distinctive feature of the property. I peek my head into the breakfast room to see what colour of gloop is on the menu this morning. It's a more frightening shade of rusty taupe than yesterday. I croak a sleepy order for tea and leave it at that.

An hour later, I report to a soggy tent in Mills Park. Dan looks critically at me, rummages in a bag and pins a Clan Smith tartan sash and his mother's silver thistle brooch on me. Suitably adorned, I am left in charge of the festival's merchandise concerns. Dan has stressed the importance of my job today; not only am I representing Gatlinburg Scottish Festival and Games, but I am in charge of generating some vital income for the organisation. I inspect my wares. Having sold out of everything any reasonable human might possibly want yesterday, my entire stock consists of six t-shirts from the last few years' festivals and five commemorative pins from 2002. Parton's Deli seems like a clothing megastore by comparison.

I do not do a brisk business. It's pouring and around 7 people wander around the field in the rain. Every so often, a 50-something clansman sidles over and shows me his military medals, swords or membership cards of various Transatlantic armaments societies. To a man, they frown darkly when they see me in my Smith sash. Dan gloats, having claimed me for his clan. A feisty Fraser presents me with a tartan hat in his colours and I dutifully don it. Dan's brows crease as the Fraser limps victoriously off to try his hand at battle-axe-throwing with the Scottish American Military Society on the other side of the park, sword clanking against his knobbly white knees. A MacDonald approaches with a tartan waistcoat for me and I feel a bit like a prize heifer, a Christmas tree or the groom at a polygamous Highland wedding.

Since I'm now running short on personal surface areas for tartan decoration, I sneak off to a nearby corral where a few Highland cows droop about. Descriptions of the merits of the various animals include splendid details such as 'She has terrific feet!' and 'Luckily, she is a wide heifer!' I know one isn't supposed to anthropomorphise mammals, but it really is very hard to imagine Highland cows having anything other than a rather morose take on life. Or it is until I see a tiny hairy face peeking out from under her mother's scraggy underbelly. Perky wee Pearl is the colour of milky porridge and as fuzzy as a stuffed toy. Or an angora rabbit if it was multiplied by a mohair goat. Or a really, really long lost mint from down the back of the couch. She butts me playfully with her tousled wee oatmeal head as I cautiously stroke her. She's wiry and quite damp, so a couple of pats is enough for me to feel that I have achieved the milestone of meeting my first Highland cow up close. Also, her mother, Opal, a more traditional ginger Hielan' heifer, is examining me balefully from behind a curtain of coarse orange hair, while angling an impressive four-foot rack of horns in my direction.

The American Highland Cattle Association states that Highland cows come in folds and not herds and that they can be red, black, yellow, dun, white, brindle or silver. They don't mention porridge as a common hue. Their information says that the first recorded Highland bovines in the US got off the train at Moorcroft, Wyoming in the early 1900s and were trailed to the Powder River in the northeast of the state. I imagine them stepping daintily off steam locomotives, fetching carry-alls clutched in one hoof. The AHCA also informs me that there are an estimated 25,000 of the burly beasts registered in the States today. On the way back to my post, I catch a glimpse of my reflection in a truck window. Today's constant rain and a lack of early morning effort on my part has taken its toll on my own hair, making it dispiritingly similar to Pearl's mother's lank fringe.

In a sales lull that stretches from shortly after 10 am to late afternoon, I read through a lot of literature about clan activities in the midsouthern states and then move on to festival pamphlets. Today's event leaflet says, 'Grab your kilt and head for the hills!' It also says, in much smaller print, 'Games will be held rain or shine, unless conditions are dangerous.' Tennessee is prone to tornadoes, but today the most dangerous conditions anyone needs to look out for are the possibility of losing footwear in the thick mud, the risk of being skewered by a sword- or axe-wielding clansman or being mistaken for an appetiser and gnawed by a cow needing a haircut. There is also, of course, the very real threat posed by an increasingly bored and fractious Scotswoman, weighed down by her bodyweight in tartan paraphernalia and silver occasional jewellery.

To celebrate having sold a 2002 Gatlinburg Games badge, I do a lap of the field, taking in many Confederate flags and a plate of delicious haggis and chips, before coming to a halt at the Scottish Tartans Museum stand. The museum itself is in Franklin, North Carolina and the angular guy in his mid-30s behind the table is Matthew, the museum director. He is amused by my competing tartan wear and identifies my ineffectual soaked outer garment as a 'Blue Stuart, except that no such thing exists.'

I've never felt any particular bond with the McDonnell tartans, the official clan colours of our branch of Mulhollands. They've never felt relevant in my life. As today's tartans are a largely 19th-century invention and as there were few situations that required tartan attire during my childhood back in Scotland, I just can't see how any such arrangement of colours could mean anything to me. But Matthew says he thinks he's seen a Mulholland tartan in his files and I humour him by saying I'd love to see it. Ninety seconds later, he produces a crumpled print-out: gold threaded through a blue as deep as Loch Awe and a green as fresh as the first ferns that flourish up the banks of Loch Lomond and the name 'Mulholland' printed above it. I'm caught off-guard. I know that this was something cooked up two, maybe three years ago. I know this is something woven together for the sake of a sale. I can even see on the line for 'Pattern Description' that this colour configuration is suspicious enough for someone to have typed in 'needs investigating.' But it doesn't matter. I feel a rush of pride, of ownership, of joy at the sight of the colours, my colours, my tartan. My eyes fill with tears as this strange sense of belonging to something bigger than myself strikes. Finally, for the moment before I realise that one flip-flop has got irretrievably stuck in an ankle-deep trough of mud, my first and last names coincide and I feel truly radiant.

The Blessing of the Tartans has just started in the field, as has a major downpour. I look at the stall with some desperation. I know Dan will never consent to let me go while there's even one chipped badge or a single 1983 t-shirt left. There's nothing else for it; I buy all the wares myself and squelch through the muddy field and into a waiting taxi back to the motel. I'm ready and it's time to end this.

As I leave the motel, I meet Chip smoking outside. 'Where you goin', Miss Scotland? Which traffic light you hitting today?'

From the festival programme, I read out, '"All Scots are invited to gather in front of the restaurant near the National Park entrance at traffic light number 10." I'm off to gather.'

'Aw, I miss all the good stuff. Traffic Light 10, yeah, that's a good light.'

I wave goodbye to Chip, retrace my steps back up the puddle-dashed Parkway, past Parton's and a crowd of people in Great Smoky Mountain National Park raincoats at Traffic Light 2. At Traffic Light 3, I smile at the driver of a pickup with a huge yellow neon cross on its bumper. I walk past the Living Faith Manger and Rose René, The South's Number 1 Psychic. I pass Traffic Light 4, pausing for a car with faith plates that proclaim 'In God We Trust' and paintwork dotted with yellow army ribbons. I pass all the t-shirt shops, tattoo parlours and gun stores and continue on up the Parkway. I follow slowly behind a truck as it carefully plants US flags all the way up the parade route. The only one wearing tartan, I walk past the animatronic T Rex, past Ripley's Haunted Adventure, past MacPherson's Sweet Fanny Adams Theatre. I outpace multigenerational family groups in Harley Davidson gear, couples in matching sweatpants and a push-chair holding two miniature schnauzer dogs. A Gatlinburg Trolley bus, filled with tourists, shuttles past the aquarium. People bustle in and out of the Mirror Maze and Smokyland Motel. A lone Scottish flag flies at one of the many pancake emporia. Otherwise, Gatlinburg seems far less excited about this parade than I am.

Finally, I reach Traffic Light 10 and realise why I saw no tartan on the way up: all the tartan in Tennessee is here. As are all the kilts, bagpipes and knee-length wool socks in a three-state radius. Hundreds of kilted, tartaned and sock-clad Scots throng the car park opposite Shirley's Texaco Station. Still feeling emotional after my tartan turnabout this afternoon, my eyes fill with tears at the sight and sound of my people, at being a part of this. The sky above the Smokies is the precise shade of bruised grey that promises an imminent downpour. As a lone bagpiper wails the stirring opening chords of 'Flower of Scotland' I feel entirely in tune with the weather.

I exchange a few words with the Reverend B Sharp and his wife Tracy from Kingsport, Tennessee. A MacDonald, Reverend B tells me his family left Glasgow for Tennessee in 1822. His daughter sleeps soundly in her pushchair.

His wife says shyly, 'She's definitely got Scottish blood. She falls asleep to the sound of the pipes.'

A mutt that could be a serious contender for the title of oldest dog in the world sniffs around various clusters of clansfolks. Vintage cars rev, Scottie dogs yap and the mutt and I wander about in a bit of a daze. Around us, there's a lively sense of anticipation coupled with an urgency to get going soon that comes from everyone who didn't bring raingear. Bagpipes tune up discordantly and the oldest dog in the world totters away towards the Texaco, ears cringing at the sound.

The unruly hordes fall into order. Clans line up alphabetically, led by an elderly couple in matching kilts and identical plaid bonnets. I look for Clan Donald, but they all turn away from me and fiddle with their banners and flags when I approach. There is no room at my ancestral inn. I try to get absorbed into another clan, initially avoiding ones I know were frequently at war with the MacDonnells and MacDonalds. But as clan after clan blanks me, I realise I may have to form a new strategic alliance.

Forty-one clans, a clutch of 70-year-old cars, a scattering of dogs and one orange Gatlinburg trolley bus are now lined up and ready to march from Traffic Light 10 all the way to Traffic Light 3.

An organiser announces, 'Anderson! Buchanan! Campbell! Donald! Douglas!' and each clan steps smartly forward and onto the Parkway as its name is called. The Parade is underway.

'Fraser! Gordon!'

I can't see Dan or anyone I recognize from the hike or the festival as I search the crowd, increasingly desperately. Many clans starting with Mac are called forward and I still haven't found a clan willing to ally with me. There are just a paltry few left now and I begin to fear I'll be forced to cancel my jubilant parade down the Parkway and instead coast down on board the trolley that's waiting to follow with those too infirm to walk.

'Ramsay! Ross! Smith! Stewart!'

Finally, the Wallaces, the last clan in the alphabet, are the only ones left. I approach the five of them.

'Can I march with you?'

'We'll take anybody!' says a cheery woman with flowing red hair and a Clan Wallace banner.

'That's the Wallace way,' agrees another.

'Join us! The Wallaces are always trying to put together an army!' says the third.

I take my place beside the women.

'I didn't have room for my swords. It was my husband or my swords,' my new redheaded friend, confides. 'I know, it was a mistake.'

'Give us the new recruit!' yells one of the two guys, and I'm shuffled to the front.

I find myself between two large kilted men, one with a leather waistcoat and a huge carved sword, the other with a claymore strapped across his back and calves of a circumference that would shame the average tree trunk.

The six of us wait, a few feet in front of the Trolley, poised, ready.

'Wallace!' calls the announcer.

This is it.

'Freedom!' cry the three Wallace women behind me.

'Freedom!' shout the men either side of me with a clank of their swords.

'Freedom!' I say softly.

I get a rough nudge from behind.

'Freedom!' I bellow and they all cheer as I take a first step and I'm marching, five Wallaces striding in my wake.

The Parkway is at a standstill. People stand four deep on the sidewalks and stare. The occasional child or seated grandmother cheers. A non-parading Scot or two waves guiltily as we troop past. A few clap or shout out, 'I'm a Wallace.' Camera phones capture us to show back home in Oklahoma, West Virginia, Kentucky. But most people simply look perplexed and point or stare and chew vacantly, much like Pearl and Opal chomping on their bale of hay. For the majority of bystanders, we're just a sideshow in between Gatlinburg's 3D animatronic dinosaur displays and Believe It Or Not's wax wonders. But for me, beaming and resplendent in my Blue Stuart, this means so much more.

Wallace 1 brandishes his broadsword at several terrified children clustered around Traffic Light 9. At Traffic Light 8, Wallace 2 whisks out what he insists is a traditional 'Isle of Spey' whiskey in a cell phone-shaped flask and offers it round. Warmed by the dram from this imaginary island, I think about all the people I've met on my way to this traffic light, so many people who have changed how I think about Scotland, Scottish-America and the proportion of tartan items in my wardrobe.

I've encountered such an incredible cast of characters on this quest: William and Cheryl Duncan at the Kilt and Thistle in Salem; Mick and Tammy at the Highland Stillhouse in Oregon City; Gus Noble at the Scottish Home in Chicago; many, many charming Memphians; Scottie dog devotees in Georgia; Lillian, Alex and the trio of Japanese Scottish Country dancers in Honolulu; Princess Kaiulani in her Waikiki glade; Don P McDiarmid Jr on the windward side of Oahu; Charlie from the Snakehole Golf and Country Club in Apache Junction; the indomitable Jonquele and my fellow Texas Gaelic student Lisa; Pipe Major Bob, bagpipe fiend Luke, sweet Amery and Mr Mississippi in Louisiana; Dan from Clan Smith and my current companions, the warring Wallaces, here in Gatlinburg; and all the other people who've let me into their lives, taught me something or allowed me to share some part of my Scotland with them along the road.

Between traffic lights 7 and 6 and between enthusiastic gulps of whisky, the Wallaces strike up a ragged but rousing chorus of 'Scotland the Brave. '

'Land of my high endeavour,
Land of the shining river,
Land of my heart for ever,
Scotland the brave.'

Those watching might think I'm crying because the harmonies are so shockingly out of tune, the lyrics so out of synch and because a drunken Wallace just unintentionally flicked a tartan sash in my eye, but the tears are happy ones.

As we pass Traffic Light 6, the Wallaces start bickering about who finished the whisky. Wallace 2 is beginning to look a bit scabbard-happy.

At times I've wondered why I'm doing this, when staying home sometimes seemed preferable to setting off for yet another airport. But I've found an unexpected joy in America's celebration of Scottishness, in celebrating who we are and what we have in common, even if it's simply the fact that our ancestors all came from the same small, draughty northern land with a penchant for patterned, wraparound attire. Today I'm celebrating this shared ancestry and fashion sense, along with the satisfaction of having checked off an 11-state inventory of Scottish skills, experiences and encounters.

I think about all the Scots who crossed the ocean to this vast unknown continent in the 1600s, 1700s, 1800s, 1900s. And how they straggled off on their own, dispersed throughout the US and Canada, and got absorbed into new communities. Pockets of Scots fanning out and building new lives across this land. How, all these generations later, they've been gathered together again by Scottish festivals, games and organisations like this one.

At Traffic Light 3, the Parkway splits. The parading Scots hesitate as they approach, unsure which way to go. They slow and separate into clusters on different sides of the road. The sound of the bagpipes peters out. The line of tartan sidles in silent fits and starts until it reaches the fork in the road. The clans stop, wondering whether to go east towards the car park or north towards the edge of town. The parade doesn't end, it simply begins to straggle away.

I quietly separate from my argumentative adopted clan and walk towards the traffic light. I look back at the Scots in their isolated pockets as they peer around, scanning for direction, preparing to go off on their own now that the parade is over. Then, from behind all the people, pipes and terriers, behind the drooping banners and dipped tartan flags, the orange trolley trundles into sight. The knots of Scots see it, too. They brighten and clear a path for it to come through. The trolley stops for straggling clan members to clamber gratefully aboard, then bustles decisively past me towards the east fork. A lone drum strikes up a marching beat, banners are hoisted high once more and the clans fall back into formation, following in its wake, united once again.

I don't join them. I walk on to the split in the road and see the trolley inching away up the East Parkway, followed by hundreds of happy Scots. I hesitate, torn for just an instant. But I have come to the end of my parade and I know which direction to take. As my people disappear around the corner, I take the other fork and I keep walking.

Aefa Mulholland is an award-winning travel and food writer. She was born and raised in Glasgow and now divides her time between Toronto and Glasgow.

Aefa has worked with national broadcasters in the UK, Ireland and Canada, and with a plethora of publications from *The Miami Herald* to *The Irish Times.* She has been published or broadcast on four continents, writing or presenting on subjects from mule racing to the hazards of bingo to partying with The Pixies.

Her work has won a Northern Lights Award for Excellence in Travel Writing and an Irish Film Board award. Other things that Aefa has won include a national poetry competition (aged 6) for her heartfelt effort about a dead deer, three pounds betting on a mouse race in North Tipperary in 1982 and $12 in the New York State Lottery.

She writes strange hotel reviews and unlikely destination guides for Angry Sea Turtles and is working on a documentary about career options for seahorses. She often tries to persuade people to eat haggis.

She is the author of the short *Chicken & Hen,* also published by Ponies + Horses Books.

www.aefamulholland.com

NOTE FROM THE AUTHOR

I have so very many people to thank for their help, encouragement and G&Ts.

My sister, Orla, for her painstaking editing and impeccable knowledge of punctuation and obscure Scottish things. My dad, Joe, for everything. My nephew and youngest reader, Wee Joe. Readers, editors and all-round wonderful humans, Joan Brou, Aimée Kleinman, LoAnn Halden, Melissa Egan, Stuart Clark, Tara Robertson, Kate Gleeson, Kyra Faber and Tracy Craig for repeated encouragement and re-readings of chapters.

Those who accompanied me on various parts of this adventure or met me en route (including those who joined me on excursions that, alas, had, to get edited for length and/or excessive gin consumption): Erin Abler, April K. Randhawa, Arran Liddel, Maggie McLean, LoAnn Halden (again!), Erika J. Harvey, Berglind Hafsteinsdottir, Michelle Loh, Adam Menendez, my brother Mark, Dan Allen and Manuel Quinto-Pozos.

And those I met along the way—and who truly made The Scottish Ambassador what it is: Mr Limo, Veronique Meunier, Gus Noble, William and Cheryl Duncan, Lillian Cunningham and the Honolulu branch of the Royal Scottish Country Dance Society, Bob and the members of Pipes & Drums of New Orleans, Jonquele and Lisa in Texas, Dan in Tennessee, Charlie in Arizona, Amy Richert Griglak, Toni Smith, Nancy Black, Tony Lopez, Mick and Tammy Secor, Jennifer Swizenski, McT, Webb Carroll, Tennessee Tim and Kim, Lovell, Sevilla, Amery and Mr Mississippi in Louisiana and the Wallace Clan. I feel very fortunate to have met those two charming Scottish-Hawaiians, Alex Pratt and Don P McDiarmid Jr, gone now, but not forgotten.

Pip Christmass and Jason Salzenstein for their fashion advice.

A few names in the book have been changed for reasons of privacy.

Cliff Hanley's lyrics for 'Scotland The Brave' are reproduced with the permission of the copyright holder James S. Kerr, music publishers, Glasgow.

The Humber School for Writers, and particularly my mentor John Metcalf, for the praise, the criticism and the push to be the best writer possible. Alisdair Gray for his encouragement.

My mum, Claire, who died just a few months before I wrote the final page. One of the last things she said to me was 'Finish that bloody book.'

And, of course, Adrian, who didn't accompany me on any trips, but who has had to live and relive and relive the journey with me at home.

CHILDHOOD

TANIA
KATAN

ANDREW J.
FITT

SOPHIA
BLACKWELL

HILLARY
SAVOIE

AEFA
MULHOLLAND

TRACY
CRAIG

CHILDHOOD 6 OF 1

Available as individual, standalone books or as an anthology, **CHILDHOOD 6 of 1**, the first collection of short memoirs from P+H Books, takes a look at childhood from all directions. The funny and moving series of stories features unconventional fathers, unexpected kids, challenging childhoods and plenty of triumph over adversity, expectation, small city limitations and potato sack races.

TRAVEL 6 OF 1

Available as individual, standalone books or as an anthology, **TRAVEL 6 of 1**, the first series of short travel essays from P+H Books, contains stories that stretch right from the moment of birth to the sometimes surprisingly colourful business of death. There are tales of arrivals and departures, ships that have sailed and ships that have come in. There are stories of festivities perched on the brink of a war zone, on the brim of the Mediterranean and on the banks of the Mississippi.

24484974R00164

Printed in Great Britain
by Amazon